A Web of Words

A Web of Words

Pattern and Meaning in Robert Jordan's *The Wheel of Time*

HEATHER ATTRILL

Fastnet Books

2012

Fastnet Books
227 Donnelly Street
Armidale, New South Wales, 2350
Australia

www.fastnetbooks.net

publishing@fastnetbooks.net

First published 2012

National Library of Australia
Cataloguing-in-Publication entry:

Attrill, Heather Anne, 1943 —
A Web of Words: pattern and meaning in Robert Jordan's
The Wheel of Time

ISBN-13: 978-0-9871712-4-5
ISBN-10: 0987171240

For Dennis.

ACKNOWLEDGEMENT

I gratefully acknowledge Robert Jordan's encouragement of my research for this project and his patience in dealing with my queries about *The Wheel of Time* sequence.

Like his colourful character Thom, the Gleeman, Jordan was a great teller of tales. He will be long-remembered by the millions of devoted readers of his books as a magician with words.

IN-TEXT ABBREVIATIONS

Robert Jordan

EOTW..*The Eye of the World*
GH.. *The Great Hunt*
DR.. *The Dragon Reborn*
SR.. *The Shadow Rising*
FOH.. *The Fires of Heaven*
LOC.. *Lord of Chaos*
COS.. *A Crown of Swords*
POD.. *A Path of Daggers*
WH.. *Winter's Heart*
COT.. *Crossroads of Twilight*
KOD.. *Knife of Dreams*

Robert Jordan and Teresa Patterson

Companion.. *The World of Robert Jordan's 'The Wheel of Time'*

J. R. R. Tolkien

LOTR..*The Lord of the Rings*
Fellowship.. *The Fellowship of the Rings*
Towers.. *The Two Towers*
King.. *The Return of the King*

Ursula K. Le Guin

Wizard.. *The Wizard of Earthsea*
Farthest.. *The Farthest Shore*
Tales.. *Tales from Earthsea*
Wind.. *The Other Wind*

CONTENTS

Acknowledgment i

In-text abbreviations ii

Introduction 1

Chapter One: Revisiting Interlace: The Author as 14
Storyteller and Pattern Maker

Chapter Two: Unravelling the Pattern: The Magus 64
Figures in *The Wheel of Time*

Chapter Three: The Patchwork Hero: Jordan's 113
Patterning of Heroic Motifs in *The Wheel of Time*

Chapter Four: Heroic Interlace: The Jordan Hero 139
as Destroyer, Builder and Preserver

Chapter Five: Virtual Storytelling: *The Wheel of Time* 181
World Wide Weave

Afterword: 'Wheel' World/Real World, The Quest of 219
the Fan/Critic

Notes 224

Bibliography 230

About the Author 251

INTRODUCTION

A phenomenon characteristic of late twentieth-century high fantasy literature is the writing of sprawling 'history rich' and philosophically complex stories that span many volumes. Perhaps it is because of the sheer size of such works that, to date, a writer such as the American, Robert Jordan (1948-2007) and his widely acclaimed and ongoing high fantasy series *The Wheel of Time*, have attracted only a limited amount of critical scrutiny. With more than 44 million books in print throughout the world and translations currently in over 25 languages, Jordan has obviously attracted enormous global appeal in little more than two decades. Indeed, during the last twenty years, his work has generated a trans-global following of fans who have spawned a burgeoning network of web sites, virtual-communities devoted to the *WOT* series. Such cyber-extensions of the written (as opposed to other media) texts represent a type of never-ending story and are a new and fascinating aspect of literary work and fandom that also, to-date, has received but little critical attention, although initial interest has increased in recent years, especially in pop-culture areas.

I use Robert Jordan's *WOT* sequence as the focus texts to explore the role of both the writer of fantasy, and the role of his online following of fans as storytellers and pattern makers, and the motif of patterning in the novels. Jordan's epic *WOT* sequence is worthy of study also because he enacts the dilemmas and challenges of the contemporary 'second-wave' fantasists. I use this term, in particular, to distinguish those authors who began to create their high fantasy cycles in the latter years of the twentieth century. Thus, they follow in the footsteps of earlier renowned fantasy authors such as Ursula Le Guin, Susan Cooper, Lloyd Alexander, Alan Garner, Diana Wynne Jones, Stephen Donaldson and many others. All of these, from the late 1950s on, were writing in the wake of C. S. Lewis's *Narnia* books and J. R. R. Tolkien's *The Hobbit* and, in particular his benchmark fantasy text *The Lord of the Rings*[1]. The sources for the intricately tangled 'web of story' are indeed vast.

Tolkien's own trilogy drew on a wealth of earlier material, and also had influential precursors of complex antecedents such as the prose romances of George MacDonald and William Morris, or the works of E. R. Eddison and Lord Dunsany.

All writers, to some extent, reveal influences of earlier authors, but in the genre of fantasy Tolkien was the first to create a completely autonomous fictional world, one that the reader could enter imaginatively and believe in fully. Thus, authors like Jordan are conscious that they are not pioneers in the creation of discrete and coherent Secondary World fantasies and that their writing is informed by both more recent and ancient conventions, narrative structures and motifs, which are drawn from an immense, traditional story-hoard. Instances of the under-girding patterns that inform the narratives of high fantasy include the imaginary landscape; magical objects and powers; the binary struggle between the forces of good and evil; a world in crisis; and the heroic quest that can save it. Yet modern fantasy writers not only draw heavily from the literary past, they also utilise an increasingly eclectic array of cross-cultural material, gleaned largely from diverse myth, legend, fairy tale and history. They thus have complicated the (timeless) narrative structure and pattern of the quest paradigm as displayed by Tolkien. The challenge facing Jordan and his contemporaries is the need to find methods of writing within a well-mined, popular tradition while imparting some sense of originality to the patterning of their own work, and to do so in ways that will hold the attention of their postmodern readers. I argue that Robert Jordan achieves this through his application of an older narrative form, the intricate literary art of 'interlacing' – a mediaeval narrative technique that Tolkien had found particularly suitable to his purposes in his construction of *LOTR*.

JORDAN'S *THE WHEEL OF TIME* SEQUENCE

From the latter part of the twentieth century it has become common for authors of high fantasies to build a template world and to use this clearly delineated and fixed landscape as a setting for an on-going series of volumes. Clute and Grant have observed that these texts, generally speaking, belong to 'genre fantasy', the more 'formulaic' end of the mode of fantasy, and that their Secondary Worlds can more accurately be described as 'fantasyland'. It is a landscape that is 'fixed in place; it is inherently *immobile*, it is a backdrop not an actor'. Therefore, it is not a setting wherein 'landscape and story are inherently intertwined; one cannot exist without the other and each modifies the other'. Clute further suggests that normally, the stories set in 'fantasyland' are structured so as to 'defer completion indefinitely, to lead readers into sequel after sequel' (1999, 341; 339). Clear examples of this type of storytelling are David Eddings's *Belgariad* series, Terry Brooks's *Shannara* and *Landover* series, or Terry Goodkind's *Sword of Truth.*

Thus the writers of high fantasy narratives may be accused of following a common pattern too slavishly. Although there are some negative responses to Jordan's *WOT,* Kaveney and Clute agree that he uses the conventions in a manner that is only 'superficially a genre fantasy' because of the way he builds his story. 'The Wheel of Time is built from conventional fantasy sequences, but these sequences are assembled with notable architectonic skill into an epic fantasy whose momentum (despite longueurs) is very considerable'. (Clute and Grant 1999, 524)

Jordan's *WOT* sequence is serial; the individual volumes are not discrete. To date it consists of thirteen books, each of which should be regarded as very substantial, interdependent chapters, and 'despite longueurs', the author is definitely weaving the narrative towards a final closure. During an interview in 2003 with Bill Thompson of *The Charleston Post and Courier* newspaper, Jordan made it clear that it would be a mistake to view the *WOT* cycle as a series, countering:

> I'm doing something that hasn't been done, I guess since [English novelist Anthony] Trollope. I am writing a very long, multivolume novel. You can read the first book, *The Eye of the World,* and stop, and feel you've read something that has enough resolution that you don't feel you have to read more. But you still have to start there. (2003)

The *EOTW* is the only volume in the series that possibly could stand alone, and the one that most clearly reflects the heroic quest paradigm of J. R. R. Tolkien's influential *LOTR*. The story-lines of each successive volume are increasingly dependent upon and interlaced with those that have gone before and purposely designed to be read and interpreted in sequence.

The titles for the *WOT* sequence, in order, are as follows: vol. i *The Eye of the World;* vol. ii *The Great Hunt;* vol. iii *The Dragon Reborn;* vol. iv *The Shadow Rising;* vol. v *The Fires of Heaven;* vol. vi *Lord of Chaos;* vol. vii *A Crown of Swords*; vol. viii *The Path of Daggers;* vol. ix *Winter's Heart;* vol. x *Crossroads of Twilight,* vol. xi *Knife of Dreams,* vol. xii *The Gathering Storm,* vol. xii *Towers of Midnight* (the last two books were completed after Jordan's death by Brandon Sanderson and will not be considered in my discussions; a final volume, *A Memory of Light,* is awaiting publication.) The first volume of the series was published in 1990 and the thirteenth in 2010.

SYNOPSIS OF *THE WHEEL OF TIME*

In traditional style the story is set at a time when survival of the Wheel world is at grave risk. Lands are now fragmented, the seven seals on the Dark One's prison are weakening, and as a consequence, some of the Forsaken (male and female) have escaped and the Shadow Lord can use them as surrogates to strengthen his own influence on the world. Human Darkfriends, traitors to their own peoples, are growing in numbers across the lands and it is once again prophesied that the Last Battle is approaching and that the Great Pattern needs a hero known as the Dragon Reborn. The background story reveals that, in this fictional world, for the past 3000 years women have largely been in control. Thus the reader does not actually get to see how well or otherwise a world dominated by females has functioned, although from fragments of history it is revealed that, since the tainting of the male side of the One Power, there has been the First War of the Trollocs and the One Hundred Years War.

The primary characters are in their late teens or early twenties at the opening of this vast tapestry epic. Five of them come from the tiny hamlet of Emond's Field in the Two Rivers, a quiet area where the Old Blood of the long forgotten Manetheren still runs strong. In the village itself – much like Tolkien's 'Shire' – the calendar of significant customs and traditional events still follows the orderly rhythm of the seasons. It is a tranquil place that has been largely forgotten by and uncorrupted from influences of the wider world. However, the Wheel world at large is at risk and as the young protagonists learn through Moiraine, their Aes Sedai mentor and guide, their village is no longer a safe haven.[2] The 'Web of Destiny' (in the Old Tongue *Ta'maral'ailen*) forms around the three youths, Rand, Mat and Perrin, who are known as *ta'veren,* as their life-threads have been spun out by the Cosmic Loom to bring change. The young village women Nynaeve and Egwene are also drawn into the web. Thus Jordan's story is concerned to show how ordinary young men and women from this small village can go out upon the world stage and how their engagement with it can be heroic and of universal significance. By the end of the first book Rand accepts that he must be the fearful Dragon Reborn, the one destined to face the Dark Lord at the Apocalyptic 'Last Battle' and that for him there can be no turning back. Suffice to say that with each book that follows, Jordan's narrative becomes increasingly complex as his teeming and various world is revealed to the reader, and further complicated through a web of political nuances and political intrigues, as the repercussions of the background story are revealed and influence the behaviour of the main protagonists, and their dark adversaries.[3]

CONSTRUCTING A STORY-SHAPED WORLD: ESCHATOLOGY

In the construction of his world Jordan draws on many and varied sources from the storied European past, and it is of interest that for an author who presents a society with no formal structure of religion he employs so much biblical allusion. The nemesis notion is provided by the movement towards a type of Armageddon – Jordan's representation of the mediaeval apocalyptic beliefs in a final cataclysmic battle between the forces of Light and Shadow. (A cyclic conceit in the Jordan texts is that in the ever-turning Wheel of Time, each of the seven repeating

Ages faces the catastrophe of a Last Battle.) His use of a 'War of Shadow' and *Taimon Gai'don* (the Last Battle) parallel mediaeval prophecies foretelling Armageddon'.[4] The continual appropriation of religious apocalyptic writings for apparently secular literary purposes would seem to indicate our persisting belief in, or desire for, a final reckoning between the powers of good and those of evil – between the polarities of the Light (service, selflessness and duty), and the Dark (power, greed and selfishness).

Jordan posits an alternative world picture strongly reminiscent of early Europe. The depicted society has no stated formalised religion and the polarities of Light and Dark have no overtly practised religious dimension, but they are believed in. In such a world, change is simply a pre-determined part of the mechanism and reincarnation is but an aspect of the cycle. However, through the development of the main protagonists, and the changes they wrought in the pattern of the Age, the author does put forward the notion of a measure of free-will and also the possibility of personal spiritual development.

The Wheel is a world in which the Creator, having set the Cosmic Loom in motion, appears to stand outside and to play no obviously active part. Jordan suggests that in his world the human inhabitants can expect no miracles or interventions; they must sort out their own dilemmas and take responsibility for their own actions. It is likely that Jordan is responding to the mindset of post ethical/post Christian Western society of the late twentieth or early twenty-first centuries, a society that is sceptical about faith. Although he presents a secular society, it is one that stresses the paramount need for his characters to choose a moral code of conduct. Oath taking and binding, selflessness, honour, duty, service, order through societal hierarchy, regard for the environment, and like concepts are held in great store and are clearly needed if the Great Pattern is to be preserved.

THE MAN WHO TURNED THE WHEEL

Robert Jordan was the pseudonym of James Oliver Rigney Jr, an American writer who lived in Charleston, South Carolina. He was a decorated soldier (for service in Vietnam) with a degree in physics from

The Citadel military school in South Carolina (1974), who worked as a nuclear engineer until 1978 when he became a freelance writer. He had a keen interest in both history and genealogy. He wrote his first novels, an historical family saga, *The Fallon Blood*, *The Fallon Pride* and *The Fallon Legacy* (1980-82), using the name Reagan O'Neal. His western *Cheyenne Raiders* (1982) appeared under the name Jackson O'Reilly. As Chang Lung he wrote theatre criticism and dance reviews. During the 1980s, under the Robert Jordan pseudonym, he wrote a number of fantasy volumes, which were based on 'Conan' the barbarian – a character created by the American writer Robert Howard. The *WOT* sequence was his first independent fantasy series. Jordan died in September 2007.

Jordan has stated that his use of the fantasy genre allowed him to explore the great moral issues. He strongly believed that there is essential 'good and evil' in the world, and that although 'sometimes it's hard to tell the difference' it is worth trying to do so. He also felt that most people 'want to believe in something, [and to] have a set of rules in life or guidelines for life and behaviour' (Lilley 2008). As Jordan likened himself to an Old Testament God who has control of his characters, he therefore posited a pre-determined world. The Wheel weaves as he willed. However, while certain characters, known as *ta'veren*, are destined to have life-threads that can alter the pattern of an Age, whether such disruptions to the 'Age Lace' favour the Light or the Shadow will depend on how the *ta'veren* rise to the challenge. Thus, Jordan was able to create an impression of conditional determinism so crucial to narrative tension.

His production of a collaborative companion book, *The World of Robert Jordan's 'The Wheel of Time'* (1997), can be viewed as an exegesis to offer detailed guidance to his complex world and enormous cast of characters for the reader (Jordan and Patterson 2000). Although the philosophical concept for Jordan's world is creatively brilliant, at times the sheer mass of work can partially obscure the underlying metaphysical level. Herodotus-like, and like Tolkien, he displays an almost antiquarian pleasure in giving extensive ethnographical detail of his various races, their societal mores, traditions, etiquette, clothing and such. Thus, he becomes an ethnographer for his peoples: the joy of reporting over and above the details of the plot is a hallmark of his style, which a number of readers and critics are beginning to question. Yet such elaborations are appropriate in their context and consistent with the literary art of interlace, and aid in the fleshing out of the characters and the landscape of an imaginary world that is remarkably convincing, richly nuanced and with a great depth of detail. For an enormous number of captive readers, although the Wheel world is clearly a place of the imagination, it is nevertheless quite remarkably real.

Jordan, as the author/creator of the *WOT* series, is clearly engrossed in weaving an extremely complex and colourful tapestry of words. From his initial book he has begun a careful threading of plot and sub-plot within the framework of a daily human struggle between Light and Shadow – a conflict that is revealed to have cosmic significance. And this is predicted to culminate in the long prophesised 'Last Battle', at which time the Dark Lord, if victorious, will recast the world of the Wheel in his own image, thereby creating a world in complete Shadow. Each of the books that follow the initial volume is interlaced with those that have gone before through the unfolding and increasingly diverse actions of the main characters and by means of their fate-determined links to each other. These links will determine the outcome of the Last Battle and the necessary balance and continuation of the Great Pattern.

The Jordan world is both encyclopaedic in its myriad of consistent details and diffuse in its sprawl, and it is richly textured and layered. Because of their reuse of traditional material, storytellers like him are continuously laying one version of story over what has gone before. Thus Jordan's work is like a transparency or overlay, one that is echoic of rich social and political history and tradition, but also reshaped to his own contemporary purposes. He has created an imaginary world where the previous Age fades into myth and legend as another comes about, and through his concept of a Wheel of Time and the continual repetition of seven Ages, it is temporally representative of what was, what is, and what may come. Janus-like, the world of the Wheel looks both back and forward. Jordan's world thus enacts many traditional fantasy conceits, while remaining consistent with itself.

HIGH FANTASY, SECONDARY WORLD,
AND SECONDARY BELIEF

High fantasy is the type of narrative that forms the focus of this work. It is a type of popular literary fantasy that critics have found easier to identify, for it operates within a shared cluster of clearly recognised conventions, that is, an imaginary landscape, an imperilled world, and a heroic quest in which the hero's growth to maturity is tied to the fate of the imaginary world. The underpinning framework is formed by the polarities of Light and Dark. Generally speaking, such narratives reflect on and respond with varying degrees of success and originality to Tolkien's *LOTR*. The settings for high fantasy texts are discrete 'other' or Secondary Worlds and the narrative is concerned with 'matters affecting the destiny of those worlds' (Clute 1999, 466). As the protagonists of such texts are faced with a world-changing crisis these stories are also often referred to as epic fantasy. Thus high (or epic) fantasy is the mode of the fantastic in which Robert Jordan's *WOT* can most suitably be situated.

A further important characteristic of the functioning of many high fantasy texts is its interconnected nature, the way in which 'acts ... are always meaningful, because everything connects with, or signifies, everything else. The least detail may be an omen of the future, and the smallest action may bring that future to pass' (Attebery 1980, 13-14). Manlove also addresses this point in regard to Tolkien's world building, observing that *LOTR* is 'founded on interconnections', for Tolkien believed the more 'internally consistent' and 'densely interwoven' he could make his sub-creation the more 'thoroughly realised' it became for the reader (Manlove, 1999, 54). Richard West picks up on this point as well and presents a convincing argument that in the construction of his Secondary World Tolkien had returned to an earlier form of narrative formation, 'interlacing'. West further stresses that interlace, for all its 'complexity', is 'a very natural literary form' and one that offers 'a direct reflection of the way life is lived' (1966-67, 22). Thus it is a useful technique to give a Secondary World the necessary sense of verisimilitude that gives rise to Secondary Belief in the reader.

INTERLACING:
THE PATTERNING OF A SECONDARY WORLD

A central component of Jordan's storytelling technique and a useful tool by which to evaluate his work is the mediaeval motif of *entrelacement* or interlacement.[5] This motif is a literary structural device in which several simultaneous themes are inter-woven into one large narrative, akin to the intricate knot work so characteristic of early Anglo-Saxon art. In its literary application this technique allows for separate but inter-related plot digressions and presents the writer with opportunities for the simultaneous development of a multiplicity of characters, a variety of viewpoints and themes, and a range of landscapes. In regard to *LOTR* it was George H. Thomson who pointed out that Tolkien's use of interlace allowed for a 'detailed yet panoramic view of a whole world in movement and turmoil', a structure also relied on by Jordan in the *WOT* sequence to similar effect (West 1966-67, 78).[6] West's own description of the effect of this mediaeval mode of working is worth quoting at length. He suggests that:

> interlace ... seeks to mirror the perception of flux of events in the world around us, where everything is happening at once. Its narrative line is digressive and cluttered, dividing our attention among an indefinite number of events, characters and themes, any one of which may dominate at any given time, and is often indifferent to cause and effect relationships. The paths of the characters cross, diverge, and recross, and the story passes from one to another, and then another but does not follow a single line ... Yet the apparently casual effect of interlace is deceptive; it actually has a very subtle cohesion. No part of the narrative can be removed without damage to the whole, for within any given section there are echoes of previous parts and anticipations of later ones. The mediaeval memory ... delighted in following repetitions and variations of themes, whether their different appearances were separated by scores or hundreds of pages ...

> Moreover, though events are in flux there is a pattern underlying them. In the Old French *Queste del Saint Graal* we pursue not only the Holy Grail but the ideals of knighthood through the adventures of Gawain, Bors, Lancelot, Galahad, and others, our response to any one adventure being molded ... by comparison or contrast of that adventure with the others ... while "unified" narrative generally isolates a single cause of an event to achieve a frequently powerful and intense effect, interlaced narrative usually assigns numerous causes for any event thereby reflecting the complex interrelatedness we actually see in life. (1966-67, 78-80)[7]

The use of interlace enhances the complexity of the foreground story and imparts a multi-dimensional quality to the overall narrative adding depth and solidity to characters and events, all of which works to enmesh the reader more firmly within the imaginary world. Thus, interlace forms a bridge between the reader and the fictional world that helps in the evocation of Secondary Belief. In effect, the author's shaping of words is taken up by the reader who imaginatively unfurls the narrative patterning and in so doing becomes enmeshed in the fictional world and so assists in bringing it to life. Through the technique of interlace the author draws the reader into a more intimate relationship with both the characters and the landscape itself. The sense of the Secondary World being a tangible place where the inhabitants exhibit real human joys and fears, and face real dangers is heightened and in turn evokes reader empathy and concern.

The use of interlace serves another purpose as it is one means by which successive generations of writers can braid traditional materials into their own patterns, to continuously reproduce story tapestries that, depending on the skill of the writer, can appear both comfortingly familiar, yet strangely new. A meaningful symbiosis of reader and text is formed when the writer builds a Secondary World that the imaginative reader can readily enter and sustain belief in for the duration of the tale. The phenomenon of the world wide web has created a new dynamic to interlace and to literary criticism, as it has given reader/fans the autonomy to extend the finite words of the original text by creating an infinite cyber-realm of story, one framed by the author's imaginary landscape, a topic that forms the focus of my final chapter.

In examining Jordan's work my intention throughout is to use the metaphor of patterning, weaving and even patchwork, as it dovetails nicely with the mediaeval concept of interlacing. I am also indebted to Faye Ringel's thesis on the heroic quest, in which she observed the similarity of the motif of interlace between mediaeval verse romance and modern prose fantasy:

> The working method known as *entrelacement* characterizes both the medieval verse romances and the modern prose fantasy novels. In both the interlaced narrative proceeds not in a flat and linear direction, but through separate, curving and intersecting paths. Stories of adventures are never interpolations or digressions; instead they are part of the narrative flow. Each is an essential curve in the Celtic knot work of the whole. (1979, 4)

Examining the interconnected patterning is a compelling and interesting way of looking at contemporary high fantasy fiction, especially narratives such as Jordan's *WOT*, in which, like Tolkien's *LOTR*, the 'main story ... involves many other stories, all more or less independent yet linked at many points, and occurring simultaneously' (West 1975, 22).

Robert Jordan, who once described his *WOT* as a 'fantasy War and Peace', is writing the 'history of a world, as well as a story of people' (n.a. 2000, 7). He shows much knowledge of earlier literature and of European history, and through his use of the working method of interlacing draws consciously on material from the past to create his characters and his Secondary World. But what is vibrant and distinctively interesting about his work is the manner in which he arranges this inter-textual material into new and interesting patterns.

The metaphor or image of patterning itself offers a compelling way to look at the contemporary fantasist's refashioning of traditional materials, which some critics still continue to dismiss. Yet part of the power of fantasy for readers is the ways in which it both reduplicates and adapts familiar conventions and motifs, so that the narratives become more complex in style and meaning. Although in its form and content high fantasy fiction such as Jordan's *WOT* traces over similar ground as earlier writers it still has something original and worthy to offer.

14

1 REVISITING INTERLACE: THE FANTASY AUTHOR AS STORYTELLER AND PATTERN MAKER

Modern literature is an immensely variegated fabric: its themes have been woven, and rewoven, in threads of illusion. (Wilson 1990, 123)

Writers such as Robert Jordan, who have been influenced by Tolkien's form of epic heroic fantasy, as presented in the *LOTR*, can be described not only as storytellers in the vein of the mythic or oral tradition but also as pattern seekers and, perforce, as pattern makers. As such they are writers who display a sensitive awareness of the notion that it is in the realm of the imagination that our greatest fears and greatest joys can be given satisfying and meaningful form. As in 'diverse ways myth and ritual loosen the grip of the temporal world upon the human spirit', so it is 'under the spell of the storyteller's art that the range of what is possible in this world is transcended', and those intangible qualities of life or truth can be explored more freely through the power and freedom of the seemingly fantastic (Rees and Rees 1961, 342).

Writers of fantasy traditionally construct imaginative Secondary Worlds that not only explore perennial, core philosophical concerns such as time, fate, the dualities of mortality/immortality, good/evil, and our place and meaning in the world, but, within the worlds of their fiction, bring an order to life and resolution of the kind of major societal and personal dilemmas that continue to plague the world of primary reality. Brian Attebery has written well that such resolution 'as a deliberate choice of form in a manifestly unreal setting ... says more about the ways [in which] we seek for order than our expectations of finding it in the real world' (1992, 15). Robert Jordan himself is clearly aware of this literary tradition and he uses it to advantage in his world building and in his interpretation of time, space, traditional story material and form.

Narratives such as Jordan's *WOT* continually draw on the vast story base or word-hoard of the past, both oral and written, and follow a structure that is akin to the morphology of the traditional fairy tale described by Vladimir Propp (1968): a circular quest into the unknown, testing of the hero, crossing of thresholds, supernatural intervention, confrontation, flight and establishment of a new order at home. However, in the telling, the traditional elements are infused with the author's own self-knowledge and contemporary cultural and societal influences, so that traditional 'story lives on in the reader; becomes the reader's history and spiritual domain' (Timmerman 1983, 7). Attebery explains further:

> The first fantastic literature was collective, its symbols shared by entire cultures. The motifs of traditional oral narratives, though probably the product of individual storytellers' imaginations, were selected, altered and recombined by generations of retellers, each of whom was faced with the necessity of pleasing a live audience. Thus the stories came to represent the desires and perceptions of the group, though the group may not have been consciously aware that it so perceived and desired. Myths, supernatural legends and ballads, magical folktales – all these express a group interaction ... Hence Jung speaks of the collective unconscious, as if human kind shared a single psyche. (1992, 8)

It is this rich heritage that provides the core paradigms for fantasy writers so that this ancient word-hoard is constantly being reworked into new stories and so brought forward in time, thereby retaining its relevance to the interests and concerns of the reader.

A STORY-SHAPED WORLD

The elements of story in high fantasy literature are here characterised in order to situate Jordan's *WOT* in terms of his use of the conventions of fantasy, and thus, to demonstrate how he complicates the traditional heroic quest paradigm through his use of the mediaeval literary technique of interlacement. Richard West suggested that through the use of interlacement the imaginary world is given a greater sense of reality and he characterises some of the features by which this is achieved:

> No single protagonist but a great many individual stories that cross one another; coherence among the interwoven stories; the appearance of a pattern behind the flux of events; recurring themes and motifs providing aesthetic and intellectual satisfaction; the events of the imaginary world gaining the illusion of depth and solidity by their mutual interaction and weight of detail ... The effect of what might be termed openendedness, whereby the reader has the impression that the story has an existence outside the confines of the book so that the author could have begun earlier or ended later, if he chose. (West 1975, 90)

The sense that there are many other stories to tell in connection with the imaginary world as presented is enhanced by constant reference to parts of a vast historical background story. For example, in Jordan's conceptualisation of a cosmology which forms a repeating cycling of seven Ages, the reader is aware that the events of the present Third Age not only look back to the past but are always endlessly weaving towards the future.

Jordan can be seen to be turning back to Tolkien's use of interlacing in the *LOTR*, as it is the form of narrative most able to accommodate the teeming and various elements of his imaginary world, in which the 'history, geography, and cultures' of many peoples 'cross one another which such complexity that we have the impression that the fantasy has life-like depth and solidity' (West, 1975, 84). Although in high fantasy, it is typical for the quest story of the hero to be interwoven into the lives and fates of other people and to be linked to the survival of the depicted world, the panoramic sweep of Jordan's epic-style work, and the eclectic nature of his carefully interwoven traditional material make it a particularly rich example of a contemporary application of an older narrative technique.

PATTERN MAKING IN FANTASY LITERATURE

Overall, the pattern in high fantasy concerns a quest for order and harmony in an imaginary world, which is pitted against the forces of dark that threaten to disrupt it. Typically, it depicts a dualistic conflict between the forces of Light and Dark and the story begins at a time when the balance is in jeopardy due to the shadow side of the world gaining in power. The catalyst that triggers the encroachment of this darker side of life is inevitably caused by some form of human folly, typically connected to greed, lust for power over others, arrogance, material gain and/or the persistent human desire for immortality on earth, and thus supplies the impetus for the hero's quest.

It is common for the events that initially brought about the imbalance to be revealed in a historical background story, thus distancing the blame for this catastrophe from the time frame of the current story and its protagonists. For instance, in the *LOTR*, Sauron's long-ago forging of the One Ring that down the ages becomes a vehicle for unleashed human power and corruption. In Jordan's *WOT*, in the Age of Legends, a group of Aes Sedai heedlessly sought to enhance their channelling abilities and so brought about a dangerous thinning in a section of the Great Pattern. It is through their over-reaching for power that the Dark One's prison was weakened, and from that time on he once again began to influence the world.

By contrast, in Le Guin's original *Earthsea* trilogy it is the main protagonist, Ged, who upsets the equilibrium of the archipelago through pride and arrogance and chants an unlawful spell to summon the dead, inadvertently releasing his own Shadow self. But when Le Guin revisits Earthsea some twenty years later in *The Other Wind* (published 2001), the setting is at a time when the equilibrium so vital to the survival of the imaginary world is again endangered and to account for this she introduces a previously unknown background story. It is revealed that ancient wizards of the Archipelago in their desire to defeat death had, long before Ged's lifetime, built a spell-wrought stone

wall beyond which they could 'live ... in the spirit forever'. (*Wind*, 228)
Foolishly, their actions brought into being the stagnant Dry Land of the
Dead, and so caused a dangerous schism between the human spirit and
the natural world. In this shadowy, artificial realm the spirits of the dead
are denied their proper dispersal within the natural world, creating a
dire disruption to the necessary and integrative cycle of birth, life and
death. Thus all of these authors posit stories in which cause and effect
are linked across eons of time to provide an interweaving of past and
present that is of cosmic significance in the depicted worlds.

In regard to immortality the consensus among the writers of fantasy
is that the hunger for eternal life is far from desirable, and that the
seeking of it involves an irreversible forfeiting of one's soul to the
Shadow. Yet in these stories the forces of dark can never be totally
vanquished since they are depicted as always being inherent in human
nature, two sides of the same coin, for in an imaginary world that pivots
on the notion of balance, there cannot be light without shadow, and this
underpinning dualistic pattern of fantasy provides much of the possible
and, indeed, necessary narrative tension. Consistent with the emphasis
on balance, the realm of high fantasy is one that privileges the natural
world and places humanity, not above, but within the vast social and
ecological web of life. As it is human action that causes the imbalance in
nature, it is up to humanity to effect a solution, which seems to
constitute a literary rejection of Divine Purpose or the trope of the *Deus
ex Machina*. The heroic quest to save the depicted world must be
achieved through an earned journey and must display plausible cause
and effect within the logic of the fictional world, throughout the
narrative. For the reader an unexpected, convenient resolution wrought
by an outside God figure (the author) would cheapen the worth of the
heroic journey and undermine the integrity of the (imaginary) human
world. Of his own sub-creation Jordan has stated firmly that the
protagonists can expect no 'miracles' or intervention from the 'Creator'
who 'shaped the world and set the rules, but does not interfere'. Instead,
as mentioned in the introduction, the human inhabitants of the Wheel
world must fix their own mistakes (Noren 1995). (Similarly in Le Guin,
Ged must right the wrongs he has committed.)

Some of the Wheel world inhabitants do appear to live within the prescripts of the Great Pattern, and so can be described as keepers of the word of the 'Creator', and perhaps they also provide a covert, persuasive textual voice for the authorial point of view. For example, in the world of the Wheel, the gentle gypsy-like and nomadic Travelling people (*Tuatha'an*) accept death as part of the fate of living and believe that all things have a cyclic pattern and must grow and fall like leaves. If attacked, they raise no hand in self-defence, nor do they bear weapons. Instead, they accept utterly the will of the Pattern. Their ancient and much-revered philosophical ideology is known as the 'Way of the Leaf' and is in keeping with Jordan's stated concept of reincarnation in their world:

> The leaf lives its appointed time, and does not struggle against the wind that carries it away. The leaf does no harm and finally falls to nourish new leaves. So it should be with all men. And women. (*EOTW*, 370)

Such philosophy is also akin to that of Le Guin's mystic Master Patterner of Earthsea, who intuits the future from the leaves, or from designs of twigs, sand and pebbles in the sacred grove on the island of Roke, a place where even the great and ancient trees that hold all knowledge of the pattern of life, live and die again and again, and will do so until the end of time. The Patterner explains that 'what goes too long unchanged destroys itself. The forest is forever because it dies and dies and so lives'. (*Tales from Earthsea*, 254) The philosophy of both these fantasy worlds suggests an acceptance of a fated pattern that weaves towards change, an allotted time span and a rejection of immortality. Yet in the Wheel world Jordan also uses the passivity of the *Tuatha'an*, which leaves them open to extortion and cold-blooded slaughter, to emphasise the fact that in a flawed world their idealistic 'Way of the Leaf' offers no (personal) solution to the encroachment of the Dark Lord. In this way the author suggests that, in a cosmic pattern that is woven from Light and Dark, the necessary change to heal the world cannot be achieved through inactive acceptance. Thus he reinforces the urgency of the fated quest of the three *ta'veren* youths, whose life-threads have been spun out (fated) by the Cosmic Loom specifically to bring necessary change to the pattern of the Age.

Weaving of threads is an old destiny motif going back to Greek, Roman and Germanic mythology and, despite the diversity and evolution of these cultures and languages, they have all retained basic ideas of fate as being personified by a trio of women (Wyrd, the Norns, the Parcae, or the Morai) who control the life-threads of all mortals, a concept of a destined pattern for existence that has survived many literary permutations without losing its potency. Jordan, with his concept of an inexorable Cosmic Loom spinning a Great Pattern from the life-threads of all living creatures and a metaphor for time itself, is drawing on an age-old association with mortals' fate that is common to both fantasy and realist literary texts. In regard to the inhabitants of the Wheel world the frequently-voiced folk saying, 'the Wheel weaves as the Wheel wills', reveals a popular belief in, and resignation to, the dictates of the Pattern or fate. (*EOTW*, 92) And even the powerful magus figures, despite their considerable knowledge of old prophecies, cannot totally read the pattern before it is spun, as shown by Moiraine Aes Sedai's frequent acceptance that an incident or a person has now become 'woven into the pattern', and not merely by chance, following an event she has not expected or foreseen. (*EOTW,* 140) An example of this occurs in the initial volume when Egwene and Thom unexpectedly join in the three *ta'veren* youths' departure from Emond's Field. (*EOTW,* 140-142) This recurring motif also allows Jordan (the pattern maker) another discreetly insistent and authoritarian voice within the text that works to instil in the reader's mind the sense of purpose or a higher design, behind the flux of events. Such a higher purpose or design is further strengthened by Jordan's use of an interconnected motif of game-playing within the texts.

THE PATTERN OF LITERARY GAMES

The ancient games played by characters within the world of the Wheel, and which form an analogy for the greater and cosmic 'game of life' between the forces of Light and Dark, perform a pivotal role at both a physical and a more metaphysical level in the Jordan texts. In this matter he is drawing on the earlier tradition of literary games, a narrative device employed in some mediaeval narrative literature. A good example is *Gawain and the Green Knight*, which is structured through a 'complex network of overlapping, interlocked games' to form 'an endless knot, like the pentangle design on Gawain's shield', and that, despite comic moments, function to test Gawain's pride and his seemingly incorruptible code of honour and truth (Leyerle 1975, 57). Leyerle explains that:

> the seeming paradox of serious play is widely encountered in the literature and culture of the Middle Ages. Examples are fortune's roulette wheel, the dance of death, tournaments, the mortal chess game, and the dance of the seven deadly sins. (1975, 60)[1]

Jordan's interpretation of literary games presents a variation on the concept of the mortal chess game so that, while he is writing within a recognisable literary 'paradigmatic structure', he is able to tailor events and meaning within it to his own specific purposes, and so to engage in a form of word game:

> Such literary games allow great scope for individual expression because they establish patterns that are widely understood and therefore allow great scope for individual variation. In this process of variation the paradigm of the game tends to be changed and developed ... because poetic play allows for great freedom with a given form and almost a limitless number of forms. (Leyerle 1975, 68-9)

Thus a theory of literature, one developed on the 'model of game-playing', is a fruitful means of textual analysis. It recognises that while a narrative paradigm is identifiable by the literary use of 'regularly-occurring elements' and rules, they are to be seen as 'descriptive, not prescriptive' and therefore, over time, a succession of writers are relatively free to rework them into individualistic but still recognisable traditional patterns. (Leyerle 1975, 68)[2]

A full analysis of game theory lies beyond the scope of this work as much of it is viewed through a sociological, not a literary lens. But it is pertinent to note that Johan Huizinga, in his influential study of play elements in culture, posited the hypothesis that the 'great archetypal activities of human society are all permeated with play', and suggested that one of the main characteristics of play is that it creates order by establishing 'rules' that are 'absolutely binding', so that if the rules are broken 'it spoils the game' (Huizinga 1970, 22, 29-30). In a literary application of his theory, a parallel can be drawn with the fantasy writers' building of Secondary Worlds that are maintained through order and balance, worlds wherein the catalyst for the heroic quest is caused by a breaking of societal rules that plummets the depicted landscape into a state of disorder and chaos.

At the level of narrative construction Jordan as master patterner sometimes uses an entire volume in his sequence as a type of literary chess board, in order to set up moves for the major pieces to be played out in the following volume; in particular books eight and ten follow this format. In the latter, *COT*, he concentrates on chronicling social intrigues and transformations which, at least on the surface, appear to do little to advance the primary plot, and little of the action is brought to full completion. He characteristically leaves the reader with intriguing hints of future developments, as with Mat's long-awaited entanglement with the Daughter of the Nine Moons, Egwene's kidnapping by the sisters of the White Tower, when under siege by her army, and Rand's negotiations with the Seanchan invaders. (In book eleven, *KOD*, some of the narrative threads are resolved and the author seems to be weaving more tightly towards the Last Battle and the long awaited finale of the sequence, although his plot twists and turns are as devious as those of the fox-like *Aelfinn* and snake-like *Eelfinn*.) This authorial manipulation in turn is repeated by the actions of various protagonists and antagonists within the texts, and in the fashion of interlacement, linked to the higher purpose of the narrative as shown by the following examples.

A commonly played Jordanesque board game is known as 'Stones' in which the major piece 'The Fisher' is analogous to the legend of the Fisher King and is in turn linked to Rand as the Dragon Reborn. Moridin, an ancient and powerful servant of the Dark, has played this game for centuries, and as he studies the pieces on the board he draws a distinct parallel between the central figure 'The Fisher' and Rand, musing that whilst 'The Fisher' piece awaits his move, in the 'greater game' al Thor [Rand] already moved to his wishes'. It is revealed that 'The Fisher was always worked as a man, a bandage blinding his eyes and one hand pressed to his side, a few drops of blood dripping through his fingers'. (*POD*, 34) In a mirroring of this figure, Rand bears a half-healed and often bleeding wound in his side inflicted during an encounter with Ba'alzamon, one of the Forsaken. Furthermore, Perrin, in a prophetic dream has seen Rand dressed as a beggar with bandaged eyes, thus tying him even more closely to the figure of the board game. (*SR*, 898) His viewing also resonates with an earlier vision of Min's where she saw a 'beggar's staff' swirling around Rand's head. (*EOTW*, 216) As will be discussed in the chapters on the hero figures, the prophecies of the Dragon further tie Rand to the legend of the Fisher King. The mysterious figure of Moridin, who slips in and out of the Great Pattern, and therefore in and out of Time, may be a surrogate for the Dark Lord. But he could also be representative of the shadow side of Jordan, who as author/creator stands outside the Pattern and firmly believes that he is in complete control of the lives of his characters.

Another popular children's game in the Wheel world, known as 'Snakes and Foxes', particularly favoured by the orphan boy Olver, is analogous to human dealings with the slippery *Aelfinn* and *Eelfinn*, who are encountered by stepping into their strange realms by means of twisted Redstone doorframe *ter'angreal*. Their untrustworthy natures are suggested by their appearance, as both foxes and snakes bring to mind traits of great animal cunning and deviousness. As it seems highly likely that Olver will prove to be the reincarnation of the legendary hero, Gaidal Cain, he too, like Moridin, will have participated in this game in other lives, so there may come a moment when he discards the naïve belief that he can win by adhering to the stipulated rules.

Adults are well aware that it is a game that can never be won except by breaking the rules (which are never explained), and it is Birgitte Silverbow (a legendary hero) who supplies us with the formula for doing so. She cryptically explains that what is required to win the game is 'courage to strengthen, fire to blind, music to daze, iron to bind'– magical sounding words with the distinct ring of a chanted spell – and that the game itself is a 'remembrance of old dealings' with the *Aelfinn* and *Eelfinn*. (*SR*, 466) With the addition of light, fire, music and iron are all items forbidden to be carried when humans seek answers from these strange creatures. Yet their use, against the prescripts of the treaty (and the rules of the game), perhaps holds the key for the future rescue of Moiraine. For in *KOD* the long-awaited contents of her letter to Thom suggest that following her disappearance she may not have died, but has become trapped in the realm of the *Aelfinn* and *Eelfinn*, and Gandalf-like may return in a more highly evolved state.

On a more worldly level, the various nations of Jordan's land are depicted at a time of great political and social flux, highlighting the ever-changing patterns of the boundaries and ruling classes of the nation states. As the sequence unfolds he increasingly foregrounds the petty political intrigues that are rife throughout the various royal courts by demonstrating the political plotting, lies, half-truths and manoeuvring for advantage between powerful families of the realms, activities which are deployed by means of the 'Game of Houses'. Rand has the unenviable task of uniting the feuding and fragmented nations, as their aid is sorely needed in the lead-up to the Last Battle, and the political 'Game of Houses' dramatically foregrounds the difficulties he faces, and also the way in which ethics and loyalties, as in contemporary life, can become warped in the scrabble for individual gain and power.

Overarching it all is the cosmic game of life, the eternal conflict between the powers of Light and Dark which, in the world of the Wheel, is repeatedly enacted on a temporal level through the use of human surrogates. As Ishamael, one of the Forsaken, claims:

> this struggle had gone on since the Creation, an endless
> war between the Great Lord and the Creator using human

surrogates ... [and] in the past, the Creator's champion [had been] made a creature of the Shadow and raised up as the Shadow's champion. (*LOC*, 179)

Semirhage, another of the Forsaken, and a powerful servant of the Dark Lord, is aware that his 'Chosen were no more than pieces on the board; they might be Counselors or Spies, but they were still pieces'. (*LOC*, 194) Is this the final irony for humans in the world of the Wheel – a realisation that they are but pawns to be manipulated to play out the moves of an eternal conflict between the greater polarities of Light and Dark? Such a bleak, nihilistic outlook denies any true spark of life, of aspiration, or pathos and ecstasy, so it is far more plausible that the image of the board-game allows the author to give concrete form to the intangible, archetypal impulses of good and evil that appear to inform human nature. The interconnected strands of game-play also provide the author with a subtle means of reinforcing the concept of an underlying fated patterning to his depicted universe, one that is largely beyond the control of the human characters.

TELLING TALES: STORY AND EMBEDDED STORY

Jordan's narrative is formed from a complex interlacing of stories. (This is where Jordan's genius lies, for his mastery of plot is what hooks his fans.) The focal narrative of the world-saving quest proceeds through a variety of interweaving stories (i.e. the journeys, actions, and the development of the primary and secondary characters), these often occurring simultaneously, so that the events gain lifelike depth and solidity by their mutual interaction. Rosemond Tuve explains:

> events connected by *entrelacement* are not just juxtaposed; they are interlaced, and when we get back to the first character he is not where we left him as we finished the episode. [We return] not to precisely what we left, but to something we understand differently because of what we have seen since. (1966, 369, 370)

In other words, the reader's conception of the world and of the characters is built up by a close following of the many strands of the story, so that information gained from the events in one strand is woven continuously into and alters another, as they cross and recross. In turn, these stories are threaded through with a vast historical background story, and complicated even further by the addition of story-like prophecies, dreams and foretellings.

Storytelling is seen as an art both inside and outside of the texts. The reader is deeply engrossed in reading a story in which the characters often are listening to stories; together, they gradually piece together the history and legends of the Wheel world. Thus, on an imaginative level, the reader is drawn into the depicted world and shares in the inhabitants' emotional reactions. In a similar fashion as the main protagonists take up the quest and journey away from their known setting the reader, too, is exposed to the wider world of the Wheel through their eyes, and is similarly affected by the wonder they express as they traverse new landscapes, and meet an array of different peoples and creatures whom they had hitherto considered to be make-believe. Jordan has said that he wanted 'his characters, like Candine, to see their world through fresh eyes' (Lilley 2002). As the characters of the Secondary World are 'captivated by the marvels of their own world ... [so] their response ... heightens and deepens our own' (Senior 1995, 118). A good example occurs when the reader vicariously shares Rand's sense of strangeness and wonder when he first encounters 'Ogier and Trollocs. Myddraael, and things from the dark corners of midnight tales ... stories walking in the flesh', and he realises that 'all the stories are true'. (*GH*, 30) Similarly in Le Guin's Earthsea, as Arren journeys to the far reaches with Ged, his 'joy of fulfilment that was like pain' at his sighting of the flight of 'dragons on the wind of the morning', is an emotional response to a marvel in his world that also catches at the heart of the reader. (*Farthest*, 147)

Thus a connecting thread between the Primary and Secondary Worlds is formed by what William Senior refers to as a 'yoking of the reader's experience to that of the characters'. For their world is one of discovery as well so that as each character uncovers the new and the marvellous, his or her reaction is passed on to the reader. Senior further explains that an 'appreciation of the marvellous world must be crafted through both external and internal expressions of wonder', and stresses the importance that Tolkien had placed on this dual emotional response to the depicted world, and his belief that the 'evocation of wonder' provided one of the 'operating principles of fantasy in connecting the primary and secondary worlds and thus involving the reader's perceptions' (1995, 120,118, 115). It is the interweaving of internal and external responses to the unfolding of marvels in the Secondary World that helps to sustain the reader's own sense of wonder and adds to his or her pleasure in the story.

Senior also points out that 'wonder, however, is a two-edged sword' and that not all fantasists wield it with enough caution. Internal wonder must be 'filigreed into the structure of things' within the Secondary World. It cannot be successfully achieved through an over-abundance of 'prodigies at which the characters ooh and ahh in bathetic reverence'. In the more formulaic end of the genre, the danger is that the use of 'preestablished or pre-approved conventions' render 'the things that produce wonder in other stories ... [to] windowdressings'. In other words, for the reader there is no sense of the characters engaging with their world on more than just a superficial level, or of exposure to unknown events and marvels that have relevance to, and underscore, the greater task at hand: the saving of their world. Instead, the landscape, despite a profusion of seemingly 'wondrous beings, objects and events' remains a playground of make-believe, for the writer has failed to inject any illusion of real life or to convince the reader of its validity (1995, 121-2).

Jordan sets up a field for fruitful contemplation of the interplay between story and life. He regarded himself first and foremost as a storyteller:

> When it gets down to the core of it, I still feel that connection with the wandering storyteller, the guy who strolls into town and sets up in the village common ... and

> he tells some stories. And if he tells entertaining stories, he
> gets dinner. (n.a. 2000, 76)

Various stories embedded throughout his own narrative highlight the importance of story-telling, especially since, within the texts, they provide one of the major tactics for plot advancement. Thus the ambiguity between the boundaries of 'story' and 'reality', already apparent in the sub-creation of the world of the Wheel, along with reader acceptance of and affinity to it, is repeated within the texts themselves. In the initial volume of the sequence (*EOTW*), Two Rivers folk, hobbit-like, delight in the boundless repertoire of stories of myth and legend, concerning romance, talismanic objects, battles and heroic deeds, which are usually recited by visiting gleemen. Thom, the gleeman who is a pivotal character in the texts and a surrogate for Jordan (as discussed in the next chapter), promises to regale them with 'wondrous stories of strange people and strange lands, of the Green Man, of Warders and Trollocs, of Ogier and Aiel'. (*EOTW*, 51) The villagers, too, savour the news of the outside world, gleaned from the gossip of visiting pedlars and merchants' guards:

> Ghealdan. Tar Valon. The very names were strange and
> exciting ... Aes Sedai and wars and false Dragons: those
> were the stuff of stories told late at night in front of the
> fireplace, with one candle making strange shapes on the
> wall and the wind howling against the shutters. (*EOTW*,
> 39)

But when their small village of Emond's Field is attacked by Trollocs and Fades and they discover an Aes Sedai priestess from the fabled White Tower in their midst, the age-old stories, and 'made-up creatures' from stories suddenly turn out to have an undreamed-of presence in real life. (*EOTW*, 49) Demonic creatures that generations of village children had believed only resided in the horror of nightmares are found to actually exist, and, like the monster Grendel, in *Beowulf*, to be abroad in the waking world. Furthermore, Moiraine Aes Sedai reminds them of their ancient blood ties to the long fallen kingdom of Manetheren, and of past heroic deeds performed by their people when they had fought beneath the 'Red Eagle banner'. She thus scorns them now as being reduced to 'little people squabbling for the right to hide like rabbits'. (*EOTW*, 132; 131) In a voice that holds the 'sound of cold tears', she recites the forgotten tale of their ancestors' heroic last stand against the Trolloc hordes at Emond's Field:

> Trolloc dead and the corpses of human renegades piled up in mounds, but always more scrambled over those charnel heaps in waves of death that had no end. There could be but one finish. No man or woman who had stood beneath the banner of the Red Eagle at that day's dawning still lived when night fell. The sword that could not be broken was shattered. (*EOTW*, 134)

This tale in its turn stirs old and buried memories, floating disturbing fragments of story to the surface of the villagers' minds. As a result they can no longer sustain the view of themselves as being just 'honest farmers and shepherds and craftsmen', simple 'Two Rivers folk'. (*EOTW*, 131) Ironically, the main protagonists, Rand (a farmer), Mat (son of a blacksmith), and Perrin (an apprentice blacksmith), repeatedly remark that their adventures are nothing like those of the ancient heroes in stories, and that they themselves are not heroes, while through their very actions and deeds, the reader is aware that they are actually growing to fit the 'traditional' heroic mould, and so to enter the realm of on-going story like the legendary adventurer Jain Farstrider. In this fashion, through the gleeman, Moiraine and later her fellow sisters of the White Tower, fragments of the vast background story are gradually revealed and interlaced into the present time frame as needed to progress the focal story, so that, together, the inhabitants of the imaginary world and the reader gain in knowledge and understanding of the Jordan world and of its complex and layered history.

Archaic prophecies, dreams and visions, snatches of legends and songs, and scraps of ancient manuscripts tell other pieces of story and can also provide tantalising clues to the pattern of the future – puzzles to be pieced together or unravelled, by both reader and protagonists alike. The cryptic prophecies of the Dragon (found in the Karentheon cycle, in particular) which are akin to the ancient motif of riddling, are open to a variety of interpretations, suggesting that there are different outcomes possible for the inhabitants of the Wheel world, depending on which set of interpretations are acted upon. Indeed, one of the few known Shadow prophecies states boldly that the Dragon Reborn has two choices, one leading to eternal life, the other to eternal death:

> The man who channels stands alone.
> He gives his friends for sacrifice.
> Two roads before him, one to death beyond dying,
> One to life eternal.
> Which will he choose? Which will he choose?
> (*GH*, 105)

The two roads refer to Rand's options of choosing to fight for or against the Dark Lord. Should he be persuaded to take the path to 'life eternal' (immortality) he will break the known Pattern of existence and, as a consequence, plunge the Wheel world into Shadow.

These words are scrawled in human blood by a Trolloc on a wall in the dungeons at Dal Farra Keep, following the cold-blooded slaughter of prisoners and guards, and are a dramatic and chilling reminder to the protagonists and the reader of the knife-edge on which humanity stands, and the heavy burden the Wheel weaves for its heroic figure, the Dragon Reborn. Already in the recent past several false dragons produced by the Great Pattern have taken the prophecies to relate to themselves, and their vanity has resulted in chaos and the loss of many lives. The people are increasingly afraid of any man proclaiming himself as the messiah, or true Dragon Reborn. And while the Aes Sedai of the White Tower are determined that the current Dragon incarnate shall be guided by their interpretations of the Karentheon cycle, and follow their path towards the much prophesied Last Battle, the hero Rand perversely evades such control and seeks to interpret destiny in his own way, increasing the sense of fear that he will take the wrong path. Through the scattering of such clues, the author constructs a pattern that guides the interpretation. The reader, too, is thus encouraged to construct meaning from the fragments, thereby to assist in the weaving-together of the pattern of the text, and so is emotionally drawn into the world instead of remaining a detached, passive observer of events. Timmerman suggests that in this way the 'story' becomes the reader's 'own story to the extent that his imagination interpenetrates the framework of the story and lives for a time in the world of the story' (Timmerman 1983, 8). So, in his or her response the reader vicariously participates in the quest of the protagonist.

Another important variation of embedded story is used by the author to anticipate events to come, providing further clues in the pattern to be unraveled. Rand's young female companions, Min and Egwene, offer small windows into the future through aura readings and prophetic dreams, as do the infrequent and spontaneous foretellings of the Aes Sedai. All of these extra-sensory readings produce vivid flashes of envisioned stories that cannot always immediately be understood by the reader or the inhabitants of the Wheel world, but that fall into context as the narrative unfolds. In the depicted world they afford pre-knowledge of 'pieces of the pattern', both good and evil, that are set and cannot be altered. (*EOTW*, 215) By contrast, the Dreamwalkers of the Aiel tribes have dream-visions that function as precautionary warnings of events that the pattern is weaving towards which could be altered – providing segments of story that the protagonists appear to have the freewill to rewrite the outcome of or to erase from within the text. (*Companion*, 299-300) An example is their dream about 'rain coming from a bowl', and the 'snares and pitfalls' surrounding the finding of the legendary 'Bowl of the Winds', which reveals two possible outcomes, and offers a cryptic clue to aid in its recovery: 'If the right hands pick it up, they will find a treasure perhaps as great as the bowl. In the wrong hands, the world is doomed. The key to finding the bowl is to find the one who is no longer there'. (*LOC*, 448)

Jordan thus utilises the tension between the pattern of fate already woven and the choices offered that can sometimes alter the weave.

Jordan's narrative, like that of Tolkien's *LOTR*, 'creates an infinite series of echoes and anticipations, [clues] by which the work gains coherence', which is one of the characteristics of interlacement (West 1966-67, 84).

THE PATTERNING OF LIGHT AND DARK: PHILOSOPHICAL CORE

In the tightly patterned sub-creations of the fantasist, the basic framework is usually not so complex, although it does not follow that the narratives themselves are simplistic. As outlined earlier, they deal with large and perplexing philosophical questions about the human condition and have strong moral purpose. At its core the narrative typically is built around a never-ending battle between representations of the abstract dualities of good/evil; there is general consensus among high fantasy writers that both are inherent and indeed necessary components in the invented world. In the case of Jordan's world of the Wheel – and as also depicted in Le Guin's *Earthsea* – some equilibrium between the two is crucial if the pattern of existence is to be maintained. It is usually shown to be the responsibility of particular characters (i.e. Jordan's Aes Sedai, and Le Guin's wizards of Roke) to keep a balance between them.

Along the way the assumption of absolute good is often shown to be as dangerous as the evil it fights against. Jordan clearly reveals this through his portrayal of the sect of pseudo-religious zealots, the warrior-priests known as Whitecloaks, who in their pursuit of what they perceive to be absolute good, and due, too, to their narrow and blinkered approach to life, actually foster evil, and perform cruel and murderous acts in the name of the Light. They have attitudes similar to those of Reformation-period Protestants/Puritans, being moralistic, militaristic, heavy-handed, bigoted and fanatical. They must parallel for many readers the Puritans and other much later splinter groups such as the Klu Klux Klan or Hitler's early Brown Shirts. Thus Jordan, in looking at their 'excess', is inviting readers to reflect on the Puritan inheritance in America, which has continued repercussions in contemporary society, although it is certainly not new for a society to do 'evil' in the name of good.

Even the main protagonist Rand, the Dragon Reborn and champion of the Light, in the lead up to his final battle with the Dark Lord must harden himself to use others against their will, and to hurt personal friends for his own purposes, as his focus is increasingly upon his destined role to save the world from the Shadow. At one point his friend and companion Egwene sadly observes that she has the 'feeling he doesn't see people anymore, only pieces on a Stones board' to be manipulated. (*SR*, 577) (Rand himself is later referred to by Moridin, a minion of the Dark, as a piece on a cosmic games-board, a point to be enlarged on in a later section.) As often proves to be the case with Jordan, and other fantasy writers, the duality of Light/Dark becomes blurred by ambiguity, perhaps suggesting that both are also ever-present in the Primary World and that the continual task for us, like the hero figures of story, is to find not so much the right balance between them, as to somehow identify their core purposes.

PATTERNING THE FANTASTIC FROM THE FAMILIAR

In the creation of a Secondary World a fantasy writer draws on the Primary World but will seek to change elements of our reality. Such a writer uses 'the fantastic mode, to produce impossibilities, and the mimetic, to reproduce the familiar' (Attebery 1992, 16-7). Thus the 'story itself is a window into another world with a quasi-existence of its own' (Pratchett 2000, 159), and it is both like and unlike reality. In the words of Rosemary Jackson:

> Fantasy re-combines and inverts the real, but it does not escape it: it exists in a parasitical or symbiotic relation to the real. The fantastic cannot exist independently of that 'real' world which it seems to find so frustratingly finite. (1988, 20)

The fantasy mode must have some recognisable point of reference to the Primary World in order to be understood. As these stories in fantastic guise actually mirror very real concerns of day-to-day human existence, although they are not perceived by the reader to be 'real', they are found paradoxically to be incredibly true to experience. Thus fantasy literature is not merely 'escapist' but rather through a braiding of the strange and the comfortingly familiar offers its readers illumination of the Primary World through releasing them from its confines. Fantasy is not so much an escape from reality as an escape to an imaginative realm from which the reader may emerge to view the mundane world with fresh vision.

As Tolkien wrote in his essay *On Fairy-Stories*, '[the word] spell, means both a story told, and a formula of power over living men', a combination which strongly suggests that a successfully constructed fantasy story has the ability to hold an audience spellbound. Moreover, in the use of traditional motifs and archetypes (i.e. the quest, the hero, the magus, legendary creatures, numinous objects and magical realms), he believed 'it is the effect produced *now* by these old things in stories as they are ... [that is of importance as] they open a door on Other Time, and if we pass through ... we stand outside our own time, outside Time itself, maybe' (1964, 32-3). In a similar vein of thought, Mircea Eliade had stated that performing acts which form a repetition of archetypes automatically removes us from the present time and into another sphere as 'any repetition of an archetypal gesture, suspends duration, abolishes profane time and participates in mythical time' (1954, 36). In other words, we willingly enter the realm of 'story-time' and, if the writer succeeds, empirical disbelief in what we find there is overcome.

Tolkien believes that the skill of the writer 'produces a Secondary World into which both designer and spectator can enter, to the satisfaction of their senses while they are inside' (1964, 48). While it is the writer's use of traditional motifs, formulae and archetypes that initially can help to trigger this state of mind, more importantly, it is the skills of the particular storyteller that must then work to keep us entranced for the duration of the narrative. The success of this will depend on how the writer utilises the traditional material and uniquely designs the narrative. For although in the wonderful realm of 'story-time' an enormous range of things become possible, and there is 'freedom from the domination of observed fact', these events must accord with the ground laws of the sub-creation, if some consistency of inner reality is to be sustained and if it is to command Secondary Belief. (Tolkien 1964, 44)

Like other writers of this narrative mode Jordan utilises a synthesis, an eclectic selection of cross-cultural material and traditional motifs, in order to create resonance and a rich layering of meaning. But in his conceptualisation of a Secondary World he retains some physical relevance or points of reference to our own, and peoples it with figures who reflect a range of recognisably human emotions, morals and motivations. Otherwise the construct would be rendered meaningless, and the affairs of its inhabitants would evoke little or no reader empathy or concern. As was also observed by Ann Swinfen, while the Secondary World needs this similarity of structure, 'physical laws of nature and vegetation need not be the same ... but they should have a reasonable cause-and-effect relationship'. And that in a Secondary World the 'fundamental physical laws of gravity, heat and cold, dark and light', are usually observed (1984, 77).

Thus, having built an imaginary world from recognisable components of ours, so that the landscape, flora and fauna, despite exotic additions, appear reasonably familiar, and impart greater depth and resonance to our 'collective unconscious' through the mining of elements of traditional story, Jordan has added another layering to the structure. Within the sub-creation, he fabricates a seemingly 'factual' yet entirely imaginary though substantial history, along with elaborate traditions of valued societal mores and customs, and a wealth of colourful regional myths and legends for the several peoples. So there is an intricate interweaving, patterning within patterning, or of worlds within worlds, like the array of inter-related cogs and wheels in the back of an old clock, which together create a way of marking the intangible flow of time, and in the narrative create, alike, both a sense of time and place. The invention of such detail for the Secondary World further adds to its credibility and through its historical and mythological depth imparts a larger-than-life quality to the main protagonists.

The writing of 'spin-off' short tales that provide prequels to the existing sequence of texts further deepens and strengthens the internal framework of historic/mythical reference. In relation to his *WOT* sequence, Jordan has written a short piece titled, *The Strike at Shayol Ghul* (1996), which reports on the finding of long-lost historical manuscripts providing details of events prior to and during the 'Breaking of the World' that destroyed the Age of Legends some 3000 years before the depicted time-frame. He has also written another short story titled *New Spring* (1998), which tells of Rand's mentor/guide Moiraine Aes Sedai's initial meeting and mental bonding with her warder Lan (1998).[3] As suggested by West, it is the 'digressive and cluttered' narrative line of the interlace technique, where 'the narrator implies that there are numerous events he has not had time to tell' that lends itself to threads of the story being taken up at a later date:

> We feel that we have interrupted the chaotic activity of the world at a certain point and followed a selection from it for a time, and that after we leave, it continues on its own random path. The author, or someone else, may perhaps take up the threads of the story again later and add to it at beginning, middle or end. (West 1966-67, 79)

Although Le Guin's original *Earthsea* trilogy – which she has described as 'a pattern in the form of a long spiral' – is not as intricately interlaced as the Jordan texts, the richness of her material has enabled her, Tolkien-like, to revisit her imaginary world, and to write both prequels and sequels to her original work (*Tales* and *Wind*), (Le Guin 1989, 41).[4] There is also the sense that there is much more to discover about the Archipelago and its various peoples. In Jordan's Wheel world the teeming diversity of the depicted age with its enormous cast of characters and nations suggests that there are an infinity of things about the world that could be expanded upon. In the cyber-construction of Jordan's *WOT*, the fans' role-play gaming and their fan fiction writings based on the Wheel world demonstrate well just how they can take up the his narrative at different points of time and either expand a particular thread in his work or integrate new ones of their own invention into the original pattern (as is discussed in the chapter on cyber storytelling).

In addition to the prequels mentioned, Jordan, in collaboration with Teresa Patterson, has also produced a series companion for his sequence, *The World of Robert Jordan's 'The Wheel of Time'*, thereby providing an extensive 'compilation of the world's [complex] geography, sociology, and history' (2000, xiii). As with Tolkien's embedded narrative in *LOTR*, 'The Red Book of Westmarch', Jordan's own companion volume is compiled from putative manuscripts and surviving fragments of writings that contain records of the world of the Wheel. Thus the reader is made more fully aware that the current *WOT* volumes concern but a small section of the stories that could be told about the history of the Wheel world. As well as this, the documented history of the depicted world is designed to impart such an air of context, of consistency and of authenticity that it might very well relate to some forgotten but real or actual historical epoch of the world in which we live. Moreover, in an unusual move for a high fantasy writer, Jordan's Secondary World is not named, and as at times the chronicler addresses the reader in a direct and intimate manner, it seems analogous with our own reality, some other and plausible echo of Earth's own history. Thus there is a continual blurring between 'story' and 'real life', by which means the author seeks to foster credibility and the reader's willingness to sustain Secondary Belief.

Not only does the use of earlier motifs and archetypes enrich such narratives by linking them firmly to a vast storied European past, but they also provide significant sign-postings for the reader. For the reader who likes traditional patterning, there is also the pleasure of recognising these recurring elements. An excellent example is Jordan's character Thom Merriman, the gleeman who from his age, white hair, beard and name is strongly reminiscent of a Merlin figure. The use of this archetypal figure alerts the reader to the fact that his role of protector/wise advisor to Rand, Mat and Perrin must surely signify extraordinary changes in their lives that will thrust them from obscurity onto their world's greater stage. Yet it is the creation of imaginary myth, legend, and history for the peoples within the invented world that imparts a quality of great antiquity, and authenticity. It is not just an entertaining but fanciful nostalgic fabrication of faerie, carefully rewoven from significant traditional material, but a believable world with its own genuinely long, rich and traditional cultural and mythic past.

WIZARDRY WITH WORDS

Attebery asserts that storytelling of itself usually relies on the properties of language:

> Language can refer to absent objects, designate different layers of time and represent transitions between them, evoke memories of sensory experience, and provoke emotional reactions. The fantastic strain of storytelling is particularly dependent upon the open-endedness of language: the fact that there are always more sentences available to the native speaker than there are situations to call for them. Thus we can, even with the most elementary vocabulary and grammar, name objects that we have never seen, like Tolkien's green sun. (1992, 6)

In regard to language Tolkien has also written that the 'invention of the adjective' is as 'potent' as a 'spell or incantation in Faerie'.

> We may put a deadly green upon a man's face and produce a horror; we may make the rare and terrible blue moon to shine; or we may cause woods to spring with silver leaves and rams to wear fleeces of gold, and put hot fire into the belly of the cold worm. But in such 'fantasy', as it is called, new form is made; Faerie begins; Man becomes a sub-creator. (1964, 25)

This transcendent and creative power of words provides an intriguing conundrum that a language, which evolved in and is firmly rooted in our world and culture, can so easily be used to create imaginary worlds that break the ground-rules of what is perceived to be possible in our own, and can describe things or thoughts of non-existent cultures. On some imaginative level we can actually believe in their existence, although in the Primary World they only appear as cleverly constructed words on the page.

Because of the shifting, chameleon-like nature of word groupings, one constrained only by the framework of grammar, a skillful writer can use them to construct a sub-creation that is a compilation of the known and the exceedingly strange, producing a perceptible world of such substance, that, in our minds, it becomes as tangible as the world around us. If anything, it can appear to be more vibrant, and more desirable than our reality. For 'story-time' gives the author license to introduce many elements that evoke and help to sustain a great sense of 'wonder' in the reader – that is, supernatural powers, wizards, mythical beasts, talismanic objects, larger-than-life heroes, quests of cosmic importance and such-like, whilst retaining enough ties to our own world to impart meaning and credibility for the reader. The philosopher David Hume believed humanity to have a persisting propensity towards 'wonder', to believe in events and things for which science has no logical explanation. Ann Swinfen in her book of the 1980s that was written in defence of fantasy, a then far more marginalised genre, chooses in Tolkienian fashion to link this intangible, inherent yearning for wonderment to 'primordial desires':

> Fantasy draws much of its strength from certain 'primordial desires' for the enrichment of life: the desire to survey vast depths of space and time, the desire to behold marvellous creatures, the desire to share the speech of animals, the desire to escape from the ancient limitations of primary world condition. (1984, 7)[5]

It is in this overwhelming human desire for transcendence of the limitations of reality, and the quest for an order and meaning to the mysteries of life that the appeal of fantasy (for those who enjoy it) must in great part lie.

PATTERNING A SECONDARY WORLD

In the Jordan world each of the seven recurring Ages has a separate and unique pattern, one which forms the substance of reality for that Age, and is referred to as the 'Age Lace'. Because the pattern is woven from all lives and actions, 'good and ill are the warp and the woof', so that society's behaviour is never wholly one or the other. (*DR*, 378) Therefore, the Secondary World of the Wheel is not portrayed as a place of perfection and the characters continuously reveal very human flaws, and this adds to our sense of affinity with them. As part of the patterning the fantasist presents a more obviously hierarchical world, one that Ringel notes is often based on 'medieval ideals of kingship and class structure'. She further suggests that 'on the page or on the Internet, neomedieval fantasy posits a great chain of being with everyone – human, hobbit, dwarf, or elf – in their proper place'. (2000, 166) Thus the imaginary world is one in which each of the various strata of society has a function and a defined place, that is, farmers, craft makers, merchant guilds, seafarers, warriors, nobles, royal rulers and wizards. Writers such as Jordan then draw on this ordered hierarchical framework of society to depict dramatically the imbalance and disorder that occurs in everyday life as a result of the Shadow's tightening grip on the land. For instance, the growing poverty, squalor, and mistrust among the poorer sections of the urban populations in his imaginary world, along with a loss of moral ethics across the social spectrum and an alarming increase in the number of Darkfriends abroad. (Similarly, in Le Guin's *The Farthest Shore* the danger of the imbalance between light and dark is dramatically depicted by the growing poverty, and mistrust among the peoples of the Archipelago, the increase in 'hazia' addicts, and the now shoddy goods produced by the dyers and weavers.)

In the prologue to the second volume, through the eyes of Bors, one of the Forsaken, the reader learns of the alarming global spread of those who follow the Dark. Bors prides himself on seeing beneath the disguises of those gathered to receive orders from their master:

> He could read them all, to class and country. Merchant
> and warrior, commoner and noble. From Kandor and

Cairhien, Saldaea and Ghealdan. From every nation and nearly every people. His nose wrinkled in sudden disgust. Even a Tinker, in bright green breeches and a virulent yellow coat. (*GH*, prologue, xviii)

The black masks and cloaks, beneath which Bors catches glimpses of national dress or distinctive pieces of jewellery that lead to their wearers' unmasking are a metaphor for the greater Darkness that has enveloped them all. Jordan sets this against the portrayal of beautiful young servants at the gathering clothed in 'tight white breeches and flowing white shirts' to reflect their guilelessness, but their 'blank eyes ... eyes more dead than death' are a horrific reminder to both those present and to the reader of the cruel power to reduce to zombies that can be wielded by the Dark Lord who rules through paralysing fear. (*GH*, prologue, xvi)

The use of disguise forms another recurring pattern in the texts that lends itself to critical analysis in the light of game theory. John Huizinga notes that another general characteristic of human play is, that 'games often involve masks, disguises and costumes, aspects [of play] that shade off into deception, trickery and fraud' (Leyerle 1975, 60-1). In a literary application of this characteristic of 'human play', disguise constitutes a form of play-acting that is frequently used for some sort of gain. In the cosmic game that is being played out in Jordan's world, the Dark Lord seeks to win by destroying the Great Pattern and thus the cycle of Time itself. Disguise then, is a repeating motif that is threaded through the narrative and is taken up by protagonists and antagonists alike, and used by the author to highlight their opposing motives of selfless and self-seeking behaviour. Members of the Forsaken change their physical appearances or character to beguile those around them; for example, Queen Morgase is besotted by Rahvin (disguised as Lord Gaebril) and so he gains control of her kingdom; Lanfear puts on the guise of a young, sensuous woman or that of an ugly, fat merchant in order to tempt or to spy on Rand; Asmodean puts on the distinctive trappings of a gleeman in an attempt to gain access to Rand in order to destroy him; and Padan Fain's outward appearance is that of an innocuous travelling tinker, but it hides the true blackness of his soul as he is one of the Dark Lord's most dangerous agents.

By contrast, the protagonists use a variety of innocent changes to their ordinary appearances and identities to gather information that will assist in the saving of the Great Pattern, and so the survival of their world. To this end Egwene and Elayne's shape-changing abilities while in the World of Dreams give them the necessary anonymity to visit the White Tower and search for clues to the plans of the Black Ajah. By changing their hair colour and clothing in the waking world, they seek to evade discovery by Darkfriends as they search for long lost numinous objects to be used to foil the machinations of the Dark. Thom the gleeman, too, is something of a shape-shifting personality as will be discussed in the next chapter. This emphasis on play-acting and identity-change in the narrative highlights for the reader the illusionary nature of appearances and offers a warning that all may not be as it seems; it also presents another set of interconnected clues or patterning to be unravelled by the inhabitants of the world and the reader.

Following on from this, the inn, the innkeeper and the conventions of public hospitality form an important trope, for throughout, Jordan uses the inn as a barometer of the state of the surrounding society. Thus in the unspoiled Two Rivers region the inns are prosperous, warm and welcoming, places central to the social life of the whole community and places of sanctuary for the traveller. In a reflection of their establishments, the innkeepers are invariably plump, honest, good-natured and spotlessly clean. By contrast, in areas where the Dark is encroaching the inns become ill-kept, places of potential danger to honest wayfarers, while the innkeepers are thin, mean, dishonest and inhospitable, and their regular patrons are uncouth and menacing. Strangers are greeted with surly suspicion and their safety cannot be guaranteed. This trope is employed to similar effect by Le Guin in the third volume (*Farthest*) of her *Earthsea* series, to emphasise the disorder and madness that troubles the inhabitants of the Archipelago once the balance of life and death is disrupted, and also echoes the differing atmosphere of the early and late inns in *LOTR*. (Jordan has said that the 'Nine Rings Inn', in bk 2 (*GH*) is a homage to Tolkien.)

THE WEB OF SOCIETY IN A SECONDARY WORLD

The social structure and architecture in Jordan's world are largely drawn from elements of a recognisably European historical past – the author has said that if it resembles anything it is seventeenth-century Europe but without gunpowder (n.a. 2000, 76). The depicted Third Age of the Wheel world also has similarities to the post-mediaeval time of great disturbance to philosophical thought and to the structures of society. But the author's words imply that if a reader is attempting to pin his world down to some point in the historical landscape of primary reality, it may have elements that seem mimetic of the seventeenth century, but not slavishly so. It is typical among fantasists to set Secondary Worlds in ages that flourished prior to those of great technological advances – usually somewhere between the Bronze Age and the late Middle Ages. Thus they depict societies that are aligned with the natural world and in which powers or creatures we term supernatural may not be seen as such but are accepted as natural by the inhabitants.[6] Freed from the conventions and restrictions of our reality, the writer constructs a sub-creation in which an array of the 'other' is possible, including potent magical powers, along with legendary creatures, non-human races and the like, which form part of everyday reality within that realm. The power of magic is crucial to the framework of the world, and provides the matrix of the patterning of existence. As Attebery suggests magic is 'not merely codified: it is itself a code as old as language or older' and has ethics, and 'is as rule-bound as language' (1992, 55). Certainly in the case of Le Guin's Earthsea Archipelago magic is intrinsically tied to language, as in that world it consists of the power of words and of naming, and is invoked by using the true name of each thing. Such knowledge carries heavy responsibilities, for misuse begets dire consequences for the world at large, as when Cob uses it to summon the dead and thereby ruptures the boundary between the living and the dead.

Earthsea, like the universe in *Genesis,* was created by the use of language (Comolette and Drout 2001, 116). The Earthsea myth of creation tells of the creator Sepoy who brought the islands up from the ocean by speaking the first word. He spoke the language of the Making and gave everything its true name. Therefore to utter words in the Old Speech is to be aware of the true essence of things. In a philosophical moment Ged explains to Yarrow, sister of his fellow mage Vetch, that:

> all power is one source and end ... Years and distances, stars and candles, water and wind and wizardry, the craft in a man's hand and the wisdom in a tree's root: they all arise together. My name, and yours, and the true names of the sun, or a spring of water, or an unborn child, all are syllables of the great word that is very slowly spoken by the shining of the stars. There is no other power. No other name. (*Wizard*, 182)

In Le Guin's cosmology the speech of the Making gives a kind of freedom from (later) distorting semantic, cultural bias – it is a joyous reflecting glass of the natural forces in the universe and displays a complete openness to the super-human or to the Cosmos.

By contrast, in Jordan's world of the Wheel, magic is derived from the True Source from which the One Power may be drawn or channelled by both males and females who have the talent. It is not words that trigger a linking to the One Power, but a meditative process that involves a specific clearing and focusing of the inner recesses of the mind, which over time becomes, for adepts, as automatic as breathing. Thus the magical force deployed in the world of the Wheel has a more scientifically-defined basis, being the natural energy that perpetuates the turning of the wheel of time itself, although like 'the Force' in the Star Wars saga, it has no stated origin – one presumes it began with the creation of the Cosmic Loom, which is Time itself.

It is not surprising, therefore, to find that Jordan, who had a degree in physics, said he 'look[ed] at magic as though it were technology ... as though it were science. The One Power and Channeling ... follow specific rules' (Lilley 2002). In keeping with the principle of balance in the world of the Wheel, the True Source or One Power consists of two conflicting yet complementary parts, *saidar* (female), *saidin* (male), which working together and against one another provide the driving force for the world. *Saidar* must be surrendered to, whilst *saidin* needs to be fought against, and it is their essential differences, working in tandem, that will create a sustaining whole – a mirroring of the cosmic power that drives the world of the Wheel itself. '*Saidar* is a calm ocean that will take you wherever you want to go so long as you know the currents and let them carry you'. But *saidin* has to be wrestled with to maintain control as it is 'an avalanche of burning stone, [c]ollapsing mountains of ice'. (*COT*, 535)

The two components of this cosmic power draw attention to the fact that at a temporal level neither female nor male should be privileged over the other and point to the need for equilibrium between both facets of the power, as achieved in the long past Age of Legends. The ancient united sign of the Aes Sedai is illustratively presented as 'a circle, half white and half black with the colors separated by a sinuous line' – an image drawn from the eastern concept of *yin* and *yang*. (*Companion*, 6) The Age of Legends was an era of great societal/technological advances, and one in which the word 'war' had no meaning, as testified to by surviving manuscripts, architectural marvels and powerful artifacts used to enhance the use of the One Power. Moreover, during the preceding 3000 years of female control, after the tainting of the male side of the power, the Wheel world has suffered two major wars, and currently the Dark is rapidly gaining sway, while the world spirals towards chaos and Armageddon. And this state of crisis forcefully illustrates for the inhabitants and the reader the urgency of regaining an equilibrium between the two, as had occurred in the Age of Legends.

A glimpse of the awesome potential of the One Power, and the infinite nature of its source, is given in the eighth book (*POD*) when the ancient crystal the 'Bowl of the Winds' is activated by a group of linked women (Aes Sedai and Sea Folk 'Windfinders') to form an intricate weave of power that climbs up into the sky and out of sight, and reverses the adverse weather forced on the world by the Shadow:

> That ever-changing lacework of *saidar* bent itself around
> something else, something unseen that made the column

> solid ... the bowl was drawing *saidin* as well as *saidar* ...
> Lacey spokes ... spreading across the sky ... spinning
> across the heavens, vanishing into the distance, on and on
> and on. (*POD*, 127)

This powerful *ter'angreal,* a relic from the Age of Legends, automatically weaves itself around an invisible column of *saidin*, although no men are linked to the circle of channelling women, offering evidence to the inhabitants of the depicted world and to the reader that it is natural for one side of the power to entwine with the other; the restoration of normal weather patterns is also proof of the positive outcome to be achieved by such a balanced union. This is just one example in which Jordan associates weaving with power. In keeping with the inter-connected pattern of the interlacement technique, the delicate lacework of *saidar* and *saidin* at this point anticipates Rand and Nynaeve's braiding of the threads of both sides of the power that will bring about the cleaning of *saidin* and the destruction of the evil city of Shadar Logoth.

Jordan's use of the motif of weaving is repeated in the construction of The One Power, which consists of five threads, comprising the natural elements of earth, fire, air, water, and spirit; thus, like the words of the 'Making' in Le Guin, it is an integral part of the depicted universe. Its use imparts powers of healing, weather-working, foretelling, bodily shifts in time and space, and the ability to destroy, although the Aes Sedai of the White Tower swear an oath not to use it as a weapon except against Shadowspawn, or to save the life of a fellow sister or that of a bonded warder. (*Companion*, 298) The ability to channel is an innate talent, but one that varies in quality and degree, and if a person is to safely develop their skills to full potential, correct training and supervision is required. The Aes Sedai at the White Tower play a role similar to that of Le Guin's wizards on the island of Roke, as the training and initiation of novices at both centres entail arduous and potentially dangerous forms of initiation, particularly designed to test the moral fibre of those who enter their doors. These authors make it clear that the acquisition of power to evoke changes within their imaginary worlds is not to be treated lightly. The control of power is of cosmic significance and pivotal to the maintaining of universal stability and order.

WEAVING THE PATTERN OF PLACE AND TIME IN A SECONDARY WORLD

Jordan's interwoven narrative technique is extended into his concept of place and time. The World of the Wheel, with its seven repeating ages, takes the form of a great Cosmic Loom, and it represents the cycle of time itself, since time began with its creation. Reincarnation, too, is part of the cycle. The author has stated that the concept for his series 'comes out of Hindu mythology, where there is a belief that time is a wheel'; he has also observed that 'many older cultures' have believed the pattern and meaning of time to be 'cyclic' (CNN 2000). Cosmic time according to the *smriti* tradition is measured in great cycles (*kalpas*), which are themselves divided into four ages or *yugas* representing different stages in human development, from a golden age to a slow decay followed by war and strife, in an ever repeating sequence. Jordan takes up this notion in his created world, one in which the Age of Legends ('golden age') that saw a peak in human advancement has long passed, and degenerated into an Age of chaos and strife, so that the world now stands on the brink of destruction. In this endless cycle of time, as already mentioned, it is a conceit that the Last Battle can occur in each successive Age.

In this seemingly deterministic world there is a widespread acceptance of a belief in the Great Pattern and a commonly held view that 'The Wheel weaves as the Wheel wills'. (*EOTW*, 92) Perhaps the idea of a cosmic loom and an eternally repeating pattern of seven Ages is a way of avoiding the fear of death as an absolute, and so the human fear of death is neatly negated in Jordan's world. Don Elgin suggests that in fantasy worlds 'death and destruction' are seen 'as an inevitable part of the cycle', and 'the renewal of life and the continuance of that cycle as an ever-dynamic system' (Elgin 1985, 182). Certainly, no ending, even death, is absolute within the turning of the Wheel, which is Time itself.

Within the world of the Wheel, memory is an enormous resource that conflates time present and past and enriches one's knowledge or feeling and awareness of what has been. The pattern of the past is repeated through or referred to through such things as folktales, popular songs, folk sayings, as well as the cyclic festivals of the peoples such as the universal Spring festival Bel Tine, which not only signify the turning of the seasons but are a continual celebration of the ebb and flow of life and nature. Other reference points include words of the Old Tongue, ancient talismanic objects, myth and legend and prophecy. Furthermore, ruins, abandoned cities, Ogier Steddings, Portal Stones, Waygates and the talismanic objects from the Age of Legends all help to keep much of the physical past in the present, and in some instances also contain the key to the future. For instance, consider the crystal sword *Callandor*, which only the true Dragon can remove from the fortress known as the Stone of Tear:

> And it was written that no hand but his should wield the Sword held in the Stone, but he did draw it out, like fire in his hand, and his glory did burn the world. Thus did it begin. Thus do we sing his Rebirth. (*DR*, epilogue, 675)

The central figure Rand and his taking of this sword are given deeper significance through resonance with the Matter of Arthur, thus setting up reader expectation that this young hero is destined to embark on an actual and also symbolic (kingly) quest, which will have enormous implications and consequences for the world around him. This also illustrates well how the reverberations of a myth from our tradition not only enlarge, but give a sense of authenticity to the invented myth within the narrative as one is threaded through the other.

MAPS

The use of detailed prefatory maps to the volumes helps to make it a concrete place in time and space, an autonomous, coherent world of the imagination within a fixed set of boundaries, one that also comes from Jordan's extremely tactile presentation of diverse landscapes. The concept of 'otherworlds' is not new in literature but the more fluid landscapes of mediaeval romances and epic, which often existed as an allegorical backdrop for the protagonist (i.e. the forest as a symbol of the unknown and the dangerous, a place of testing) are more clearly delineated and substantial in modern fantasy. Swinfen notes that the 'precise geography' of contemporary fantasy Secondary Worlds is quite unlike the 'shadowy and imprecise journeying of Spenser's Knights in the Realm of Gloriana':

> although modern secondary worlds share with traditional fairy-lands and enchanted forests a quality of otherness, of strangeness and wonder woven into their fabric, they also differ very widely from their literary predecessors. Strangeness and wonder are still present, but the modern concern with precision of detail and coherent scientific data has had its effect on the creation and depiction of the secondary world. (1984, 75)

In Jordan's Wheel world the reader experiences the varying textures, beauty and harshness of the landscape by following the often arduous travels of the main human protagonists, for this world is mostly seen through their eyes – and most often through the rural eyes of the Emond's Fielders with whom the story first begins. Close patterning upon the landscape adds to the substance of the world of the Wheel – its roads, rivers, ruins of past civilisations, villages, farmlands, walled cities, forests and mountains. Jordan's attention to such detail increases the realism of his world as it is extremely rich and interesting to read about. Secondary worlds, such as the Wheel, or those created by Tolkien, Le Guin and other contemporary high fantasists, all impart an air of 'a reality that is not contingent upon everyday reality, but instead is self-sustaining' (Mobley 1973-74, 118). These writers have created landscapes which the reader is imaginatively encouraged to believe in and to co-inhabit for the duration of the tale.

CIRCULAR WORLD – LINEAR LIFE SPAN FOR HUMANS

There is tension between Jordan's concept of a circular world with its endlessly repeating cycle of seven Ages, and the necessary linear line of the narrative, which is one much attuned to the life-span of its human protagonists. However, this is complicated in a number of ways, which work to draw the two concepts together. From the opening prologue in the first volume, Jordan makes it very clear that the battle between the representatives of the Light and the Dark, which began at creation, will last until time dies. At the Breaking of the World, some three thousand years before the setting of the present tale, Lews Therin, an earlier reincarnation of the Dragon, is reminded by his dark opponent that they 'have fought a thousand battles with the turning of the Wheel, a thousand times a thousand, and … will fight until time dies and the Shadow is triumphant'. (*EOTW*, prologue, xii) Through such reincarnation, which is the stated way of the Wheel, and the cycle of birth, death and rebirth, human lives actually form an endless spiralling circle, although, paradoxically, each span on earth can be drawn as a line from birth to death. The anticipation of the end of the narrative (the Last Battle) in the beginning, is also suggestive of a linking cycle. In turn, it mirrors the symbolic image for the World of the Wheel, the Cosmic Loom, featuring a sideways figure of eight in the form of a stylised serpent biting its tail, an ancient, pagan symbol of infinity.

Each volume of the series is linked by its formulaic, opening legend, which not only functions in a similar way to the traditional fairy tale phrase 'once upon a time' to release the reader from the confines of the present, but also insists on the circularity of time. As well as this it details how historical events can become imaginative stories that are themselves constantly evolving:

> The Wheel of Time turns, and Ages come and pass, leaving memories that become legend. Legend fades to myth, and even myth is forgotten when the Age that gave it birth comes again. In one Age, called the Third Age by some, an Age yet to come, an Age long past. (*EOTW*, 1)

The recurring legend reveals that the Age in question is both 'an Age yet to come and an Age long passed', so that it undercuts our conception of time as being linear and finite, and instead focuses upon its circularity. Through this poetic device, Jordan continually renews and strengthens the idea in the reader's mind that within the narrative he or she is stepping beyond the restrictions of time, as conceived here and now, and into the freedom of the more open-ended 'story-time', a realm in which it is logical for time to operate on different systems. And there are to be expected encounters, events and creatures that have no place in the more limiting world of reality. Thus, fantasy writers are able to disrupt or complicate the pattern of linear time on which we structure our daily lives, and to open our minds to the possibility of other ways of perceiving time and order.

Although the narrative drive to reach closure pushes the protagonists forward in time, through the use of multi-stranded plots, and an interweaving of events back and forward across the texts – so that time can be retarded or advanced – their progress becomes more of an interlacing that creates an intricate pattern, with each thread contributing towards the finished piece. Jordan, as pattern maker, can be likened to a weaver working on a huge, colourful and intricate tapestry. He may pick up threads at will, unravel a piece if it does not suit his artistic eye or purpose, brightly colour a section here or there, leave puzzling gaps or produce areas of darkness. Each thread builds towards the completion of the whole, and although there is an overall template (the Great Pattern of the Wheel), such poetic licence allows the author some leeway.

Furthermore, as the narrative unfolds, the threads which are to be strengthened, or which are altered or discarded are shown to depend to some extent on the reactions of the main protagonists. In particular Rand, Mat and Perrin, the three *ta'veren* who are destined to bring change, are presented as having some freedom in their reactions to the situations and challenges that the Great Pattern has designed for them. In turn the suggestion is that the final outcome will be governed, too, by how well they respond to any tests and trials and to the antagonists they may encounter. Although Jordan is writing within the conventions of the quest paradigm and the reader may anticipate a happy ending, by setting up elements of doubt, times when the heroic figures could make selfish or inappropriate choices, the author adds narrative tension which works to maintain suspense and reader interest.

Other threads, in the form of prophecy, foretellings, prophetic dreams or visions can be introduced into the pattern as a means of anticipating important events, for instance the prediction of the rebirth of the Dragon, destroyer and saviour of the world, or Mat's marriage to the Daughter of the Nine Moons, which will surely link the Seanchan invaders with the peoples of the Dragon and change the dynamics of the coming Last Battle. Such mechanisms allow Jordan to go back later and fill them in. They are not just surface additions to the narrative, introduced as a means of plot manipulate to advance the narrative, although they often achieve this effect, but for the reader seem to naturally grow out of the thoughts and actions of the protagonists. The use of cryptic foreshadowing of events also adds a layer of intrigue and anticipation to the narrative. Despite the vastness of his canvas Jordan insisted that 'all major plot lines will be resolved … [although] some minor plot lines would have to be left unresolved as a way to let the world continue to live and breathe' (Noren 1995). This tactic adds to the feeling that there is always more to be known about the world, and that it could be re-entered at another time.

THE PATTERNING OF TIME AND SPACE

Jordan continually plays with the notion that time – and even space – are human constructs and that the boundaries between dream/reality, past/present, what is, what could be and what will be are fluid. His world is multi-dimensional with mirroring worlds of the Wheel revealing the imprint of what was, or could be, depending on the path taken by his characters. This certainly suggests to the reader that, to some extent, within the Wheel world human choices can shape the outcome of events within the Pattern of any given Age, creating tension between the author's stated view that his world is totally 'pre-determined' and his depiction of characters who make their own free choices. For instance, there are 'mirror' and 'optional' realms that can be reached by use of Portal Stones (much like freestanding, ancient monoliths) which provide spatially located gateways to alternative realities and 'mirror' worlds that might have been. As they are empty of human life, or aberrations of nature such as Trollocs, perhaps, in keeping with the philosophy of the Wheel, they are representative of the possible reincarnation of apparently historical landscape, and alternative courses available to the brave.

The typography of the mirror worlds is identical to that of the primary world of the Wheel, but here the landscape is washed out and hazy, lacking true substance, rather like the ephemeral ring that sometimes encircles the solid disc of our moon. Mirror worlds exist outside the time of the primary Wheel world, for within them vast distances can be quickly covered. In the second volume, when Rand accidentally activates a Portal Stone and transports himself, Loial and Hurin to one of these realms, although they are traversing much the same terrain they quickly find themselves to be days ahead of the companions they had left behind in the real Wheel world. (*GH*, 268-9) They find themselves in a mirror world empty of human life, with terrible scars upon the earth. Monuments raised to Trolloc triumph in battle, or desolate ruins of statues of legendary human kings or warriors offer the bleakest testimony to the frighteningly possible successes of the forces of the Dark. Such images give concrete form to the abstract concept of the horrific dangers facing the inhabitants of the Wheel world, should they, by passivity, allow the Shadow to continue to gain the upper hand.

A further dimension is added through the depiction of the inner spirit realm of the World of Dreams (*Tel'aran'rhoid*), one which mirrors the waking world. It is a place to which various characters of both sides can gain access, since even in the World of Dreams, there must be both dark and light. Twisted spiral-shaped *ter'angreal* rings can aid a sleeper to more easily reach this dimension. The one-edged, unbroken spiral that curves from the outside to the inside of the ring is symbolic of the inseparable link between the temporal world and the inner spirit world of dreaming. (*DR*, 240) Further, an injury taken in the dream realm will also exist upon waking, while to be mortally wounded in spirit brings instantaneous death to the body in the waking world. Several of Rand's major battles against the champions of the Dark are conducted simultaneously on a physical and a metaphysical level, thereby further tightening the connection between the two.

Moreover, much strengthening the link between humanity and animals of the wild who share the web of life at temporal and metaphysical level is the power of Perrin's shamanistic role. Through his ability to link with the minds of wolves in the waking world, he gains access to the inner spirit realm of the wolf-dreaming where he spontaneously takes on the form of a wolf. Le Guin draws on such a link, giving Ged the talent to shape-change to a sparrow hawk, and through her metaphysical linking of humans and dragons – creatures with the ability to 'dance on the other wind' – provides a mystical, metaphoric interface between the finite world of the flesh and the eternal world of the spirit. (Le Guin repeats this motif in *Tehanu* where Tenar unfolds a silk fan on which one side is painted with human figures and the reverse with dragons. But when the fan is held up to the light, 'the two sides, the two paintings, [are] made one by the light flowing through the silk'. [*Tehanu,* 105]) There is a glimpse of eternity in Le Guin's dragons' spiralling dance, a dance without beginning and end. This concept is mirrored in the universal 'long dance', in which all peoples of Earthsea participate at the winter equinox. In the archipelago of Earthsea this dance symbolically integrates land and sea, life and death, as well as light and dark, for it is performed from sundown to sunrise – a celebration of the endless cycle to which all things must submit. Fantasy worlds are presented as realms where people are less separated from the landscape and other life forms and where spirituality forms a complex and delicate web between them.

Le Guin's notion of a spiritual eternity is also glimpsed in Jordan's metaphoric night sky of stars that reflect the immeasurable number of individual dreams. As they flicker in and out of an infinite realm that lies between that of the waking world and the inner spirit realm of *Tel'aran'roid*, they also provide a metaphysical interface between the two, a brief intermingling of the finite and the eternal – a time out of time (a moment of epiphany as evoked by Eliot's 'Four Quartets'). By implication they suggest the myriad of lives to be experienced by the Wheel world inhabitants as the Wheel of Time turns, and even the possibility that life itself is but a state of dreaming or illusion:

> an ocean of stars, infinite points of light glimmering in an infinite sea of darkness, fireflies beyond counting flickering in an endless night ... dreams of everyone sleeping anywhere in the world, maybe of everyone in all possible worlds ... A vast ever-changing array of sparkling beauty. (*COS*, 200)

This sense of infinity is further strengthened by Jordan's description of the infinite and vital nature of the force that drives the Wheel of Time. During Rand's attempt to cleanse the taint from the male side of the One Power, he mentally links with Nynaeve through a pair of small statues, one male, one female, known as *ter'angreal* access keys, which in turn link to a pair of powerful giant *sa'angreal* statues of the same form. Thus he is able to draw upon seemingly unlimited amounts of both *saidar* and *saidin*, since they form the core of the universe, an invisible force that permeates every atom:

> The weave did not form at all as he expected ... [but] took on convolutions and spirals that made him think of a flower. There was nothing to see, no grand weaves sweeping down from the sky. The Source lay at the heart of creation. The Source was everywhere, even in Shadar Logoth. The conduit covered distance beyond his imagining and had no length at all. (*WH*, 659)

Clearly, the One Power is endless and boundless and knows neither good nor evil. It just is, so can be used by the Light or the Dark in the continually changing patterning of life-threads that occurs throughout the repeating cycle of Ages, yet without it the world of the Wheel would cease to exist. Jordan uses the Platonic image of the cosmic weaving powerfully here to show the very purpose of Creation itself.

PEOPLE AND TIME

In regard to time, it is apparent that, rather than pretending to represent what we conceive of as being 'real' time, fantasy allows for a number of different conceptions of the nature and meaning of time. In his recent literary exploration of mythology, Bob Trubshaw draws attention to the abstract nature of our notion of time in this world as being 'equal segments, endlessly repeated'. His comparative research reveals that recent strands of philosophical thought suggest that however 'objective' time may first appear, human perception and experience of time are always story-like. Indeed, it is from such narratives that the identities of individuals and groups emerge. He notes that:

> Modern Western ideas about time seem so obvious, so scientific, that it is difficult to conceive of alternative ways of understanding time. Yet these modern ideas about time have only dominated Western thinking in the last 150 years. Non-western societies and traditional European cultures all display wider attitudes to time. And, above all, they do so in their myths. (2003, 30)

Traditional narrative is thus a way of exploring time and of allowing people to gain imaginative control over it. (This sense of time as an 'eternal now' in which all tenses of time are held in 'equilibrium' lies at the 'heart of Oriental philosophy' where past, present and future 'are simply names in an endless circle' [Cameron 1962, 72].) In fantasy, for which myth and fairy tale have been the root paradigms, magical intervention naturally allows for temporal interruptions through time slips, pauses or a spiraling of time that allow the past, or what might yet be, to co-exist in the present. Further, as observed by Attebery in his discussion of Tolkien's *LOTR*, the characters in fantasy texts can function to present alternate ways of relating to time (1992, 60). For example, in the characters of Jordan's three main heroes, Rand, Mat and Perrin, life patterns of the past come alive in the present, through a condensing of time that links their minds to old talents or memories of previously lived lives, in ways that enhance their abilities and contribute to their self-knowledge, maturity and status. In turn these personal experiences are linked to their fated paths that are being woven in the present and on which the success of the quest is reliant. In his conceptualisation of a pattern of time in which the mythical or historical past of his imaginary world re-occurs in the present, Jordan, like other fantasists, is drawing on Mircea Elaide's concept of the 'eternal return', whereby through archetypal events and motifs 'the past is but a prefiguration of the future. No event is irreversible and no transformation is final' (1965, 89).

Compounding this telescopic sense of time, in Jordan's work we also view the world through the eyes of inhabitants who are granted far longer life spans than those of his human characters. Ogier giants, within their Steddings (groves of ancient trees), are immune to the One Power that drives the world of the Wheel, so that for them time passes at a different rate than in the outside world, although they share the same spatial location. When relating a story, like Tolkien's Ents, they are extremely long-winded; and similarly when their Elders meet, they ponder questions at great length. They also retain memories of the past that extend well beyond those of human capability, thereby providing a living link to historical events long since lost to the recall of most humans in the Wheel world.

The Aes Sedai priestesses of the White Tower, too, have enhanced life spans that exceed those of normal humans by several hundred years, which not only gives them a great depth of knowledge of their world and its history, but also the time in which to perfect their arts in the use of the One Power, and to build a strong moral and political power base. The great ring that each woman wears, depicting a serpent biting its tail, is a metaphor for the infinity of the power they possess, as well as serving as a reminder that the repeating cycle of birth and death may be extended for them, as for the Ogier giants, but it can never be entirely circumvented. These women are easily identified by a quality of 'agelessness'. They seem to stand still as time flows by, an image symbolically reflected by the antiquity and unmarred beauty of the Ogier-built White Tower, the stronghold of their learning, as it stands on an island in the river, impervious to the constant ebb and flow of the tides around it.

Moreover, legendary heroes in some extraterrestrial dimension are fixed to the great cosmic Wheel Pattern, destined to be spun out (reborn) again and again through the seven repeating Ages at times of need. Thus they are immortalised both at a temporal and at a spiritual level through their repeating cycle of famed and newly-enacted deeds. Because they are reborn throughout time, they are known not only on a metaphysical, mythical level through the old stories, but also within time to people of the various ages in which they reincarnate. When Birgitte Silverbow is torn from the Pattern and flung into the world as an adult – due to a fight with one of the Forsaken – she is a notable legendary figure who instantly brings heroic story to life. So, too, do the legendary warriors of the past who can be summoned by the call of the numinous Horn of Valere to aid in present day battles. But as they are compelled to fight for whoever first sounds the Horn, they can be summoned by either the Light or the Dark. Such disruptions of any patterning discernible in time add to the complex layering of the narrative and reinforce the validity of the circular nature of time itself.

With regard to such legendary figures, personality traits, proficiency with certain weapons, and even emotional or martial relationships are perpetuated from one reincarnation to another, so in a sense they are constantly re-enacting themselves or reinforcing their necessarily timeless heroic/legendary status. In our contemporary world popular heroes such as Superman and the Phantom share a similar role, as there is a general conception that they never age or alter in appearance as well as a public expectation that they can be relied upon to perform their super-hero roles for successive generations of readers.

The Seanchan invaders from across the Aryth ocean, descendants of the army of the legendary mainland king/warrior Artur Hawkwing, who in the past had invaded their shores, not only bring actions of the past to bear on the present, but through their genealogy they are also representative of the past in the present. They refer to prophecies of the Dragon, which have become altered over time to encompass aspects of their own distinct culture, thereby showing the many-faceted nature of myth and legend and the instability of truth as an absolute in cultural memory. As the Seanchan view themselves not as invaders but as peoples with a right to return to what they regard as their homeland, their invasion and resettlement is a metaphor for the physical interweaving of cultures and nations and so another facet of interlacement.

On the Shadow side we see a number of interesting temporal disruptions to time. The mysterious figure, Moridin, who appears to have lived for thousands of years, has the ability to tear a hole in the Great Pattern and so step out of time, and to come back again at will. Mordeth, the ancient bane of the fallen city of Shadar Logoth, and one of many manifestations of evil, long ago through his own misdeeds became entrapped in a strange time warp, and although the city has naturally weathered and crumbled around him with the passing of time, he remains bound within its precincts, and is denied either true life or true death. He exists in the temporal world of the Wheel, yet outside the true cycle of time. Similarly, the thirteen Aes Sedai of the Dark known as the 'Forsaken' did not age during their three thousand years of entrapment at the site of the Dark Lord's prison at Shayol Ghul. The concept of escaping the ravages of time through sleep is an old literary motif (i.e. Sleeping Beauty, Snow White, Rip Van Winkle) and as Jordan applies it only to his antagonists, by linking it to evil he brings to the fore the dangers inherent in seeking immortality.

TIME AND LOCATIONS

To add to the complexities of Jordan's vision of time, within the world of the Wheel the cycle of time can differ in a number of locations. In the hidden Aiel city of Rhuidean, in the numinous forest of crystal spires initiates of the Aiel tribes can relive events of the past, while ter'angreal archways offer access to realms and events that stand beyond any known time. Various devices such as Portal Stones, the Ways, or travelling by opening gateways with the One Power, allow transport to other planes of existence, or the ability to step from one place to another without crossing the usual surfaces of the intervening space. Moreover, Ogier Steddings and the Green Man's enchanted grove alike symbolise the lost

60

Paradise once accessible on earth. Ogier giants, akin to Tolkien's ents, a long-lived but dying breed are the gentle guardians of trees. And the Green Man (reminiscent of Tom Bombadil) represents the last of the race of Nym, constructed sentient beings from the Age of Legends, made from living plants which utilised the One Power for the benefit of all plants and growing things. The Green Man's enchanted grove is only to be found by the pure of heart. Although it is sought by many, few succeed in their quest, for unselfish need to serve others and not glory, is the key to its discovery. As it is not the grove that moves, but the necessary approach towards it of the person who needs it, this enchanted place, like the Garden of Eden, is both of but apart from the everyday world of the Wheel, both in and yet outside time. It holds the grail-like 'eye of the world', an untainted pool of *saidin*, hidden against contingent time of great human need. It also holds the legendary and talismanic Horn of Valere and the banner of the true Dragon – aids that will be needed at the Last Battle. A further parallel to the Christian loss of Paradise is that, as the Dark One's touch on the world strengthens, due to human over-reaching for power, one of his minions, serpent-like, gains entrance to the Grove, and so brings about its destruction and the death of the last of the Nym.

Ogier Steddings, much like the open temple groves of classical antiquity, are scattered across the landscape and can be easily found by all travellers and none are denied entry, although Darkfriends find even their proximity uncomfortable. They consist of groves of the most ancient trees, lovingly tended by the remaining Ogiers, and they are both in but apart from the everyday world, since within them the One Power that drives the world of the Wheel cannot be accessed. Therefore, within the Steddings time also has a different meaning, which accounts for the longevity of the Ogier as a race. The grove of each Stedding stands as a sacred, primaeval but living cathedral of the natural world, one from which the human inhabitants of the Wheel world have turned aside, and so can only provide for their race a place of temporary sanctuary and healing. The reverse is true of the Ogier, almost the priests of the trees, who can spend only limited amounts of time in the world of humans without developing a wasting sickness. In his portrayal of the Ogier Steddings, as with the Green Man's grove, Jordan is drawing on the ancient and potent motif of groves as being places of sanctuary and sacredness, as does Le Guin with the grove of the Patterner on the Island of Roke.

A WEB OF WORDS

In summary, Jordan's construction of intricately tangled multi-stranded plots draws on the mediaeval literary techniques of interlacement and game-play. Landscape is vividly portrayed and also used as a metaphor/mirror for the encroachment of evil; for example, the deepening drought reflects the rise of darkness of spirit throughout the Wheel world, and perhaps also our current crisis of global warming. Different points of view are used – sometimes from the side of the Shadow – to provide a broader picture. His world is given concrete form and depth by the use of maps, historical records, ruins, legendary tales of the gleeman, folksongs, folk sayings and a cast of distinctly recognisable characters from numerous cultures. Prophecy, dreams, and visions foretell the future. Legendary, talismanic objects add to the sense of magic and wonder. Synthesising of an eclectic array of cross-cultural material and traditional motifs (e.g. Arthurian Romance, Celtic and Norse myth, Greek myth, Christian myth, Buddhist concepts, Samurai swordplay, and Native American lore) imparts another rich layering of meaning. Evil is manifest not only in people but in places (the abandoned city of Shadar Logoth, Shayol Ghul site of the Dark One's prison, and the Tower of Ghenji) and in tainted objects, especially weapons (daggers and swords). Self-conscious protagonists are aware they are not like the heroes in 'stories' but that they are part of a greater pattern of life and so exhibit a strong sense of destiny and duty.

A plethora of skillfully manipulated sub-plots have allowed Jordan to embrace a great diversity of peoples, locations, dimensions and time-frames to flesh out his story and to give his world complex substance and so historical credibility. This structural tactic also enables the placement of the main protagonists in a variety of situations, which all aid in self-growth and so prepare them for the responsible tasks that lie ahead. Places of sanctuary, such as the Ogier Steddings, also bring important environmental issues to the fore. Rand's battles occur on both a temporal and a metaphysical level, which increases the depth of his character and elevates him to a larger than life and more symbolic heroic status.

Through the myriad of differing rumours and tales that spread about Rand's exploits, Jordan also highlights the constant creativity of language, and of mortal thought, there being many shadings of reality and truth, depending on how individuals experience events and interpret them to others. In his imaginary world he shows us how easily fiction can become part of the fabric of 'reality', and colour people's perception of life in a way that influences memory of the past and must influence the behaviour patterns for the future:

> Across the nations the stories spread like spiderweb laid upon spiderweb, and the men and women planned the future, believing they knew the truth. They planned, and the Pattern absorbed their plans, weaving toward the future foretold. (*POD*, epilogue, 643)

As time passes, such stories turn to myth and legend and the weaving of them becomes so intricate that it is virtually impossible to separate the strands of truth from those of imaginative hearsay. Perhaps, it is on such history-like stories that the fabric or meaning of our own post-Christian world is to be creatively reconstructed and maintained through time and, in part, this may account for our receptiveness to earlier style worlds of the imagination. In the perceptive words of Peter Brooks:

> Narrative is one of the ways in which we speak, one of the categories in which we think. Plot is the thread of design and its active shaping force, the product of our refusal to allow temporality to be meaningless, our stubborn insistence on making meaning in the world and in our lives. (1984, 232)

Moreover, as Timmerman suggests, 'fantasy relies upon the age-old tradition of story-telling' and that 'most properly fantasy is a kind of myth, a story which stands in opposition to the iron-clad pragmatism of the age and seeks to return [us] to a sense of origins and divine significance. It affirms a meaning which is the ground of reality for humankind' (1983, 28). Accordingly, the thrust of this chapter has been to explore, through patterning and interlacement the ways in which writers of epic-style high fantasy, particularly writers like Robert Jordan, reweave traditional materials to build Secondary Worlds that disrupt our concept of time and space. Thus they are enabled to form an imaginative, literary coalescence of past, present and even future, and to use it as a means to explore the eternal human dilemma, and to create an alternative blueprint for existence which challenges the disorder and uncertainty of the Primary World. Within the world of the Wheel it is only a special interpreter who can comprehend the whole meaning of the Great Pattern. Accordingly, the analysis must turn to the subtle presentation of the several magus figures in the pattern of the stories.

2 UNRAVELLING THE PATTERN: THE MAGUS FIGURES IN *THE WHEEL OF TIME*

A significant plot or pattern element in contemporary high fantasy is the use of a range of superhuman characters (i.e. those of a higher nature or possessed of magical powers) who function as helpers to or opponents of the hero. The *magus* as a superhuman character, whether male or female, who is given or progressively assumes a role of responsibility for keeping the pattern of mortal existence in balance, in order to save his or her world from destruction by the forces of the Dark. Although the trope of the magus has been much written about, as a kind of magical warrior, less attention has been paid to the role played by this figure in high fantasy as an interpreter of the discernible patterns of the heroic quest. It takes an extraordinary interpreter in the text to make sense of the pattern of destiny that forms around the central characters in works such as Robert Jordan's *WOT*. It is in the light of pattern interpreter and keeper, or of pattern disrupter, that I wish to explore the dualism of Light and Dark that Jordan assigns to the stock figure of the magus, which continues to play such a pivotal element in the fantasy genre.

Accordingly, this chapter provides an exposition of Jordan's patterning of Light and Dark in his presentation of three female magus figures. Moraine symbolises 'good' and rationality. She is dedicated to keeping Rand within the pattern that will bring victory for the forces of Light. Lanfear, an agent of the Dark Lord, is dedicated to seducing Rand to other darker paths. Cadsuane, who appears once Moiraine and Lanfear are removed (from the narrative), is an inscrutable figure who symbolises balance, but may have mixed motives – a combination of the attributes of Moiraine and Lanfear. Her unfinished tapestry of Rand is a metaphor for the hazardous nature of his heroic journey, a reminder that either the Light or the Dark could be victorious. These three characters are constructed to provide the necessary guidance and testing of the hero.

Jordan also utilises a magus-like figure, Thom, a travelling bard, as a means of projecting himself into the narrative. Thom stitches together stories from fragments of all manner of heroic tales, past and present, and so represents the hero as an interlaced character. Thus Jordan is the storyteller both inside and outside the text, providing yet another facet to the patterning of his already complex work, and highlighting the feature of the magus as both pattern-keeper and interpreter.

BRIEF HISTORY OF THE MAGUS FIGURE

As was documented by E. M Butler in *The Myth of the* Magus, this legendary figure of superhuman powers is an archetype central to myth and religion across many cultures. This well-respected theoretical work identifies the anthropological origins of the magus in ancient rituals performed by a shaman or wizard to ensure the prosperity of the tribe. Butler traces the figure's subsequent development through pre-Christian religious and mystic philosophers, through mediaeval sorcerers and alchemists, and on into the eighteenth and nineteenth-century occult revival. Traditionally, too, in literature this figure has repeatedly appeared as a seeker, prophet, seer, teacher, guardian, shaman, and conduit for the forces of both good and evil. Moreover, much Western fantasy literature – and many post-mediaeval writers in particular – are indebted to the more specifically Celtic tradition of this archetype for one of its most enduring and enigmatic figures.

Merlin – seer, magus, mentor and shape-shifter – has performed many roles and re-appeared in many guises since his earliest appearance in the fabled court of Camelot, while always maintaining his magical powers and aura of mystery. Despite his pre-Christian origins, tales of Merlin's life evolved from within the mediaeval Christian tradition as did those of other Dark Age figures such as Beowulf. For writers of fantasy like J. R. R. Tolkien, and later writers such as Robert Jordan, who have been strongly influenced by the *LOTR*, one of the most crucial topoi of their narratives is that of the magus. In a variety of guises, this chameleon-like figure forms part of the matrix on which the stories are created, and functions as an important, even crucial, intersection between the human and the supernatural. In works of high fantasy it is this figure who has been given, or has acquired, knowledge of the true path that the hero must follow for the good of the world; it is also this figure who takes up the responsibility of mentor and guide to the main protagonists in an effort to save their world from imminent annihilation.

In Jordan's world of the Wheel, the pattern of the Third Age weaves relentlessly towards *Taimon Gai'don* (the Last Battle) but, as mentioned in the previous chapter, while the Age Lace is to be woven by all life-threads, some strands in the web are not yet set, and so the final outcome can be influenced by the choices and actions of the hero Rand, who is the Dragon Reborn. Because he is *ta'veren*, Rand is one of the key characters whose life-thread is spun out by the Great Pattern specifically to bring change to the emerging weave. For a time, like the ripple effect of a pebble dropped into a pond, he will influence the weaving of the life-threads of those around him. As explained by his Ogier friend Loial:

> sometimes the Wheel bends a life-thread, or several threads, in such a way that all the surrounding threads are forced to swirl around it, and those force other threads, and those still others, and on and on. (*EOTW*, 554)

Rand may, to some extent, alter the Pattern of the Age and although his destiny continually pushes him towards a final confrontation with the Dark Lord, it is not yet certain if he will stand as a champion for the Light or for the Shadow. Ba'alzamon, one of the Forsaken and mouthpiece for the Dark Lord, can taunt Rand by suggesting: 'You have served me before. Serve me again ... or be destroyed forever'. (*GH*, 588) Therefore, if the depicted world is to survive, it is imperative that the young hero be brought to accept some measure of guidance from the magus figures who serve the cause of the Light, and so to develop the strength to resist the lies and temptations which are offered by their Dark counterparts.

As noted by John Timmerman, the Manichaean dualism which forms the underpinning framework for many high fantasy texts such as

Tolkien's *LOTR*[1], Le Guin's *Earthsea* and Jordan's *WOT*, also dictates that the 'magic and presence of supernatural powers' must be 'inescapably allied with the [eternal] problem of good and evil' (1983, 72). Manichaeism, which survived until the thirteenth century, was a 'religious system with Christian, Gnostic, and pagan elements ... based on a supposed primeval conflict between light and darkness, and representing Satan as coeternal with God' (*Shorter Oxford English Dictionary* 2002). Thus, it offers the writer of high fantasy a useful cosmological framework in which light and dark can be presented as essential, eternal elements, one in which an imbalance between the two precipitates the hero's call to adventure.

The Buddhist cosmology in which a universal equilibrium must be sought through a harmonising tension of light and dark also suggests a similar pattern, and in the eclectic manner of fantasy writing both Jordan and Le Guin's work also reflect the influence of this Eastern thought. In regard to fairy tale, to which fantasy is related, Le Guin has remarked that 'evil, then, appears ... not as something diametrically opposed to good, but as inextricably involved with it as in the yang-yin symbol' (1989, 56). In *Earthsea* the Equilibrium is to be kept through a balancing of light and dark, for one cannot exist without the other. Similarly in the *WOT*, both light and dark are woven into the Great Pattern.

Writers of high fantasy assign to the trope of the magus as wielder of magic or superhuman qualities, a dualistic role, creating figures that can become powerful conduits for either good or evil, as portrayed in the characters of Tolkien's Gandalf the Grey and Saruman the White. Magi can also provide powerful surrogates on earth for the cosmic polarities of Light and Dark – as depicted in the *WOT*. Such figures of the Light may be swayed to the side of evil, if hunger for knowledge or improper power negates either caution or the judicious use of their special abilities. Then in turn the inherent danger in the use of power can become a useful literary device for heightening the tension of the on-going struggle between good and evil that provides the driving impetus for the onset of the protagonist's quest. So, for example, the refraction of pure white light into the colours of the spectrum, glimpsed when Saruman swirls his white cloak, is a metaphor for his fall to the Shadow through his insatiable desire to obtain forbidden knowledge and power. When Saruman sneeringly tells Gandalf that the 'white page can be overwritten; and the white light can be broken', Gandalf sagely replies, 'in which case it is no longer white ... [a]nd he that breaks a thing to find out what it is has left the path of wisdom'. (*Fellowship*, 252)

Jordan's response to this famed Tolkienian scenario is realised in the *WOT* through the leading female figures of Moiraine Aes Sedai and Lanfear (Daughter of the Night), a former Aes Sedai, who during the Age of Legends chose to turn to the Shadow for personal gain. In the Jordan sequence the traditional concept of the central magus figure as being solely male shifts to incorporate figures of either sex, which is in keeping with the concept of balance in his imaginary world. But insofar as Moiraine and Lanfear are presented as opposing representations of mind/body, purity/sexuality the author is here again drawing on stock motifs.

Le Guin, too, seeks to redress her earlier presentation of a masculine domination of magical powers when she revisits Earthsea in the novella *Dragonfly*. (2001, 197ff) In this more recent tale Irian, a young woman from the Island of Way, unexpectedly gains admittance into the male-dominated and sexually sterile world of the wizards on the island of Roke, where she is recognised by the Patterner of the Sacred Grove as being the catalyst of unprecedented change:

> All this year the patterns of the shadows and the branches and the roots, all the silent language of his forest, had spoken of destruction, of transgressions, of all things changed. Now it was upon them, he knew. It had come with her. (2001, 256)

Le Guin's text reflects both personal and contemporary societal changes in regard to feminine and masculine stereotyping. Jordan gives strong and important roles to his female characters and even presents a world in which females have held the power for three thousand years, but his work is not entirely free of gender stereotypes.

In Jordan's *WOT*, in keeping with his Manichaean framework, the magus figures fall into two main groupings, being either of the Light or of the Dark. Those of the Light are presented as the interpreters of the Great Pattern (through prophecy, archival manuscripts and foretelling), desperately needed if the world is to survive in its present form. Jordan's world is depicted in its Third Age, and looks back to the Age of Legends, a golden era that was destroyed by human greed and over-reaching for power.[2] These figures act, with limitations, as mentors/guardians to the main protagonists. Their Dark counterparts, too, are interpreters of the Great Pattern as they seem to have knowledge of the prophecies. But they seek to disrupt the cosmic pattern in order to replace it with an alternative one, which would bring chaos and fulfil the Dark Lord's promises to them of limitless power and immortality. Indeed it is prophesied that, if the Dark Lord gains control of the Wheel of Time, he will recast it in his own image and bring into existence a world of eternal Shadow. Jordan's light and dark patterning of the magus figures, who are so constructed to both test and encourage the development of the main protagonist, is interlaced with a type of pseudo-magus figure, one whose magical ability lies solely with words; a mercurial character, through whom the author gains entry into the realm of his own story-world.

THE SPELL OF THE STORYTELLER: MAGIC WITH WORDS

A wandering minstrel I –
A thing of shreds and patches,
Of ballads, scraps and snatches,
And dreamy lullaby! (W.S. Gilbert, *The Mikado*, Act 1)

Jordan's re-working of the traditional archetype of the magus or wise man is given a twist as Thom the gleeman provides a surrogate or alter ego for the author, which allows him not only to co-inhabit the world of the Wheel, but also to keep to the fore the importance of 'story' itself in maintaining the pattern of life within his depicted world and, by implication, its important role in our own lives, whether in oral or written form.

Through his portrayal of Thom Merrilin, also a prominent mentor/guide to the central protagonists, Jordan anticipates and then undercuts our expectations of the stock figure of the magus. On the one hand Thom appears to fulfil the traditional role of the superhuman wise man, but on the other his carnality and fallibility eventually reveal him to be a very human and much less romantic or elevated figure. Nevertheless, his essential goodness is not tarnished and his human warmth and foibles make him a character of great appeal, so he functions as a kind of 'rogue' wise man figure, but one whose unfailing sense of higher moral purpose in life puts him firmly on the side of the Light. The gleeman, who from his age, white hair, beard and name is strongly reminiscent of Merlin or Gandalf, has to date in this on-going series displayed no magical powers. Yet, paradoxically, early on he is introduced as an imposing and seemingly magical figure for even his 'deep voice … sounded in some way larger than that of an ordinary man', and 'in the open air it seemed to fill a great room and resonate from the walls'. (*EOTW*, 47)

The following word picture of Rand's first sight of him at his home village of Emond's Field, brings this character to life and imparts a sense of great age and of a certain grandeur:

> The white-haired man whirled, cloak flaring. His long coat had odd, baggy sleeves and big pockets. Thick mustaches as snowy as the hair on his head, quivered around his mouth, and his face was gnarled like a tree that had seen hard times. He gestured imperiously at Rand and the others with a long-stemmed pipe, ornately carved, that trailed a wisp of smoke. Blue eyes peered out from under bushy white brows, drilling into whatever he looked at. (*EOTW*, 46)

This stereotypical description, and the fact that Thom declares he is 'there for his art' – which includes not only his storytelling, but also his juggling, sleight of hand and fireworks – must draw some comparison with the representation of the wizard Gandalf and with his arrival in Hobbiton. (*EOTW*, 49) Gandalf was initially introduced in *LOTR* as 'that old wandering conjuror' and his fame throughout the Shire is mainly brought about through his 'skill with fires, smokes and lights'. (*Fellowship*, 24; 25) But the narrator soon warns the reader that Gandalf's business is 'far more difficult and dangerous', thereby cloaking him in an air of mystery. (*Fellowship*, 25) Since Thom must trigger echoes of Gandalf, this account sets up an expectation in Jordan's reader that Thom the Gleeman, too, could well have hidden superhuman talents. This thought is strengthened by Thom's wariness at Moiraine Aes Sedai's arrival in the village and his seemingly deceptive remark to her that he is but 'a simple Gleeman, that and nothing more'. (*EOTW*, 52)

Jordan repeatedly stated that he was in control of his narrative, likening himself to an 'Old Testament God' with his 'fist in the middle of [his] characters' lives' (Lilley 2002). Therefore, the character of Thom can feasibly be considered as a covert persona for the author, a way of giving himself not only a voice in the text, but also an active 'physical' presence and a further measure of control. For the author/creator is also the teller of great tales, an artist, like the gleeman, who creates magic with words, and in the depicted world the old gleeman's mind is said to be the repository of '*all* stories ... of Ages that were and will be'. (*EOTW*, 51) Upon arrival in the small village of Emond's Field, Thom assures his eager audience not only that he has 'all stories' but that he will 'make them come alive before [their] eyes'. (*EOTW*, 51; 50) Furthermore, he wears the distinctive garb of his trade, the gleeman's coat of many patches and colours, which is a marvellous metaphor, and signal for the reader, of the way in which Jordan's own *WOT* narrative is to be pieced together from many different bits of story, that in the end will make a coherent pattern and a strongly woven whole. Such a concept is strengthened by the fact that, despite the village innkeeper's dismissive observation that like the garments worn by all gleemen, Thom's 'is more patches than cloak' (*EOTW*, 16), and by inference flimsy, the opposite is true for it is revealed to be an article of some substance:

> His cloak seemed a mass of patches, in odd shapes and sizes, fluttering with every breath of air, patches in a hundred colors. It was really quite thick, Rand saw, despite what Master al'Vere had said, with the patches merely sewn on like decorations. (*EOTW, 46*)

In this way Jordan is able to privilege the role of the author as a teller of tales and to emphasise the importance of 'story' by suggesting that it provides the framework for a storehouse of collective human memory, and that, over time, like a patchwork garment, it is continuously being added to and altered, so that history as 'story' is timeless and never-ending and becomes part of the rich fabric of life.

LEGEND AND STORY

Jordan also said that, on one level, the *WOT* series gave him the chance to explore the source of 'legends and how they alter over time' (Sukul 2004). He seems to be referring to the way that fantasists are continuously drawing on an eclectic selection of traditional motifs, myths and legends, or the re-workings of these things by other writers, which they in turn reshape anew to suit their own purposes. On this recurring literary braiding of plot motifs and character types, Northrop Frye, in *Fables of Identity,* asserts that 'every literary work catches the echoes of other works of its type in literature, and so ripples out into the rest of literature and thence into life' (1963, 36-7). This view is also suggestive of the way in which 'story' and 'reality' continuously bleed into one another, blurring the boundaries between the two. Jordan's view of the transmutability of legends and other traditional material is echoed in the world of the Wheel by Thom, when he explains to Elayne about stories changing through the ages and reveals how the gleemen take up and preserve important events by continuously weaving them into their repertoire of tales, so that reality is constantly in the process of becoming 'story':

> My epic ... and Loial's book – will be no more than seed if we are both lucky. Those who know the truth will die, and their grandchildren's grandchildren will remember something different. And *their* grandchildren's grand-children something else again. Two dozen generations, and you may be the hero of it, not Rand. (*SR*, 327)

As the gleeman tells tales of 'what has been and what will be', he imparts a sense of time in his world as a continuous spiral that allows for a confluence of past, present and future, an idea frequently explored by the writers of fantasy, whether in totally Secondary Worlds like Tolkien's, Le Guin's and Jordan's or, as in the magical-realism works of writers like Susan Cooper, Alan Garner and Diana Wynne Jones, through an intersection of mythical past ages with the depicted mundane world of the characters.

Furthermore, writers of high fantasy work to keep the reader under the spell of the story and, indeed, they invite the reader to believe in and imaginatively co-inhabit their Secondary Worlds. So Jordan's introduction of a subtle narratorial voice that speaks from within the text, in the guise of an important and entertaining character, ensures that the pattern of the narrative is not disrupted nor the spell of the story broken.[3]

In the world of the Wheel it is through story that information is gathered and distributed and this is largely done through the gleemen, who 'travel like dust on the wind'. (*EOTW*, 309) By this means, the history and mythology of the world are preserved and retain a vibrant, on-going presence. The gleemen also speak of what may come to pass through the recital of long-memorised verses of ancient prophecy that have been handed down by word of mouth from one generation to the next. It is through the repetition of story that the inhabitants of the Wheel world retain a sense of place and self, for it is the threads of story that weave a pattern of life by drawing the past into the present, and foreshadowing the future. This sits well with Jordan's cosmology of a patterned and fatalistic world, one in which the inhabitants accept without question that throughout the repeating Ages 'the Wheel weaves as the Wheel wills'. (*EOTW*, 92) Story in Jordan's imaginary world is universal, and so it percolates throughout all levels of society via the public performance of the gleemen or by rumour. The hierarchical nature of the world of the Wheel is reflected in the different registers used by Thom in his recitals, from the 'High Chant' of the Old Tongue, used in the Royal Courts, through to the popular 'Plain Chant' of the taverns, down to 'Common'.[4] Thom's pride in his performance of story and his 'contempt' for 'Common' which 'meant simply telling' a story the way you might 'tell your neighbour about your crop' perhaps reflects an authorial vanity shown in the preference for the work of the artist as opposed to that of the layman. (*EOTW*, 210-11) A measure of the beauty of Thom's craft is captured during his one of his recitals in 'Plain Chant'. This performance occurs during a brief stopover in the city of Baerlon with the Emond's Fielders a few nights after they first flee their home village, where, at the Stag and Lion Inn, he re-tells an old favourite of cavalcade titled 'The Great Hunt of the Horn':

> 'prancing, silver hooves and proud, arched necks', Thom proclaimed, while somehow seeming not only to be riding a horse, but to be one of a long procession of riders. 'Silken manes flutter with tossed heads. A thousand streaming banners whip rainbows against an endless sky. A hundred brazen-throated trumpets shiver the air, and drums rattle like thunder. Wave on wave, cheers roll from watchers in their thousands, roll across the rooftops and towers of Illian, crash and break unheard around the thousand ears of the riders whose eyes and hearts shine with their sacred quest. The Great Hunt of the Horn rides forth, rides to seek the Horn of Valere that will summon the heroes of the Ages back from the grave to battle for the Light'. (*EOTW*, 210)

Thom's recital is imitative of Jordan's own range of styles and voices. For Jordan's purpose, as is shown through Thom's recital of the ancient tale of the legendary Horn of Valere, the gleeman is a versatile and extremely useful vehicle for imparting all kinds of knowledge, both fantastic and true, not only to the inhabitants of his own world but to the reader. Thus a deeper understanding of the depicted world grows naturally from within it, in a way that not only encourages the reader's belief in the reality of this realm, but heightens the emotional involvement in it.

The gleeman's extensive repertoire is a particularly useful literary tool for revealing many details of ancient battles and heroic deeds that help to flesh out the background of his world's long and glorious history. In a sort of parallel, the recital of verses taken from the prophecies of the Dragon highlights the urgency of the role the reincarnation of this figure must play in the approaching Last Battle, if the destruction of their world is to be averted. Thom's sharing of cryptically worded and riddle-like verses of ancient prophecies also provides puzzling clues to be unravelled by both protagonist and reader, thereby adding to the dramatic tension as Rand slowly moves towards an acceptance of the mantle of Dragon Reborn being thrust upon him by fate. The gleeman's remark that 'a prophecy that was easily fulfilled would not be worth much' reinforces the importance of story and adds to the epic sense of Jordan's own narrative, as well as suggesting that the hero's quest will take him upon a long and arduous path, for maturity and self-knowledge are not easily to be won. (*EOTW*, 190)

Jordan also highlights the fact that, in the depicted world, the inhabitants' acceptance of information is selective; they tend to relegate unpalatable although true stories (such as those indicating the existence of Trollocs and Fades or a Dragon who is both destroyer and saviour) to the realm of fable. Thereby, they would dismiss them as part of 'a great sackful of gleeman's tales', for Thom openly admits that some of his 'stories are exaggerated, in a way'. (*EOTW*, 233; 100) When the gleeman first makes mention to Rand of the prophecies of the Dragon, as found in the *Karaethon Cycle*, Rand is quick to reply that 'nobody tells … those stories in the Two Rivers, [n]ot in Emond's Field' and that the village Wisdom (i.e. healer) would 'skin them alive if they did'. (*EOTW*, 189) In other words, unduly alarmist stories that could disturb the villagers' peace of mind are to be ignored. But, as in our own world, denial of disturbing aspects of life does not negate them, nor does it preclude the changes they may bring; and eventually fears of the unknown need to be confronted and overcome, a lesson the main protagonists must master on their painful paths towards maturity. Yet, on the whole, Thom's travels throughout the lands over a period of many years make him a credible eye witness and chronicler of events, so that when he first warns Rand, Mat and Perrin to beware of entanglement with the 'Aes Sedai witches' of the White Tower because their true motives cannot be fathomed, his words have the ring of truth. And his words alert the reader that the role of these women is ambiguous and not always to be taken at face value.

Thom's identity as a gleeman and teller of fantastic tales is also linked to his trademark cloak of patches, worn in all weathers, hot or cold, as 'he always' wants to ensure that 'everyone' knows he is 'a gleeman'. (*DR*, 352) Moreover, when forced by circumstances to remove this garment, chameleon-like he reluctantly shrugs off this colourful persona to reveal other aspects of his character. Throughout the narrative the absence or presence of his cloak signals either the mental tucking away or opening up of his bottomless 'bag of gleeman's tales'. An excellent example of this occurs early in the first book when he prepares to flee from the city of Baerlon with Rand and Mat because the two youths are being stalked by a deadly 'Fade'. He removes his gleeman's cloak and, significantly, folds it 'into a bundle around his instrument cases, inside out' so that the patches are 'hidden', thus signalling a putting away of 'story'. In its place he dons a drab 'dark brown' cloak, becoming a stranger whom his two companions view as a scary 'tall man' who menacingly approaches them 'with the hood of his cloak pulled up to hide his face'(*EOTW*, 397; 396).[5] Although at this point, after aiding Mat and Rand's escape, he is thought to be killed by the Fade, because they carry his bundled up cloak and instruments to safety, hope remains that Thom and his stories will return – which of course, in time, they do.

When Mat next encounters Thom in the village of Salidar, stronghold of the rebel Aes Sedai, where he has temporarily become guide and protector to Elayne and Nynaeve, the youth muses that he 'did not know what to make of him without his gleeman's cloak'. (*LOC*, 803) On another occasion as he and Thom make plans to escape from the city of Ebou Dar, where Mat has been held as the sexual 'toy' of the Queen, he muses that the one-time gleeman seems 'positively drab in plain bronze-coloured wool and a dark cloak'. (*WH*, 341) The gleeman's change of apparel throughout the narrative clearly signals a change in the role that he will adopt: a device that enables Jordan to bring out different aspects of this character's personality to suit the pattern within his own greater narrative. Such changes fit well with the fact that essentially Thom, who with his oral performances brings story to life, is a highly experienced artist or illusionist. By this method Jordan creates an intriguingly adaptable character, whose multi-faceted personality metaphorically mirrors his gleeman's coat of many colours. Furthermore, Thom's ability to influence the way in which people perceive him, merely by the wearing or not wearing of his cloak, presents a type of shape-changing, an art that traditionally has been one of the supernatural abilities attributed to the magus figure. Thus Jordan, like so many writers before him, adapts traditional archetypes to fit his own purpose.

In line with the author's use of multi-stranded and intricately interlaced plots and sub-plots, and like other leading characters, Thom is woven into and out of the pattern of the narrative, playing a more prominent part in some books than in others, but always maintaining a presence, albeit only briefly, in volume ten (*COT*). As the later volumes in the series become increasingly concerned with the intrigues and politics of the various nations and the Dragon Reborn struggles to unite them before the Last Battle, so too Thom's role changes and he is portrayed as a less romantic and far more worldly-wise figure. Moiraine Aes Sedai reminds him that she is aware that he is no 'simple gleeman' (echoing his earlier words), but a man who is purported to be able to 'play' the deadly political 'Game of Houses in his sleep'. (*SR*, 272) His prowess in the chess-like moves of the popular game of Stones has already hinted at his ability to manipulate tricky situations to his own advantage. Moiraine, as if 'reading from a page', recites other details of his past:

> Thomdril Merrilin. Called the Gray Fox, once, by some who knew him, or knew of him. Court-bard at the Royal Palace of Andor in Caemlyn. [Queen] Morgase's lover for a time ... It is a shame that such a man calls himself a simple gleeman. But such arrogance to keep the same name. (*SR*, 272)

Thus, Jordan is able to legitimise Thom's role as it shifts from theatrical storyteller to political spy among the kitchens of the influential and wealthy or in the city taverns, where servants are inclined to be off-guard around a gleeman and so, loose-tongued. As a gleeman Thom is an acceptable figure at all levels of society which puts him in the perfect position to gather a wealth of material. It is a common trope in many genres of literature for a spy to be characterised as a liminal figure and thus enabled to cross thresholds. But from the fifth book on Thom lays aside his cloak, and ceases to bear any significant resemblance to the earlier projection of a Merlin or Gandalf type of figure. In the second book (*GH*), his passionate love affair with the young woman, Dena, and drinking bouts following her untimely murder, along with the hints of various other females who are willing to share his bed, make him a far more vulnerable and carnal figure. In fact, he never attains that aura of otherworldliness apparently informed by a Christian concept of grace that some critics have attributed to the wizard Gandalf. Yet, Egwene's puzzling dream of Thom putting 'his hand into a fire to draw out the small blue stone' that Moiraine wore on a chain across her forehead, offers the first clue that she is not dead and that in some way he holds the key to her rescue from the strange realm of the *Aelfinn* and *Eelfinn*, and so helps to retain a hint of his formerly more mysterious status. (*FOH*, 267) And Jordan, like Thom, is fond of pulling surprises out of his bag of stories.

Thom's role may change throughout the texts, but his ability to beguile his listeners with words, like that of his creator, remains constant, whether he is in the guise of flamboyant, artistic gleeman, wise counsellor and protector to the main protagonists, lover, or cunning and persuasive contestant in the political 'Game of Houses'. By positing the gleeman as his alter ego, Jordan gains a versatile voice and presence within the text itself. Through Thom he foregrounds constantly the notion of the storyteller (both the gleeman and himself) as a type of silver-tongued magician who, through agility with words, not supernatural powers, weaves stories that have the capacity to enchant an audience (both inside and outside the text) and thus extend the bounds of what is conceived to be possible.[6]

However, despite Thom's charm and magus-like qualities, strictly speaking, he is not really a magus. The true magus figures in the *WOT* are the characters who display the talent to channel the One Power, the source of magical prowess in Jordan's imaginary landscape. But before turning to an analysis of them, and their function in relation to the main protagonists, it is worth considering their scholarly and custodial nature as they too are presented as preservers and interpreters of the stories of the past, although their purpose is one more strongly tied to the journey of the hero.

KEEPERS OF THE CULTURAL 'TREE OF TALES'

Tolkien referred to stories as leaves 'from the countless foliage of the Tree of Tales' (1964, 51), a metaphor for the way in which stories, like leaves, are not only constantly renewed through time, but also are a means of preserving the cultural heritage of a people. As the collecting, writing, telling and preservation of stories throughout time constitute one of the central motifs in the Jordan texts, those who engage in these activities can be seen as the keepers of such a cultural 'Tree of Tales'.

Book-learning is always a valued attribute in fantasy, and the scholarly nature of the magus figure is a common conceit; for example, Belgarion's grandfather in the Eddings books has a fantastic study, while Hogwarts school for wizards contains an extensive library of rare and wonderful books, and in Susan Cooper's *The Dark is Rising* all ancient and true knowledge of magic is stored in the 'Book of Gramarye'. In the Jordan world the White Tower contains extensive archives of ancient manuscripts, as well as numerous objects of power that date from the Age of Legends. Many of the Aes Sedai scholars have devoted their lives to the interpreting of prophetic documents in an attempt to forecast the future patterning of events, which may help them to guide the long-awaited Dragon Reborn to victory. A helpful comparison can be drawn with the hoard of 'scrolls and books' held at Minas Tirith, where both Gandalf and Saruman had long sought to increase their knowledge of ancient lore. It is to the recorded story-patterns of the past that Gandalf turns to seek clues to the events of the past that have contributed to the shaping of the present crisis in Middle-earth. (*Fellowship*, 245-46) In Jordan's imaginary world, book-learning is also valued by the general public: inns contain small libraries, and even the al' Thors' modest home in Emond's Field boasts a couple of treasured 'wood-bound' books, including *The Travels of Jain Farstrider* – one of the Wheel world's legendary heroes. (*EOTW*, 65) Perhaps this love of books in the imaginary world is a reflection of the avid reading habits of the voraciously curious reader of fantasy in our world. (Le Guin in her *Earthsea* novels emphasises book-learning and the potency of words. But following the death of the wizard Ogion, Tenar (former priestess of the Tombs of Atuan) leaves his precious spell-books on the 'mantle at Oak Farm' with her son Spark who 'can't read a word of them'. In this instance Le Guin uses the putting aside of long-held magical lore to subtly foreshadow the changes to masculine-held power of the wizards of Roke that will come to pass in her later additions to the *Earthsea* series. (*Tehanu*, 26)

In Jordan's *WOT* even certain non-human characters, the Ogier giants, are portrayed as notable scholars, historians and storytellers. They are known in the Old Tongue as '*alantin*' or 'Treebrother', guardians of the remnants of the old groves known as Steddings. (*GH*, 290) Because of their longevity they have gathered and preserved a wealth of stories about the world of the Wheel, which in turn become woven into the pattern of the current story. Loial ventures forth into the wider world because 'the old stories caught [him]', and '[t]he old books filled [his] unworthy head with pictures', and a longing to travel. (*EOTW*, 638) In turn, he becomes caught up in the new story-like quest of the main protagonists, and it is his store-house of old knowledge that enables him to guide his companions through places such as the labyrinth-like passages of the other-worldly Ways. He also looks forward to 'watching from close by as the Pattern wove itself around' the three *ta'veren* youths, and is constantly taking notes for a book he plans to write about their adventures. (*GH*, 644) In Jordan's world the Ogiers can be viewed as gatherers and keepers of the stories, or leaves, of a never-ending cultural 'Tree of Tales'. As the Aes Sedai women of the White Tower, a society of magi, are also portrayed as long-lived gatherers, protectors, and interpreters of story patterns, by association, they too can be viewed in a similar light.

THE ROLE OF FEMALE MAGI: INTERPRETERS, KEEPERS OR DISRUPTERS OF THE 'GREAT PATTERN'

Female Aes Sedai

> Breakers of the world. Puppeteers who pulled strings and made thrones and nations dance in designs only the women from Tar Valon knew.
> (*EOTW*, 101)

As the Aes Sedai priestesses of the White Tower are the major society of magi in the *WOT*, a brief contextualisation is necessary before I focus on individual magus characters. Jordan is among the first writers of high fantasy to give multiple strong and leading roles to female characters, although despite their high profile his three central heroes are traditionally male. The author has stated that:

> One thing I did want to explore was how things would work out if one popular thread of fantasy in the last few decades were turned on its head. There are many books about women who must struggle to become sorcerers ...

because women just aren't allowed to do that. What, I thought if it were men who were not allowed to become wielders of magic. (Personal email 2004)

The action of Jordan's sprawling chronicle takes place in the Third Age, at a time when the male side of the One Power (*saidin*) has been contaminated for 3000 years by contact with the Dark Lord, and no male has hitherto been able to channel the *saidin* force without going mad. In this way Jordan has conceived of a largely matriarchal society, one where female Aes Sedai or priestesses – as in some ancient civilisations of our world – have developed great status and power. In a review of Jordan's tenth book (*COT*), William Thompson remarks percipiently that the author's portrayal of 'a magical order predicated upon a feminine principle, with the male side associated with chaos and madness, becomes a conceit hardly envisioned by Tolkien or his immediate imitators'. (Thompson 2003)

Indeed over the past 3000 years, in the world of the Wheel, Aes Sedai priestesses of the White Tower at Tar Valon have formed the moral and philosophical controlling mechanism that the society in general has accepted. Moiraine informs Egwene that:

> [The] Tower has been a bulwark against the Shadow for three thousand years. It has guided rulers to wise decisions, stopped wars before they began, halted wars that did begin. That humankind even remembers that the Dark One waits to escape, that the Last Battle will come, is because of the Tower. The Tower, whole and united. (*FOH*, 268)

Moreover, because of the fearsome nature of the Dragon who once destroyed the Wheel world, and the fact that on his return he is predicted to be both 'saviour' and 'destroyer', many people prefer to avoid or ignore the prophecies, so it is the Aes Sedai who have sought to maintain them for the benefit of the whole world. But the Aes Sedai are not omniscient beings and as keepers of ancient prophecy – which is the key to interpreting the Pattern of the future – they must piece together, like fragments of mosaic, odd bits of highly significant information on which the survival of their world rests. Some prophecies are clearly worded and can be relied upon, such as the Dragon Reborn facing the Dark Lord at the Last Battle: 'When the winds of Tarmon Gai'don scour the earth, he will face the Shadow and bring forth light again in the world'. (*GH*, 130) And it is certain that if the Dragon Reborn is not there the world will fall to 'fire and shadow, forever'. (*SR*, 21) Yet many of these ancient writings are cryptic and subject to multiple interpretations and the Aes Sedai fear that once the Dragon is reborn, unless guided by them, the changes he effects in the Age Lace may court disaster. Moiraine warns Rand and Mat that:

> as the Wheel of Time turns ... places wear many names.
> Men wear many names, many faces. Different faces, but
> always the same man. Yet no one knows the Great Pattern
> the Wheel weaves, or even the Pattern of an Age. We can
> only watch, and study, and hope. (*EOTW*, 29)

In the possible variations of the pattern of the Age, for all their knowledge and wisdom, not even the Aes Sedai can be certain of the final outcome. Their counterparts among the people of the desert, the Aiel Wise Ones, believe 'there is no one set path to the future', although in the World of Dreams (*Tel'aran'rhiod*) 'it is possible to see some ways the future may be woven'. (*SR*, 385) Thus Jordan foregrounds the complex nature of events that can affect the weaving of the Great Pattern.

The Aes Sedai's magical powers come from channelling the female half of the True Source or One Power, the endlessly self-perpetuating life-force that drives the Wheel of Time itself. Moiraine Aes Sedai remarks to Egwene that drawing upon *saidin* cannot use it up, 'any more than the river can be used up by the wheel of the mill. The Source is the river; the Aes Sedai, the waterwheel'. (*EOTW*, 169) They are merely conduits for the eternal flow of the One Power, which is neither of the Light nor the Dark, it just exists, and can be tapped by either and so used for positive or negative purposes.

Despite the awe and fear in which the Aes Sedai are held by the Wheel world community at large, Jordan does not present them as totally 'good and pure' – instead, they share human fallibility. Moiraine warns Egwene, before she becomes a sister at the White Tower, that at Tar Valon the Aes Sedai she will find 'are human, no different from any other women except for the ability that sets [them] apart'. They are found to be 'brave and cowardly, strong and weak, kind and cruel, warm-hearted and cold', as 'becoming an Aes Sedai will not change you from what you are'. (*EOTW*, 182-3) Through them the author thus explores the temptation, loneliness, and responsibility of female leadership.

Jordan divides the Aes Sedai of the White Tower into seven groups known as Ajahs, each denoted by a separate colour: white, blue, green, red, brown, yellow and gray. For many years they have been infiltrated by a secret and subversive society known as the Black Ajah, sisters drawn from all the Ajahs who have turned to the Shadow. (Fantasy writers tend not to present characters of the Light as double-agents infiltrating the Dark. In the *WOT* the activities and plans of the Dark are revealed to the reader in sub-plots, which are presented from the viewpoint of the antagonists and so interwoven into the focal narrative.) Jordan thus blurs the distinction between the polarities of good and evil, and highlights the destructive potential of power itself, for the White Tower which outwardly stands as an ancient and pristine pillar of the Light is in fact being insidiously corrupted from within.

In the distant Age of Legends, male and female Aes Sedai had used the One Power in unison, producing an era of great technical and philosophical advancement, a time when the word 'war' was forgotten. As Jordan's world looks back to an advanced age that was eventually destroyed by human greed, a comparison can be drawn with our present Western society, and perhaps a warning that we, too, may stand on the brink of total global destruction. Since the tainting of the male side of the One Power (*saidin*) by the Dark One, which brought about the 'Breaking of the World', there have only been female Aes Sedai. And from that time, when all men who drew on *saidin* went mad, nothing has been more feared than a man who could channel. For three millennia the necessary societal control of 'rebellious' males has been carried out through a process known as 'gentling' (a severing of males from the One Power) – an obviously effective way of negating societal danger, division or disruption.

Queens and their female Aes Sedai advisors have ruled the various nation states with some degree of success, although in a flawed and falling world they have not been able to wholly prevent the insidious reassertion of the Dark. Furthermore, during that same time the numbers of female initiates at the White Tower have slowly dwindled; the fact that the Wheel world is once again in an acute state of rising peril points to the realisation that, in the long run, it is imperative to have a balance between *saidar* and *saidin*, female and male, the two principles on which rests the power (the True Source) driving the Wheel of Time itself. Jordan accentuates this point in his depiction of the ancient symbol of the Aes Sedai which, as discussed in chapter one, shows the influence of Eastern philosophy and the concept of *yin* and *yang*.

Not surprisingly in a world ruled by women for the past three thousand years, those who serve as interpreters of the Pattern or central mentors/guides to the main protagonists are predominantly female. They are drawn from a group that displays varying degrees of talents and strengths in the One Power, that is comprised not only of Aes Sedai priestesses of the White Tower but also at times Aiel Wise Ones, or the more enigmatic Windfinders of the Sea Folk. On the Dark side there are other adepts in the One Power, servants of the Dark Lord, who work against the Pattern in order to turn the hero from his destined path and so bring their Master to rule the world. In particular they consist of thirteen former Aes Sedai from the Age of Legends (five females and eight males), traitors known as the 'Forsaken', although they regard themselves as the 'Chosen'. They work with the mysterious Moridin, the *Nae'blis* (Right Hand) of the Dark Lord, and all of these characters, along with the members of the Black Ajah, can be viewed as Jordan's negative counterparts to those who follow the Light.

It is the two women, Moiraine and Lanfear, who form the focus of this exploration of Jordan's interpretation of the magus figure through analysis of the key roles they play in the world of the Wheel as, respectively, keeper or potential disrupter of the Pattern of the Age. (As Cadsuane's later guidance of the hero Rand is to temper excess, her role will also be considered.) All of these women have been chosen for analysis because of their central roles in the growth of the hero Rand and the effect they have on the pattern of his journey. Jordan may seem only to draw on the Sophia and Lilith archetypes, one representative of truth, light and rebirth, the other of temptation and destruction, but he is giving his own secularised interpretation of this type of knowledge with a freedom from the close Christian symbolism apparent in the fantasy work of nineteenth-century writers such as George MacDonald. Moiraine symbolises rationality and Lanfear sensuality. They are both magi and these different approaches are important in the reading/interpreting of the pattern and the heroic quest.

Moiraine and Lanfear

Until their unexpected and dramatic disappearance through a *ter'angreal* doorframe during a violent confrontation in the fifth volume (*FOH*), the two strong female magi, Moiraine and Lanfear, form an intriguing triangle with the hero, Rand, the Dragon Reborn. Moiraine, as good mentor/guide, seeks to encourage him to accept his destiny and the Aes Sedai interpretations of the prophecies of the Dragon, while Lanfear, the seductive beauty, plots to lure him from his true path, and thus to destruction. In her discussion of the temptation of the hero in fantasy, Karen Schaafsma recognises that 'the negative figure of Lilith never appears in isolation in fantasy (as she might in horror fiction); she is always paired with her opposite, Sophia, whose light brings true vision and heralds rebirth'. Schaafsma further notes that 'the typical hero's development depends upon his encounters with archetypal feminine figures who may be inspiring or threatening or both, but who act as catalysts for his radical transformation' (1987, 53).

This is the case in Jordan's narrative, as it is because of the choice-forming actions of Moiraine and Lanfear, to a large extent, that the hero's mettle will be tried. These actions provide the author with a means of dramatically testing the hero, both physically and spiritually, as he struggles to come to terms with the enormity of the role being thrust upon him by fate. By leaving his village home as a naïve youth and embarking on a journey to the unknown, Rand faces choice and temptation that lead to personal growth and undreamed of changes to his life and to those around him. (A full discussion of Rand's youth, naivety and need for instruction belongs to the later chapters on the hero figures.)

In keeping with Jordan's overarching framework of Light and Dark in his imaginary world, there is clear symmetry in his patterning of these female characters as being representative of the cosmic polarities of good and evil and, perhaps, as a mirror image of the two extremes of human nature. Bearing in mind that Lanfear, before turning to the Shadow in the Age of Legends, had been a powerful Aes Sedai priestess, the concept of Lanfear and Moiraine as representing the two sides of woman (body and mind) has considerable merit. Viewed in this light they can be likened to the positive and negative aspects of the High Priestess of the ancient Tarot, who has been described as a 'linear descendant of the High Priestesses of antiquity', and the 'embodiment of the lunar goddesses of combination and procreation' (Douglas 1974, 54). The history, mysticism, philosophy and psychology surrounding the Tarot are as eclectic as the motifs and other traditional material ransacked by writers of fantasy, and can be taken from the same sources and so help to explain Jordan's presentation of Moiraine and Lanfear.[7]

In the Tarot pack the High Priestess is generally portrayed as being seated between two pillars, one light and one dark, symbolising the 'the twin pillars of positive and negative power upon which the universe is founded'. It is said that she is the 'passive link between the physical and spiritual planes', or the 'great feminine force controlling the very source of life'. Under this positive aspect she is 'Divine Inspiration – Sophia, the Gnostic goddess of wisdom'. But in her negative aspect she also becomes 'the *femme fatale* Hecate, Queen of the Dark of the Moon, Lilith ... the weaver of illusions who destroys her lovers'.(Douglas 1974, 54-5) The way the 'moonlight' creates a 'nimbus' around

Moiraine, enhances the idea of her purity of spirit, while Lanfear's title as 'Daughter of the Night' links her firmly to the moon and the shadowy realm of night and so of seductive succubus-like dream. (*EOTW*, 183) Many of Lanfear's appearances in the text occur at night, in the amorphous dimensions of the Wheel's mirror worlds, or in *Tel'aran'rhoid*, the World of Dreams. In Jordan's world she is regarded as a mythical demon figure, one long 'used by mothers who only half-believed in her [themselves] to frighten children'. (*SR*, 193) A similar representation of light and dark aspects of a feminine figure is to be found in Malory's *Le Morte d'Arthur*, for the Lady of the Lake 'serves the cause of heroism and the tradition of chivalry', while her opposite the enchantress Morgan Le Fay uses her 'wiles to make [Arthur] her lover, and consistently seeks his death' (Hourihan 1997, 178). Thus Arthur's strength of character, his ability to abide by the chivalric code of truth, duty and honour on which the stability of his realm is dependent, is to be tested between the two.

In Jordan's representation both women are slender, dark haired and exceptionally beautiful, and their voices 'musical', but Moraine never invites intimacy and despite her tiny stature has an unsettling air of 'maturity', coolness, 'grace', and 'command' that engenders respect. (*EOTW*, 26) Early on in their acquaintance Rand likens her to a 'High Lady' from a 'gleeman's tale'. (*EOTW*, 25) He freezes under her gaze, and finds her 'dark' eyes are 'deep pools about to swallow him up', and muses on the frightening tales he has heard of the Aes Sedai who are purported to be '[b]reakers of the world' and '[p]uppeteers who pulled strings and made thrones and nations dance in designs only the women from Tar Valon knew'. (*EOTW*, 26; 101) Rand recalls his father Tam's warning that an 'Aes Sedai never lies, but the truth she speaks may not be the truth you think you hear'. (*EOTW*, 644)

However, Lanfear, who often disguises herself as a beautiful young woman called Selene, is deliberately provocative, seductive and flattering. (Selene of course is the ancient Greek goddess of the moon.) At their initial meeting in a mirror world of the Wheel, where Rand rescues her from a monstrous creature, she kneels to him and says demurely yet seductively, 'I am yours, Lord Rand al'Thor'. (*GH*, 253)

He believes she looks upon him as if he was 'a hero in a story', and her 'dark eyes' not only 'make him feel as if he were naked', but the 'unbidden thought' of her 'with no clothes' fills his mind'. (*GH*, 254) In her presence he seems compelled to want to constantly be 'close enough … to smell her heady scent, close enough to touch'. (*GH*, 257) When he takes her hand to help her dismount from her horse, he discovers that the skin on her hand is 'softer', 'smoother' than 'silk'. (*GH*, 255) Thereafter, from their initial meetings with the hero Rand, the two women's opposing roles of wisdom/grace and temptation in the inter-connected patterning of the narrative are firmly set in place.

Jordan further heightens his mirror-imaging of this pair of powerful women through a patterning of colour association. Moiraine's accessories are of gold, while Lanfear's are of silver and, as J. C. Cooper points out, 'gold and silver' or 'sun and moon', are the 'two aspects of the same cosmic reality' (1992, 40-1). Moiraine is also associated with blue, the colour traditionally symbolic of 'truth, the intellect, revelation, wisdom, loyalty, fidelity … coolness' and, in Christian terms, of the 'Virgin Mary as Queen of Heaven' (Cooper 1992, 40). She is of the Blue Ajah, and her commitment to guiding the Dragon Reborn elicits the comment by an old friend: 'You Blues. Always so ready to save the world that you lose yourselves'. (*GH*, 330) The clothing worn when she first appears in Emond's Field of 'sky-blue velvet' cloak, over a dress of 'a darker blue' and with 'a small, sparkling blue stone in the middle of her forehead' fastened in her hair by a 'gold chain' is typical. Her belt of 'woven gold', and the 'gold ring in the shape of a serpent biting its own tail … an even older symbol for eternity than the Wheel of Time', bring other associations of divine power, and light that help to set her apart from normal mortal beings. (*EOTW*, 27) Like Susan Cooper's mystical 'Lady' in *The Dark is Rising*, who says of herself that she is 'very old … and has in her time had many, many names' (1976, 33), Moiraine, too, is presented as an ageless protective figure, a champion of the Light and a version of the archetypal figure that Robert Graves wrote about in his book *The White Goddess* (1959).

By contrast Lanfear, although slender, is 'tall' for a woman, with 'ivory-pale skin', 'night-dark' hair and 'black' eyes. (*GH*, 253) She is always clad in 'white belted in woven silver', her hair hung with 'silver stars and crescents', linking her to the moon and the realm of night and dream. (*FOH*, 16) The association here is not with 'purity' or 'chastity', but with the beguiling and deadly white ur-witch from the myth of Lilith who is traditionally presented as being pale skinned, dark haired, and clothed in white. Lanfear's description closely resembles that of the seductress 'Geraldine' in S. T. Coleridge's mediaeval-inspired poem, *Christabel*, who is:

> Drest in a silken robe of white,
> That shadowy in the moonlight shone:
> The neck that made the white robe wan,
> ... And wildly glittered here and there,
> The gems entangled in her hair. (lines 58-65)

Jordan's employment of a worldly-wise, wily, and sensuous woman to tempt his naïve and sexually inexperienced hero increases the odds of his susceptibility to her charms and the danger that under her seductive spell he will be lured to abandon his fated and key role in the interpretation of the pattern that can save the Wheel world.

DESTINY AND DUTY: MOIRAINE AES SEDAI

> The Pattern pays no heed to human plans... our plans are precarious things. The winds of destiny are blowing ... and we must ride them where they take us. (*GH*, 64-5)

Gandalf as a template for Jordan's Moiraine

Moiraine, as mentor/guide to the main protagonist Rand plays a role similar to Tolkien's Gandalf, but unlike the wizard of Middle-earth she is not an agent of a higher cosmic force from beyond the boundaries of the world of the Wheel. Jordan has conceived of an imaginary world in which the force that provides the superhuman or magical power is an integral part of the cosmology – much as depicted in the archipelago of Le Guin's *Earthsea*. Tolkien's Gandalf is a supernatural being, for he is not explicable in terms of the natural laws or phenomena of the imaginary world in which he operates.

Gandalf's background is steeped in mystery, and to the reader is suggestive of an immortality that links him throughout the ages of our mythic lore, not only to the Arthurian Merlin, but also to the Northern God Odin. Furthermore, in the appendices to the *LOTR* it is revealed that Gandalf is one of five wizards sent by the semi-divine Valar to 'contest the powers of Sauron' and who 'came in the shape of men, though they were never young and aged slowly'. (*King*, appendix b.193) Within the narrative, although Gandalf does not explicitly say that he comes from or is directed by a higher outside force, Treebeard's words to Merry and Pippin strongly suggest this to be the case. Treebeard is the oldest living creature and yet he '[does] not know the history of the wizards', only that they 'appeared first after the Great Ships came over the sea; but if they came with the ships [he cannot] tell'. (*Towers*, 462) The mystery that surrounds Gandalf's presence in Middle-earth is echoed by Pippin who wonders: 'What was Gandalf? In what far time and place did he come into the world, and when would he leave it?' (*King*, 740) Following his defeat of the evil Balrog and the survival of his spirit through 'the fire and the abyss' he reappears on a mountain top, 'naked ... sent back – for a brief time, until [his] task is done', which suggests he is directed from a force that lies beyond the perceived confines of Middle-earth. (*Towers*, 490; 491) The giant eagle, Gwaihir the Windlord, who bears him to Caras Galadhon, now finds him to be 'as light as a swan's feather', which further suggests that although he is still incarnate he is a higher and immortal being. (*Towers*, 490-491) Having passed through 'the fire and the abyss' he has returned as Gandalf the White. Gimli refers to Gandalf's head as being 'now sacred' adding to the sense that Gandalf has been returned as an act of some divine grace in order for the destined pattern of events to be played out. (*Towers*, 492)

Throughout the narrative it is Gandalf who appears to have knowledge of a larger pattern of destiny and who acts as mentor/guide to the main protagonists. The narrator warns the reader at the beginning of the tale that Gandalf's purpose 'is far more difficult and dangerous' than the Hobbits know, thus hinting that he is to be the co-ordinator of a destined pattern of events. (*Fellowship*, 25) The centrality of Gandalf's role in the quest to save Middle-earth is borne out by Elrond who tells Frodo and his companions that Gandalf is to accompany them and that 'this will be his great task, and maybe the end of his labours'. (*Fellowship*, 268) The truth that Gandalf moves to a higher fated pattern is further strengthened by Galadriel who points out that 'needless were none of the deeds of Gandalf in life'. (*Fellowship*, 347) Unlike Jordan's Moiraine, the angel-like Gandalf has foreknowledge of the larger pattern of future events that is not to be gleaned from ancient prophecies. At his coronation, following the defeat of Sauron and the destruction of the One Ring, Aragorn refers to Gandalf as 'the mover of all that has been accomplished'. Gandalf admits: 'I was the enemy of Sauron; and my work is finished. I shall go soon'. (*King:* 946; 950) But for all his powers he is not omniscient, for he explains to Gimli: 'I can see many things far off, but many things that are close at hand I cannot see'. (*Towers*, 484) Thus, Tolkien achieves the appearance of the finer details of the pattern of destiny being subject to chance and governed by the free choices and actions of the mortal beings of his imaginary world.

Christine Brooke-Rose accuses Tolkien of using the Gandalf character as the 'great explainer' (1981, 237). But in her analysis she overlooks the deliberate interlaced patterning of the narrative, the considerable skill and artistry employed by Tolkien in his use of Gandalf, and at times Elrond or Galadriel. Gandalf's foretelling of future events and his ability to guide the main protagonists are woven into the fabric of the depicted world, for they develop organically out of an intimate knowledge of the vast storied past of the depicted world of which he is a part. (It is Gandalf and the elfin brethren who continually reinforce the concept that the larger events in Middle-earth move to a higher, destined pattern.) Gandalf has not been superimposed on the world for the convenience of the plot as Brooke-Rose's words would seem to imply, although this is not to deny that his role serves that purpose.

Moiraine: Jordan's magus of reason

In Jordan's *WOT* Moiraine Aes Sedai is presented as mortal, although long-lived, and some detail is given of her family and her younger days before joining the White Tower. Characterising her like all the Aes Sedai women, Jordan sets her apart from the ordinary through her ability to channel the One Power, that source of magic or superhuman power in the world of the Wheel, and the reason for her enhanced life span. Like a priestess or nun, Moiraine has an air of otherworldliness, and has 'dedicated [her] life' to her 'cause', to find the Dragon Reborn and see him safely to the Last Battle. (*SR*, 124) Yet there are illuminating parallels that can be drawn between Moiraine and Gandalf, for like him she is the catalyst for the commencement of the hero's quest. She seeks out the three rural youths, Rand, Mat and Perrin, and following an attack on their homes by monstrous Trollocs, decrees that they 'must leave, for the sake of [their] village' as 'in one of [them] ... or all three, there is something the Dark One fears'. (*EOTW*, 111; 113) In this manner, despite their reluctance, she sets Rand and his companions on a dangerous journey of personal growth. As they pass beyond the boundaries of their known world of the Two Rivers shire, she hints at their far greater destiny:

> You have further to go yet ... much further. But there is
> no choice, except to run and hide and run again for the
> rest of your lives. And short lives they would be. You must
> remember that, when the journey becomes hard. You have
> no choice. (*EOTW*, 185)

Similarly, when Frodo wishes to relinquish the role of ring bearer and suggests that he is 'not made for perilous quests', Gandalf replies: 'but you have been chosen, and you must therefore use such strength and heart and wits that you have'. (*Fellowship*, 60) Thus, like Gandalf, Moiraine sets Rand and his companions on the traditional path of the typical hero of fantasy, 'the sacrificial hero who must abandon the small, personal self so that he can serve as a vessel of renewal for the larger community, for life itself'. (Schaafsma 1987, 60) Jordan's portrayal of the hero harmonises well with this theoretical observation as he presents a world that is falling to the Shadow, and the Dark One has now touched the idyllic Two Rivers shire; this shatters the illusion that anywhere in the world of the Wheel can now provide a safe haven. Chosen by the Great Pattern, Rand, Mat and Perrin, as *ta'veren*, are plucked from obscurity to play their destined parts on their world stage, and how they perform will have reverberations for all living things.

Moiraine believes 'everything is a part of the Pattern', that one 'cannot pick and choose' for '[t]he Wheel weaves as the Wheel wills'. (*EOTW*, 143; 92) For instance, in the prophecies of the Dragon, known as the *Karaethon Cycle*, it is written that the 'Dragon will be reborn on the slopes of Dragonmount, where he died during the Breaking of the World'. (*GH*, 128) Twenty years before the commencement of the tale, Moiraine's own path was set when she and her friend Siuan witnessed a foretelling by an older Aes Sedai, who cried out before she fell dead:

> He is born again! I feel him! The Dragon takes his first breath on the slope of Dragonmount! He is coming! He is coming! Light help us! Light help the world! He lies in the snow and cries like the thunder! He burns like the sun! (*GH*, 128-9)

It was from this moment that the then Amyrlin Seat[8] of the White Tower, gave these two young Aes Sedai the secret task to find the child. For she knew that out of fear of a man channelling not everyone at the Tower would allow him the freedom to develop and to fulfil his role at the Last Battle. Moiraine believes that they were 'chosen for this by the Pattern', and the urgency of the task is stressed by her decree that 'we are part of the Prophecies, and the Prophecies must be fulfilled. Must!' (*GH*, 63) Over the years Moiraine scours the countryside, posing as a collector of old 'stories'. (*EOTW*, 52) It is a 'story' of a man who had found an 'infant on the mountain' that eventually leads her to the 'Two Rivers'. (This is another instance of Jordan's foregrounding of storytelling.) In this far flung quarter of the land, where the 'Old Blood of Manetheren seethes still like a river in flood', and in keeping with the prophecy that the one she sought was to be 'of the ancient blood, and raised by the Old Blood' her trail ends. (*GH*, 129) As she later explains to Rand when he first shows signs of being able to touch the One Power:

> in Emond's Field, I found three boys whose name-days were within weeks of the battle at Dragonmount. And one of them can channel. Did you think the Trollocs came after you just because you are *ta'veren?* You are the Dragon Reborn. (*GH*, 129)

Unlike Lanfear, Moiraine constantly urges the youth to accept the role thrust upon him by fate, through remarks such as: 'You were made for a purpose ... you were born to unite mankind and lead them against the Dark One'; 'you will face the Dark One, [i]t is your destiny'; and '[t]he prophecies must be fulfilled'. (*GH*, 130) From her interpretations of the prophecies she is convinced that 'the Pattern itself will see him named Dragon, whether he wills it or not'. For he has 'no more control over his fate than a candle wick has over a flame'. (*GH*, 70) Thus she acts as an externalisation of his conscience, and ever appeals to his sense of duty. A good example of this occurs in the aftermath of the battle against the invading Seachan army at the port city of Falme, when Mat sounds the Horn of Valere to summon the heroes of the past to help them. At this point, Rand engages with Ba'alzamon, a surrogate for the Dark Lord, in a metaphysical battle displayed 'across the sky ... in full view of every soul in Falme', while the ancient 'banner' of the Dragon 'rippled' behind them. (*GH*, 676) Yet, despite all evidence that he must be the much prophesied saviour, Rand rebels against her guidance and his fate, shouting: 'I don't need you ... I don't want you ... I will not be the Dragon'.[9] To this she replies:

> You are what you are ... already you stir the world ...
> Three of the seven seals [that keep the Dark One imprisoned] are broken ... when all seven are broken ...

the only hope of the world is that the Dragon Reborn will be there to face him. (*GH*, 676-77)

Despite Rand's protests, she is an insistent voice of a higher reason and never deviates from her attempts to keep him on the right path, reminding him 'it is too late to hide ... it was always too late for you to hide', for 'each of us has his part in the Pattern' and so must accept it (*GH*, 678; *EOTW*, 721):

> You must choose, Rand ... The world will be broken whether you break it or not. Tarmon Gai'don will come, and that alone will tear the world apart. Will you still try to hide from what you are, and leave the world to face the Last Battle undefended? Choose. (*GH*, 679)

Her fierce belief in her own part in the Pattern and her 'duty' has a darker side, for she warns Rand, Mat and Perrin that, 'before I let the Dark One have you, I will destroy you myself'. She also reminds them of the fact that, 'humankind, and Ogier, everything that lives [is] at war with the Dark One'. (*EOTW*, 180-1; 649) In literature a figure with this kind of tutelary role is often cast as serious and authoritarian in contrast to the seductive nature of evil offered by her opposite.

Jordan presents a world that is governed by a type of conditional determinism, so that although life's Pattern is controlled by an inscrutable outside force in the form of a Cosmic Loom, he creates the impression that the characters have some freedom of choice. If his main protagonists were perceived by the reader to be merely puppets treading a totally pre-determined path there would be no chance of failure and little opportunity for believable personal development or growth. Much of the tension in the narrative is generated by the fact that although Rand, Mat and Perrin have destined roles at the Last Battle, there are different paths that they could take along the way. Moiraine's warning to them that 'the Web can still be woven many ways, and some of those designs, would be disastrous', for them and 'for the world', raises the horrible possibility that one or all of the three youths could fall to the

Dark or be killed. (*EOTW*, 644) Moiraine's later caution to Rand that although as a *ta'veren* he is fated to bring change to the pattern, any foolhardy actions could 'rip the Age Lace for all time', reiterates the dangers inherent in exercising choice. (*SR*, 363) The survival of the world is thus poised on a knife-edge, and its people cannot trust to 'destiny' alone to keep the Dragon 'alive'. Moiraine's friend and leader of the White Tower, Siuan Sedai, in her wisdom fears that:

> This isn't a story; he isn't some invincible hero and if his thread is snipped out of the Pattern, the Wheel of Time won't notice his going, and the Creator will produce no miracles to save us. If Moiraine cannot reef his sails, he may very well get himself killed, and where are we then? Where is the world? ... Doomed ... [to] fire and shadow forever. (*SR*, 21)

Jordan's concept of a Cosmic Loom, like the Anglo-Saxon Wyrd, is that of an inexorable, impersonal force: should Rand's life-thread be cut before he completes his fated task it will blindly spin on without him. The frightening thing for the inhabitants of the world is that if they lose the Dragon Reborn they cannot appeal to a higher power and victory will belong to the Dark. And from that point on it will be the hand of the Dark Lord that 'sets the warp' and 'controls the shuttle' of the Wheel of Time. (*EOTW*, 644) Thus, Jordan uses the concerns and fears of the Aes Sedai to highlight for the reader the epic scale of the heroic quest and the centrality of Moiraine's mentoring role, which is further emphasised by her friend Siuan who believes that:

> Prophecies are meant to announce to the world who he is, to prepare him for what's coming, to prepare the world for it. If Moiraine can keep some control over him, she will guide him to the Prophecies we can be sure of – when he is ready to face them ... The Light send it's enough. (*SR*, 21)

Yet, paradoxically, Jordan suggests that the Aes Sedai are but pawns in the Pattern, as they exist in a world where all 'humankind is made for uncertainty, struggle, choice and change', and so we see that unlike Gandalf they are not helpers sent by a higher force that is external to the Wheel world. (*SR*, 387) For all the Aes Sedai women's schemes to protect and guide the Dragon Reborn to the threads of the future which they deem safest for him and the world, he increasingly fights against such control, interpreting the prophecies in his own way, and wilfully refuses to be led. Moiraine has to lament, 'why could he not have remained the amenable youngling' whom she had first found. (*SR*, 345) However, she accepts the fact that 'the Pattern pays no heed to human plans' and that with all their scheming, they 'forgot' that they were 'dealing' with a *ta'veren*, and for a time that the 'Wheel will weave the Pattern around this young man as it wills, whatever [their] plans'. (*GH*, 64-5)

Moiraine admits to her limitations, to the truth that although she has 'read every word of the Prophecies of the Dragon' in 'every translation' she does not have knowledge of all that could happen, for 'the Wheel weaves as the Wheel wills' and 'no eye can see the Pattern until it is woven'. (*DR*, 601; *EOTW*, 418) Some things are made clear to her once they have been woven into the Pattern: 'Prophecies are fulfilled as they are meant to be', not as the Aes Sedai 'think they should be'. (*DR*, 670) For instance, it is only after the Aiel warriors leave the Wasteland to assist Rand to bring about the fall of the fortress at Tear, that she realises they must be the much-prophesied 'People of the Dragon'. (*DR*, 671) She also had no prior knowledge that Perrin would develop the talent of linking with the minds of the wolves, or that Mat would first sound the Horn of Valere that summons the aid of a band of legendary warriors.[10]

Moiraine, much like Gandalf, can guide her *ta'veren* charges, but she cannot compel them, although her rhetorical advice is designed to sway their decisions, as in the first book (*EOTW*), when it is learned that the Dark One plans an assault on the legendary Green Man's hidden grove. The Green Man has long guarded a concentrated, uncontaminated pool of *saidin* that has the 'Power to mend the seal on the Dark One's prison, or to break it open completely'. (*EOTW*, 746) Moiraine appeals to Rand, Perrin and Mat's better selves, to their developing sense of obligation and duty to ensure that they take up this particular quest:

> Three threads have come together here … It cannot be chance … you three did not choose; you were chosen by the Pattern …You can step aside, and perhaps doom the world. Running, hiding, will not save you from the weaving of the Pattern. Or you can try. You can go to the Eye of the World, three *ta'veren,* three centerpoints of the Web, placed where the danger lies. Let the Pattern be woven around you there, and you may save the world from the Shadow. The choice is yours. I cannot make you go. (*EOTW*, 649-50)

In the *LOTR* Tolkien uses a similar technique, for although Gandalf and the Elven-lord Elrond believe that the carrying of the One Ring to the Cracks of Doom is a 'task appointed' for Frodo they both reiterate that he must 'take it [up] freely'. (*Fellowship*, 264) But at the outset Gandalf's rhetoric, too, is designed to emphasise the fey and terrible danger inherent in the One Ring, against which even he is not immune. Gandalf refuses to accept the ring from Frodo for he fears that the 'wish to wield it would be too great for [his] strength' and he could 'become like the Dark Lord himself'. (*Fellowship*, 60) The wizard's words are designed to frighten Frodo, to sway his thought processes in favour of accepting the fated quest. In high fantasy the hero's necessary development is linked to the ability to make such hard decisions; choices that will lead to the undertaking of arduous journeys into the unknown at both a physical and a spiritual level.

The emphasis is ever on the need for the hero figures to draw upon an inner strength, a steadfast belief in a selfless, higher good. A clear example occurs in the *WOT* when the three *ta'veren* youths' dreams are invaded by Ba'alzamon and Lanfear. It is a realm wherein Moiraine can offer but limited degrees of protection and she insists that they 'must find the strength and will' within themselves, warning 'I cannot give it to you'. Although it is not easy to stand against the Dark One 'he cannot' make them do his bidding his unless they 'let him'. (*EOTW*, 642; 643) An oft repeated folk saying in the Two Rivers is that 'the hand of the Creator shelters the world, and the Light shines on us all', revealing a popular belief in the existence of a higher good. (*EOTW*, 14) Moiraine, in opposition to Lanfear, is presented as the voice of caution and oracular wisdom, and it is shown that she fights not for personal gain, but rather uses her powers and knowledge to interpret the Pattern of the Age in ways that will assist Rand to meet his final battle with the Dark One. As these two female magus/mentor figures are divided not only into Light and Dark but also into reason/passion, gender lines mean that Lanfear's interactions with Rand are necessarily sexualised.

TEMPTATION: LANFEAR, DAUGHTER OF THE NIGHT

Daughter of the Night, she walks again,
The ancient war, she yet fights.
Her new lover she seeks, who shall serve her and die,
yet serve still.
Who shall stand against her coming?
The Shining Walls shall kneel. (A prophecy of the Dark, *GH*, 105)

The tradition of a beautiful temptress who brings about the destruction of men who fall under her spell has a long literary history, sacred and profane, as a representation of evil; for example, the biblical stories of Eve's temptation of Adam that led to the Fall, Delilah's betrayal of Samson, and Salome whose sexual wiles were instrumental in obtaining the beheading of John the Baptist, or the myth of Lilith, the destructive first wife of Adam. From classical myth there is the figure of Helen of Troy in whose beauty lie the seeds of the destruction of Troy, and later representations include Shakespeare's Cleopatra and Lady Macbeth. As Roderick McGillis observes:

she represents a source of evil, a siren who destroys those who fall under her spell. She represents the unknown and the mysterious and to turn away from her enchantments is to preserve humanity. Men fear her and love her, both terrorised and fascinated by her power. (1979, 3)[11]

Lanfear: Jordan's dark magus of passion

In his portrayal of Lanfear (Selene), Jordan makes her the arch-temptress and seductress of his hero Rand, as the most obvious means of exploring the true nature of power and love and their destructive potential at both personal and universal level. For should Rand reject the higher virtues of duty and honour and so fall, the imaginary world as it is known would fall with him.[12] Thus, Jordan uses her as a disrupter of the Pattern that is needed to lead Rand to victory. In the Age of Legends, Jordan tells us, Lanfear was known as Mierin, a respected researcher into the One Power.[13] She had been one of those responsible for finding the Dark One's prison and so for creating a weak spot, the 'Bore', in the Great Pattern that allowed Him to begin to touch the world, but she eventually sold her soul to the Shadow. (*Companion*, 78ff) She was a former lover of Lews Therin, the Dragon, who ended the relationship because she 'loved power' above all else, but she refused to accept the break and, after his marriage to Ilyena, she continued her obsessive claim on him. (*SR*, 175) As one of the thirteen 'Forsaken', trapped in the 'Bore' when the Dark One's prison was re-sealed, for 3000 years she was caught 'in a dreamless sleep where time did not flow' and so she did not age. (*SR*, 175) Upon awakening to the world, she had retained her obsession for power and for Lews Therin, through his reincarnation Rand al'Thor, the Dragon Reborn. If she can but turn Rand to the Dark and bring him to 'kneel to the Great Lord', she believes her own rewards will be great indeed. (*SR*, 176)

Lanfear appears to tempt Rand at key moments, times when if he should be swayed by her rhetoric, her beauty and sensuality, it would lead towards a breaking of the pattern of his destiny and set in motion her desired alternative dark, and destructive pattern of events. Accordingly she seeks to distract him by her sensuality and by promises of personal glory and fame. In direct opposition to Moiraine, she dismisses the power of prophecy. For example, when Rand tells Lanfear that he was 'born' to fight the 'Father of Lies', and to 'fulfil the prophecies', she counters this by suggesting that 'prophecy is no more than the sign of what people hope for'. Fulfilling them will only 'bind' him to a 'path leading to Tarmon Gai'don and ...death'. (*SR*, 177) However, if he will but 'kneel to the Great Lord ... he will set you above all others', and '[h]e will leave you free to reign as you will'. (*SR*, 176) On another occasion she also swears that 'the Pattern has infinite variation ... and every variation that can be will be', thereby implying that in the seeming randomness of the Pattern, Rand does not have to follow the prophecies of the Light, or the White Tower's interpretations of them, as being the only or best way he may take. (*GH*, 258)

Rand's first encounter with her occurs in a 'mirror world' of the Wheel, at a point when he is struggling to resist the pull of *saidin*, cannot control it and so is afraid of the madness it brings. He reveals his inner core of strength by standing firm against the surrogate of the Dark Lord, Ba'alzamon, who appears in the night with promises of teaching him to 'control that power', and of the 'Great Lord of the Dark' who can 'shelter' him from the 'madness', so that he 'can live forever'. (*GH*, 244) But in Lanfear's presence it is more difficult for him to remain resolute and clear of mind, as 'there seemed to be a scent to her, something that filled his head with her' and aroused unbidden, strange thoughts. (*GH*, 255) She tempts him to embrace *saidin*, silkily suggesting 'it is best to wrap it around you continuously, to dwell in it at all times ... and you'll learn uses for it you never suspected'.(*GH*, 260) He also has the legendary Horn of Valere in his possession, having rescued it from a group of Darkfriends, and so plans to return it to those who will ensure it is taken to Tar Valon for safe keeping. The prophecies say that the Horn is needed at the Last Battle, but they do not link the Dragon with it, implying that someone else is destined to sound it and thereby summon the heroes of the past to aid him. Lanfear constantly works on Rand's vanity, suggesting that he is 'a man for the legends' and that the 'man who sounds the Horn will make his own legends'. (*GH*, 255) In addition he can have her:

Think of the glory that will come to the one who finds the
Horn of Valere. How proud I'll be to stand beside him
who holds the Horn. You have no idea of the heights we
will scale together ... you can be a king. You can be
another Artur Hawkwing. (*GH*, 287)

It is further predicted that the finding of the Horn will be a sign that the
Last Battle is approaching. As the Horn is tied to the one who first
sounds it, whether of the Light or the Dark, the heroes of the past must
come to its call. Lanfear thus schemes to turn Rand to the Shadow, to
have him use the Horn and so become a powerful tool for her own
purposes. In her attempt to sway the hero, her flattering and persuasive
rhetoric is constantly accompanied by body language designed to arouse
and confuse him. Jordan presents her as a dangerously beautiful woman,
as changeable as quicksilver, which both deeply attracts and frightens
Rand: 'Moonshadows veiled her face in mystery as she looked up at
him, and mystery made her even more beautiful'. Her eyes seem as 'dark
and deep as night' and 'soft as velvet'. (GH, 289; 268) She flaunts her
body, '[her] legs pale in the moonlight', her slightest touch is a caress
that 'ma[kes] his skin tingle and his mouth go dry'. (*GH*, 288; 301) She
can seem young and 'vulnerable', or distant and 'as old and as cold as the
mountains'. (*GH*, 261; 300) Her bouts of 'silent coldness that made
even the morning sun seem chill' have Rand longing to regain her
approval, and so provide another way of manipulating his feelings.
(*GH*, 301)

Lanfear also materialises after Rand has fulfilled one of the
prophecies by taking possession of the crystal sword, *Callandor*, 'the
sword that cannot be touched', one that is foretold to be 'wielded by the
Dragon's hand'. (*EOTW*, 189) This prophetic fulfilment of a step on
his destined path towards the Last Battle signals an increase in his
stature and power so that she finds him 'stronger' and 'harder'. (*SR*,
172) As foretold by prophecy Rand now bears the heron sign on each
palm that mark him as the Dragon Reborn:

Twice and Twice shall he be marked,
twice to live, and twice to die,
Once the heron to set his path,
Twice the heron, to name him true. (*SR*, 172)

Yet, despite these prophetic markings, Lanfear remains intent on turning him to her and to the Shadow. But at this point her obsessions with him, past and present, converge when she reveals her true identity as Lanfear, and angrily declares that '[y]ou were mine, and you are mine', and that she means 'to have [him] forever', reminding him that in the past 'you loved me'. (*SR*, 173; 175)

From somewhere in the recesses of Rand's subconscious he replies, in what appears to be an echoing of Lews Therin's words, 'and you loved power'. (*SR*, 175) For the reader this exchange accentuates even more Lanfear's self-seeking and destructive nature. The over-reaching for power which first led to her downfall in the Age of Legends has grown, not diminished with the passage of time. She offers to have Asmodean, one of the male Forsaken, teach Rand to wield the One Power safely:

Let me help you. We can destroy the others. The Great Lord will not care. We can destroy all of them, even Asmodean, once he has taught you all that you need to know. You and I can rule the world together under the Great Lord forever ... Two great *sa'angreal* were made just before the end, one that you can use, one that I can ... Their power is beyond imagining. With those, we could challenge even ... the Great Lord himself. Even the Creator'. (*SR*, 176-7)

The great folly inherent in Lanfear's proffered delusions of grandeur is heightened for the reader as it must resonate with the Christian myth of the fall of the rebel angel Lucifer, suggesting a possible banishment to the netherworld is in Lanfear's future.

Lanfear is even driven to tempt the other two *ta'veren*, with dreams of 'power and glory', as she knows they are linked to Rand and to the Last Battle. She cunningly chooses times when they are at their most vulnerable. Thus, before the wolves guard his dreams, she haunts Perrin and warns: 'the night is always there, and dreams come to all men. Especially you, my wildling. And I will always be in your dreams'. (*DR*, 69) She also materialises to Mat in the liminal zone of the sick-room, a place where the distinction between sleeping and waking, dream and reality can easily become blurred. (*DR*, 223 ff) Jordan's repetition of the motif of Lanfear's tempting of his main protagonists draws attention to the interconnected patterning of their life-paths, and also highlights for the reader the threat she poses to the quest.

SENSUAL TEMPTATION IN HIGH FANTASY

Although in high fantasy the temptation of the hero figures is achieved in a number of different ways, the bait is always that of unlimited power and/or an immortality that is linked to an ascension of the darker side of life in a way that imperils the safety of the depicted world and can lead to its destruction. For instance, in *LOTR* Tolkien uses the concept of the 'One Ring' that has the power to bestow world control to its wearer. In her original *Earthsea* trilogy, where magic is linked to words and 'true naming', Le Guin uses the mishandling of word-spells. The young wizard Ged, through arrogance and pride, is tempted to use a forbidden spell of summoning that unleashes a darkness into the world, while in his quest for immortality, the sorcerer Cob ruptures the boundary between life and death, light and dark, and threatens the equilibrium on which the world is founded, for there cannot be one without the other. (*Wizard*, 74-75; *Farthest*, 195)

Le Guin, like Jordan, also draws on the archetype of the white witch. At the court of Terrenon, Ged is nearly seduced by the Lady Serret, a coldly beautiful young woman, 'tall', and 'dressed in white and silver, with a net of silver crowning her hair that fell straight down like a fall of black water'. He likens her to a 'white new moon'. (*Wizard*, 125-126) Her beauty and her words confused his mind and 'his mind never seemed quite to clear'. (*Wizard*, 128) In this enchanted state he almost succumbs to the temptation she offers of 'an evil way [that] may lead to a good end', by falsely suggesting he can master the ancient and evil spirit sealed in the stone that gives her husband's court its name. (*Wizard*, 126) She offers 'power over his own destiny: strength to crush any enemy... foresight, knowledge, wealth, dominion, and a wizardry ... that could humble the Archmage himself'. (*Wizard*, 133) As she tempts him further with the Stone-spirit's knowledge of the true name of the shadow that follows him and sees his 'will shaken within him', she promises, in words akin to those of Lanfear's to Rand, 'you will be mightier than all men, a king among men, [y]ou will rule, and I will rule with you'. (*Wizard*, 134) The hero's ability to resist her charms, his assertion that 'it is light that defeats the dark', and his realisation that they had 'used his fear to lead him on', signal the beginning of his self-knowledge. (*Wizard*, 135) After fleeing this 'domain of a dark power' he finally embraces the dark Shadow of himself that his foolhardiness had loosed on the world, and thus 'light and darkness met and were joined and were one'. (*Wizard*, 135; 198) As he and Vetch set sail for home from their quest to the 'Outer Reaches', on the horizon a 'new moon shone: a ring of ivory, a rim of horn', symbolic of Ged's right to re-entry into the 'Great House' on Roke, through the 'door of horn and ivory' and of his rebirth. (*Wizard*, 199; 88) This parallel from Le Guin demonstrates that Jordan is writing within the shared sense of stock figures and a traditional paradigm of the temptation of the heroic figure that haunts much of our old and new mythological, fantastic literature. Thus, the overcoming of such sensual temptation forms a necessary part of the hero figure's growth pattern.

JORDAN'S USE OF STOCK TUTELARY AND TEMPTRESS FIGURES

In his portrayal of the magi Moiraine and Lanfear, Jordan thus uses two stock female figures, one to guide the hero to accept a selfless part in a quest where personal development is linked to the healing of the imaginary world, the other to tempt him by way of her sexuality to the seemingly easier but destructive path of self-gratification and self-glory. However, it is a common quest motif that at some point the hero figure needs to be separated from mentor/guides (good or bad) to allow him or her sole responsibility of choices and actions and so room to develop independently. For instance, in Lewis's Narnia series, Aslan was not always present to intervene on the part of the children; Rowling's Dumbledore cannot be relied upon to rescue or to guide Harry Potter; and in Feist's *Riftwar Saga* the protagonist Pug must often manage without the guidance of Macros the Black. Further like examples include Susan Cooper's Mr Merriman who, in *Silver on the Tree,* is called to an emergency in another time-frame, leaving Will and Bran to rely on their own decisions in the Lost Land (1979, 115ff), and Tolkien's Gandalf who vanishes into the abyss leaving the Fellowship to make its own way. It is also common for fantasists to introduce secondary mentor figures, such as Moiraine's bonded warder, Lan (like Aragorn, a type of 'hidden monarch'), who function as an exemplar for the hero of duty, courage, and self-sacrifice for a just cause. In the *WOT* Jordan resolves this removal of the opposing positive and negative mentor figures at a significant point, after Rand has been thrice recognised as the long-awaited messiah – by his own people as the 'Dragon Reborn', by the Aiel as 'He Who Comes with the Dawn' and by the Sea Folk as 'The Coramoor'.

In *FOH*, book 5, Moiraine and Lanfear engage in deadly combat. This battle culminates in them falling through a *ter'angreal* Redstone doorframe, in a 'flash of white light that did not end'. (*FOH*, 824-5) Their mutual disappearance means they have cancelled each other out. Jordan thus dramatically removes both their positive and negative influences and Rand must now stand alone. Moiraine fought her opponent in order to save Rand's life, and to ensure that he fulfils his destiny as Dragon Reborn, putting his safety and that of the world above her own. From a letter she leaves him, opened after her disappearance, it is learned that she chose to forfeit her own life in order to save his, as she had a foretelling of 'three [possible] branches' that the pattern could weave. He reads that down one of the paths Lanfear had killed him. Down another he called himself Lews Therin and became Lanfear's devoted lover. (*FOH*, 829; 830) Moiraine chose, calmly and selflessly, to be instrumental in bringing to fruition the third branch in the pattern, the one that would ensure his survival, as she knew he would not kill Lanfear (or any woman) in order to save himself. By contrast, Lanfear is consumed with anger because Rand has not only 'let another woman touch [him] again', but publicly spurns her twice through a strange melding of his past memories and the present situation. (*FOH*, 818) As the former Dragon, Lews Therin, he declares: 'I was never yours Mierin. I will always belong to Ilyena', and then as Rand, the current Dragon Reborn: 'Your name is Lanfear, and I'll die before I love one of the Forsaken'. (*FOH*, 820) The core Lanfear, unlike Moiraine, is ever driven by jealousy and hate, and twisted by a centuries-old obsession. In her, power, love and hate are inextricably intertwined. She faces Rand, her face 'a mask carved of ice' and shrieks: 'If you are not mine ... then you are dead'. (*FOH*, 818; 820)

At this point both women are presumed to have died, as the *ter'angreal* gateway back to their world melts 'as if it were wax', and Lan, Moiraine's bonded warder, can no longer 'feel her presence'. (*FOH*, 825) But Jordan gives Lanfear a brief reappearance, in volume nine (*WH*), where it is revealed that she has escaped from the other-worldly dimension of the *Aelfinn* and *Eelfinn*, this revelation making it possible for the reader to speculate that Moiraine, too, will eventually return. As she so clearly echoes Tolkien's Gandalf, perhaps such resurrection is to be in a more highly evolved form that may well be needed to tip the balance in the Light's favour in the lead up to the Last Battle. There is also Min's cryptic vision of Rand to consider, where she saw that 'he would almost certainly fail without a woman who was dead and gone'. (*COS*, 603) The author's repetition of hints or clues that suggest Moiraine still has a part to play provides another example of Jordan's use of interconnected patterning of possible futures in the texts.

By the removal, at this point, of these two potent characters who function as a kind of living anvil on which to hammer out the hero's worth, Jordan allows Rand more choice of action to set his own path and so to develop in ways that will be dependent upon his own judgement. Just prior to her disappearance Moiraine remarks that he has already 'changed' from the 'boy' she first met, and 'is hardly the same at all' and she prays he has 'changed enough' for what lies ahead,

highlighting once again for the reader the enormity of Rand's quest and
of the real possibility of failure. (*FOH*, 813) In the beginning, Rand,
Mat and Perrin had been pliable, naïve creatures of circumstance until
they began to view themselves and the world at large through different
eyes due to their life-changing journeys and ever more demanding
actions. Within the pattern of their destinies Jordan goes to great
lengths to give them some freedom in the manner in which they will
journey along their fated paths. This is particularly true of Rand, as his
coming-of-age entails accepting the role of the Dragon Reborn and
mastering of control of the One Power. Thus, while Jordan makes it
clear that his characters' fated pattern in life cannot be side-stepped, he
creates the impression that his three young protagonists have a degree of
choice and responsibility in weaving the finer detail of its intricate
design. Thereby they may develop the attributes needed to complete the
quest.

In her letter Moiraine sets Rand free, advising him to 'trust no
woman fully who is now Aes Sedai':

> We have made the world dance as we sang for three
> thousand years. That is a difficult habit to break, as I have
> learned while dancing to your song. You must dance free,
> and even the best intentioned of my sisters may well try to
> guide your steps as I once did …. May the Light illumine
> and protect you. (*FOH*, 830-31)

In such epic-style fantasy the success of the quest is linked to the naïve
protagonist's transition from youthful inexperience and ignorance to a
state of maturity, great responsibility and self-sacrifice. But the necessary
transformation of the young hero at the hands of others can only take
him or her so far and at some point the hero must be left to take full
responsibility for decision making and actions. Rand's guilt at
Moiraine's supposed death reveals a growing self-awareness of his faults,
for it is a weakness in him that has led to this tragic scenario. Moiraine
had known he was incapable of killing a woman, even one as evil as
Lanfear, and that at Cairhien 'she had come to her death knowing it

waited'. (*FOH*, 831) To assuage his self-acknowledged guilt, Rand unsoundly reasons that in future he must harden his heart, to become like 'steel'. Thus Jordan brings into play a new lesson for his young but developing hero, for in a world that is reliant on balance he must learn to operate from both his heart and his head.

Temperance: Cadsuane Aes Sedai

'Strong endures; hard shatters'. (*POD*, 296)

The book that follows on from the disappearance of Moiraine and Lanfear is fittingly titled *Lord of Chaos,* which seemingly refers not only to the chaotic state of the world around Rand, but also to the instability of his mind as he struggles to retain his sanity and keep the increasingly insistent voice of Lews Therin, the former Dragon, at bay – a voice that 'seemed to come from some capering figure in the shadows of [his] head'. (*LOC*, 114) Although without Moiraine's guidance he continues to grow in stature, and retains an unbending sense of justice, he becomes increasingly cold, manipulative and arrogant, his choice of action now powerfully fuelled by the bitter memory of Moiraine's death.

Jordan does not introduce another female magus as the Dragon's mentor/guide until midway through *COS,* the seventh volume, where Moiraine is replaced by Cadsuane, thought to be the oldest living Aes Sedai. Cadsuane, unlike the clear-cut figures of Moiraine and Lanfear, is a far more ambiguous and more elemental figure, and it is uncertain if she has some devious purpose of her own that may stand apart from the polarities of good and evil, although she does assure Rand that what she does is for his 'own good … not mine' and not for 'the good of the White Tower'. (*POD*, 587) She is wily enough to know he 'fights guidance' and unlike her predecessor, bides her time until he asks her to be his advisor. (*WH*, 509; *POD*, 586) Cadsuane is reminiscent of one of the Three Fates of antiquity, perhaps symbolic of the future or what may be. For she constantly works on a piece of embroidery that seems a metaphor for the plan she is weaving to bring Rand to full awareness and to prepare him for the Last Battle:

The major image on her piece of embroidery was finished, a man's hand clutching the ancient symbol of the Aes Sedai. Cracks ran across the black-and-white disc, and there was no telling whether the hand was trying to hold it together or crush it. She knew what she intended, but time would tell what was truth … It would be a disturbing piece, when completed. (*POD*, 291)

In a sense Cadsuane is weaving Rand's story and through her Jordan implies that the final outcome of Rand's great quest cannot be brought to pass until she completes her work. (In this regard she is a mortal equivalent or paradigm of the Cosmic Loom that spins the Great Pattern of life.) Diana Wynne Jones uses a similar motif of weaving in *The Spellcoats*. In that narrative a spellcoat is 'a poncho-like garment woven with word pictures that either told a story or stated facts. The garment, in the weaving became the spell that made the story or the fact come true' (1979, 237). Wynne Jones's central character Tanaqui must weave the story into two 'spellcoats' in order to obtain the release of the greatest of the gods (the 'One') and her people from bondage to the evil magi. Wynne Jones makes an extensive use of the motif of weaving in her text: for example, the magi are clothed in 'spellgowns' that display woven signs of their craft and they weave 'soul-nets' to trap departing souls. The fate and fortunes of mortals are spun by the Weaver, the Lady of the Undying and even everyday apparel such as 'rugcoats' and skirts is woven with a patterning of words or phrases.

Cadsuane is a harsh taskmaster, although she says of Rand that 'she will not hurt him any more than she must'. (*COT*, 633) Min has a 'viewing' that Cadsuane is to 'teach' Rand and his Asha'man of the Black Tower something they 'will not like learning from her'. (*COS*, 716) From years of 'rummaging' in 'musty corners' of the White Tower, she has gleaned useful bits of knowledge not known to Moiraine that can assist Rand, for instance, that the crystal sword is a dangerously 'flawed' *sa'angreal* and to be used safely must be 'linked with two women', with 'one of them guiding the flows'. (*POD*, 587-88)

As a mentor figure Cadsuane is representative of a balance of reason and emotion and so very human, despite her considerable powers. In contrast to this as Rand grows in stature as the Dragon Reborn he becomes further removed from his former self, and sees himself as hardened like 'steel'. (*POD*, 311) If Moiraine's role was to teach him the pattern of his destined duty, and Lanfear's to tempt him from it, Cadsuane is surely to teach him temperance, to remind him that 'even the Dragon Reborn is flesh'. (*POD*, 297) The world needs him to be strong, for 'strong endures', and yet not hard for 'hard shatters'. (*POD*, 296) In other words, Rand must 'relearn that he's human', he must act with his head and his heart and be brought to 'laughter and tears again' or Cadsuane fears that at Taimon Gai'don 'even his victory may be as dark as his defeat'. (*WH*, 508; *POD*, 296-297)

In this way Jordan yet again brings to the fore the destructive potential of power, a common theme in fantasy, suggesting that the danger inherent in Rand's cold application of power and ruthless disregard for individuals is that, inadvertently, he may become a type of fearful Dark Lord in his own right. (It is because of their awareness of the destructive potential of unbridled power, even if wielded in the name of good, that Gandalf, Galadriel and Elrond refuse the One Ring.) Jordan's patterning of a trio of female magus figures is tailored to further the different stages of his hero's development. Moiraine Aes Sedai as interpreter of the Great Pattern is the catalyst that sets the hero on his inner and outer journeys of growth that are linked to the saving of the world. His ability to rise to the task is tested by exposing him to her counterpart, the temptress Lanfear who offers the seemingly easier path of self-glory. Cadsuane's further role is one of fine-tuning the hero to ensure that Rand the mortal human is not over-shadowed by Rand the fearsome Dragon-reborn, for the healing of the world of the Wheel depends on a balance between these two aspects of his personality. Clearly, the roles of these three women are firmly entwined with Rand and help to progress his journey. Jordan's patterning of the main hero figures – Rand, Mat and Perrin – who embody various aspects of the heroic, presents another interesting trio of interlaced characters that form the focus of the next two chapters.

3 THE PATCHWORK HERO: JORDAN'S PATTERNING OF HEROIC MOTIFS IN *THE WHEEL OF TIME*

THE HEROIC MOTIFS IN FANTASY

In general writers of Tolkienian-inspired high fantasy draw much of their inspiration for the heroic paradigm from mediaeval romance. Northrop Frye described the typical hero of the romance mode as:

> superior in degree to other men and to his environment ... whose actions are marvellous but who himself is identified as a human being. The hero of romance moves in a world in which the ordinary laws of nature are slightly suspended; prodigies of courage and endurance, un-natural to us, are natural to him, and enchanted weapons, talking animals, terrifying ogres and witches, and talismans of miraculous power violate no rule of probability once the postulates of romance have been established. (1957, 33)

However, in the modern revival of this mode the romance hero paradigm may well be interwoven with aspects of other source material much as Tolkien himself was also influenced by Anglo-Saxon and Norse epics and, to a degree, by the Celtic myths. As noted by Faye Ringel:

> the motivation for the twentieth century hero is not, as it sometimes was in the medieval romance, random chance or adventure; instead, something wrong must be put right, and the quest hero, however unlikely, seems destined to accomplish the deed. (2000, 163)

The heroic figure in modern high fantasy, such as Jordan's *WOT*, moves in an imaginary landscape that, as in 'classical epic, is ruled by Fate, its plots [often] determined by prophets and oracles speaking in riddles'.

(Ringel 2000, 165) Confusingly, it can also be a landscape in which luck or happenstance may appear to play a part, as in our own world. And, as already discussed, the hero figure's maturation and the restoration of the imaginary world itself are inextricably intertwined. This integrative concept was endorsed by Tolkien, and can also be seen to underpin the philosophy of both Le Guin's *Earthsea* as well as Jordan's *WOT* and it is constantly reflected in the choices and actions of the main hero figures, which have consequences far beyond the personal sphere. In regard to the *LOTR*, Don Elgin has suggested that this text clearly encompasses both comic (i.e. integrative) and ecological traditions:

> using a physical environment shaped by humanity's own actions, characters who affirm the imperative of survival while recognising that the system must survive if they are to survive with any degree of freedom, and a general tone that suggests the importance of experience over abstraction.(2004, 265)

Elgin's analysis is equally applicable to both Le Guin's and Jordan's concept of the need to achieve a balance between the forces of Light and Dark, life and death, in order to maintain the 'equilibrium' of the Earthsea Archipelago and the 'Great Pattern' of the Wheel world, both of which have come under threat due to foolhardy or selfish human actions.

The numerous protagonists and complex plotting of the *WOT* make it difficult to analyse Jordan's heroic figures individually in terms of either epic or romance paradigms. His main protagonists are not strictly representative of either of these modes, which respectively are tragic or comic, for he incorporates aspects of both. Jordan stitches together various motifs to construct his multiple interpretations of the heroic figure and of his or her life-changing journey, thereby creating a type of composite personality. The broad characterisation of Jordan's notion of the hero figure, which like his plotting owes a great deal to the interlace technique, shows his consciousness of writing 'secondary' fantasy epic, with Tolkien and other similar writers behind him, and the difficulty of finding his own voice. One of the interesting things about his work is what it tells us about the hero, and thus a critique of Jordan's heroic figures suggests that his composition of the hero is a more eclectic interweaving of the traditional qualities given or uncovered by various scholars, which commonly feature in literature.

Jordan, like his character Thom, in telling the story of the hero gathers up a number of figures, so can be seen to explore the qualities of the heroic (and not so much the heroic person) through a repetition of traditionally-held values such as personal sacrifice, honour, strength, and courage. Jordan's own gleeman's bag of stories, concerning the individual journeys of his various characters, becomes woven into the focal quest of Rand's larger story. Similarly, the gleeman in the *WOT* recites from an endless repertoire of heroic deeds that are stitched together over time, to collectively reveal the larger story of heroic patterning in the world of the Wheel.

THE HERO AND THE JOURNEY IN QUEST FANTASY

In regard to the centrality of the journey of the hero figure in modern fantasy Clute suggests that:

> fantasy can almost be defined as the genre whose protagonists reflect and embody the tale being told, and who lead the way through travails and reversals towards the completion of a happy ending. (Tragic fantasy exists but is uncommon.) (1997, 339)

For this purpose, fantasists frequently rely on some variation of the traditional fairy tale paradigm of the quest, a complex narrative progression from departure and experience to return, through which common persons may be brought to heroism and to maturity. Both Vladimir Propp (1976) and Joseph Campbell (1973) describe this journey in similar fashion as a circular quest into the unknown that involves the testing of the hero, the crossing of thresholds, supernatural intervention, helpers or companions, confrontation, gaining of a boon, and the return home. Brian Attebery notes that Propp refers to such 'structural elements' as 'functions', and that in fantasy they can be 'reduplicated':

> often these functions are doubled or tripled, a rhetorical
> device that emphasises their status as parts of a pattern, a
> story, rather than mimetic renderings of real human beings
> and lives. The pattern they make is usually a quest. (1992,
> 25)

The panoramic sweep and epic length of Jordan's *WOT* allow room for an unusually high degree of such reduplication of these traditional functions and, in particular, the author offers an interesting theory of a triple heroic figure – as will be discussed in the next chapter. The reduplication of structural elements complements the interlaced patterning of Jordan's work; for instance, the narrative threads of the secondary protagonists (female or male), as the trials and tribulations of their ancillary quests can both mirror and enlarge the focal quest of the main protagonist Rand. Thus, in Jordan's work we continuously see an inter-linking of stories within stories that continuously add to the complexity of his imaginary world, as well as enhancing the individual personalities of his characters.

In the creation of his male and female characters and their various roles in the *WOT*, Jordan works within the general framework of our Western cultural inheritance, but he does attempt to write beyond its confines and to confront the issue of gender restrictions imposed by (earlier) cultural expectation. In his imaginary world Jordan has conceived of a largely matriarchal society, a realm in which for three thousand years only female Aes Sedai have had control of the One Power. But it is a world in which survival is now dependent upon a rebalancing of male and female power, a reflection of the two aspects of the One Power needed to drive the cosmic Wheel of Time itself. Jordan is interested in exploring the concept of a society in which men and women come together as valued human beings for the common good of all living creatures and for the environment in which they dwell.

POSITIONING THE HEROIC FIGURES
IN *THE WHEEL OF TIME*

Jordan stated that the impetus to write the *WOT* series came from a desire to explore 'what it would be like to be tapped on the shoulder and told that you were born to carry out a great mission, and that it was your destiny no matter what you wished' (Sukil 2004). For the young protagonists in his work, as in Tolkien's *LOTR*, Le Guin's *Earthsea* series, or similar fantasy texts, the 'great mission' or quest involves both the outer journey to adventure and the inner journey to self-awareness or growth and so, in part, can be viewed as a magnified rite of passage. On the transformative nature of fantasy narratives, Clute suggests:

> a fantasy text may be described as the story of an earned passage from bondage ... and which may involve a profound metamorphosis of protagonist or world (or both) – into the eucatastrophe, where marriages may occur, just governance fertilize the barren land, and there is a healing. (1997, 338-9)

In the sub-creations of each of the above mentioned authors the psychological transformation of the protagonists is inescapably linked, and indeed is vital, to the survival of their worlds, which all stand on the brink of apocalyptic chaos.

On one level the narrative may function as a metaphor for the development of the main characters but, unlike the case in fantasy texts such as Stephen Donaldson's *The Chronicles of Thomas Covenant* series, it does not necessarily follow that the characters and landscape are merely a metaphoric externalisation of the 'inner landscapes' of the protagonist's mind (Moorcock 1987, 16). This type of literary device may well be incorporated on occasions, such as Jordan's use of Moiraine's voice to encourage Rand to shoulder the responsibility of his destined role, which can be interpreted as an externalisation of his conscience. Donaldson himself asserts that:

> fantasy is a form of fiction in which the internal crises or
> conflicts or processes of the characters are dramatized as if
> they were external individuals or events ... in fantasy the
> characters meet themselves – or parts of themselves, their
> own needs/problems/exigencies – as actors on the stage of
> the story, and so the internal struggle ... is played out as
> an external struggle in the action of the story.(1986, 4-5)

In Donaldson's work, the antagonist Lord Foul is a 'personified evil',
who is a 'part of Thomas Covenant', an externalisation of Thomas's
hatred of the leprosy that plagues him in his primary reality. The
invented world 'is an expression of the characters' and the eventual
'healing' of the Land heralds the 'healing' of the protagonist, whose
mindscape is both mirrored in and 'confer[s] reality' on his
'surroundings' (Donaldson 1986, 4-5). As a consequence, in this type of
scenario, the metamorphosis of the protagonist remains paramount.
(Yet, paradoxically, Donaldson offers his protagonists the choice of
believing the Secondary World they find themselves in to be either
reality or just a dream. [1982, 74-8]) By contrast, in Jordan's Secondary
World, as in that of Tolkien or Le Guin, the opposite holds true, for the
emphasis is laid on the ways in which the growth of the protagonists
enables them to confront and, potentially, overcome the disruptive
forces that threaten to destroy both the society and landscape in which
they dwell. At times they may even fail, as when Frodo finally succumbs
to the lure of the One Ring.

In Jordan's world of the Wheel each protagonist's journey of
personal development is triggered, not by some need or lack within
themselves, but by a disruption to the world order, and so their
subsequent development is vital if they are to restore the integrity of
their surroundings. Jordan is drawing on the conventions of the epic
and romance modes where the hero's task is to fight disruptive forces:
Rand fights an evil that has the potential to destroy the Cosmic Loom
that weaves the Great Pattern of the world. Therefore, within the
construct of Jordan's imaginary world, as in that of Tolkien or Le Guin,
the protagonists' personal choices and actions, their positive or negative

strengths, potentially have enormous societal and environmental ramifications. As noted by Myles Balfe, such heroes are 'generally defined by their deeds and [they] exist in a dialectic relationship with "their" landscapes embodying the core values that the landscape is thought to represent' (2004, 77). As a result, they are driven to save their worlds, no matter at what personal cost. Therefore Frodo, as ring bearer, does not expect to return home from Mordor, and Rand accepts that to defeat the Dark Lord he may need to sacrifice his life. In Le Guin's *Farthest*, too, the breach between the living and the dead is sealed at the loss of Ged's magical powers. All three hero figures shoulder their designated roles simply because there is no one else who can do it – and in the ever-increasing understanding that the fate of their worlds is irrevocably entwined with their own.

THE HEROIC FIGURE AND THE ETHICAL PATTERN

In general, high fantasy creates tension through the interplay between protagonists and antagonists, between the 'selfless' and 'self-seeking' principles that respectively apply to the opposing groups of characters. Through this means authors such as Jordan signal to the reader the desirability of making moral or ethically grounded decisions that are designed to foster integrative rather than selfish individualistic ends. This mode of behaviour is enacted through the actions and choices of the heroic figures as through their adventures and tests and confrontations with the enemy they are enabled to develop traits of responsibility and authority. (Yet Jordan, perhaps inadvertently, also adds a sense of moral ambiguity to the above usage of the terms 'selfless' and 'self-seeking' for at times his male hero figures, Rand, Perrin, and Mat, are in danger of losing self, of becoming 'self-less', and must partake in 'self-seeking' in order to consolidate their identities.)

Lionel Basney suggests that high fantasy asserts 'the general possibility of ethics, of ethical action, in an imaginative world specifically designed to display them' (1980, 27). His point of view accords with that of Jordan who said that he believed in the 'necessity to struggle against evil', in the desirability of a responsible and morally based society, and that fantasy literature supplies the ideal arena for exploring this: 'In fantasy, we *can* talk about right and wrong, and good and evil … discuss morality or ethics, and believe that these things are important' (n.a. 2000, 76). In other words, codes of ethical behaviour can be modelled in the imaginary worlds of fantasy texts, and solutions found to societal problems which, by contrast, remain inherently problematic in the Primary World. Francis Molson takes a similar stance by suggesting the portrayal of 'ethical choices' to be one of the 'fundamental purposes of this kind of fantasy', and that such texts often explore how 'apparently insignificant actions can bring about momentous consequences' in the invented world, at both personal and societal levels (1979, 130). An example of this is when young Ged, showing off to his rival, Jasper, at Roke, summons Elfarran's spirit from the dead, an action that releases his own shadow into the world and upsets the fragile balance of the Equilibrium of the Archipelago. (*Wizard*) Similarly, Mat takes the tainted dagger from Shadar Logoth thereby releasing into the wider world of the Wheel a latent seed of evil, which previously had been bound within the confines of this fallen city. (*EOTW*)

Within the invented worlds these texts posit a pattern or order for human existence that is integral with the natural world, a philosophy of ecological balance – one increasingly found to be absent from the fractured global politics of exploitation of our world. Elgin suggests that the modern fantasy novel has adopted an ecological, integrative or 'comic conception of humanity, placing its emphasis upon humanity as part of a total environment or system and acknowledging the absolute dependence of humanity upon that system' (2004, 264).

As discussed in chapter one, high fantasy narratives usually commence at a time of societal and moral rupture that much favours the Dark, and as the restoration of the order of the world is of most significance, in a sense, the protagonists are merely the tools of destiny, shaped for a specific purpose and driven by circumstances beyond their control to take up restorative roles. Nevertheless, the author shows that it is how they respond to the larger call of destiny and use their free will to make choices that will determine the final outcome of events, and so the story must be told through them as they comprise the central focus.

The order of Jordan's Secondary World is governed by the Great Pattern of existence, designed by a seemingly beneficent Creator, yet One who plays no further part in its destiny (in a manner analogous to the eighteenth-century doctrine of deism). At the time of creation the Dark One was shut outside the Pattern and can only gain access to the world through the actions of its fallible human inhabitants, and the only known forces outside the world and the Great Pattern are the abstract polarities of Light and Dark. The disembodied Creator (a force obliquely associated with the Light) only speaks directly once in the text when Rand is warned by a strange voice that echoes in his mind: 'I will take no part. Only the chosen one can do what must be done, if he will'. (*EOTW*, 758) In the Third Age of the Wheel, to counter the burgeoning strength of the Dark One the Cosmic Loom spins out three special life-threads known as *ta'veren*. One life-thread is fated to be the Dragon Reborn, saviour of the world, and so cosmic order is ordained by the impersonal mechanism of the Pattern, and it is believed that to correct any deviations in the Great Design the Wheel of Time will automatically spin out the necessary threads to enable partial change to the weave of the 'Age Lace'. (*Companion*, 7) Moiraine's friend and accomplice, Siuan, Amyrlin of the White Tower, reminds her that until Rand 'proclaims himself' as the 'one true Dragon', false ones will continue to appear simply because 'the Pattern demands a Dragon' as it 'weaves toward Tarmon Gai'don,' and it will 'continue to throw up false dragons' until the 'true' one is revealed. (*GH*, 66)

The inhabitants of the world of the Wheel firmly believe that if they 'tried to walk in the Light, tried to live a good life, and did not name him' the Dark One could not harm them. (*EOTW*, 107) But the author posits no omniscient god-like presence or higher cosmic order that could come to their aid, as hinted at in Tolkien's *LOTR*, which more overtly displays Christian influences. (But as Tom Shippey points out even in Middle-earth there is danger in a 'passive confidence' in external intervention. For 'if there is an external power (the Valar), it has to work through human or earthly agents, and if those agents give up, then the purpose of the external power will be thwarted' [2000, 146].)

Jordan's theory of a benign but indifferent Creator, one who sets up the world and then stands aside, may reflect the growing secularisation of contemporary Western society; the lessening of an unquestioning belief in the doctrine of traditional organised religion, and in an all-powerful God who once gave meaning and shape to people's lives.[1] Jordan chooses to suggest that the fallible/fallen inhabitants of the Wheel world must shoulder responsibility for their own actions. Solely from within themselves they need to find the means to repair the fabric of their world order, which rests on the opposing yet complementary forces of female and male power (*yin* and *yang*), and where life and death, good and evil all form part of the pattern of the cosmology. The moral neutrality of the Great Pattern, which blindly spins both light and dark threads, emphasises the need for the human characters to make ethical choices, in order to maintain a balance between these two aspects of life. In this respect the ordering of Jordan's world is closer to that of Le Guin's Archipelago, where the governing principle, the Equilibrium, displays a similarly eastern-inspired philosophy of opposites, and where it is also up to altruistic human endeavour to correct the transcendent impulse of darkness that would disrupt the balance.

THE HERO AND THE QUEST AS PATTERN

Crossing thresholds and rites of passage

It is the journey of the quest and the initiation patterns along the way that give density and structure to the characters' personalities in high fantasy texts. Therefore, in uncovering Jordan's strategies for the use of the heroic figure, analysis of some examples of his extensive use of the convention of thresholds, both physical and metaphysical, should prove fruitful. Traditionally, thresholds are seen as places of liminality where identity is fluid, and it is in these 'between' places where normal boundaries or limits do not apply that the protagonists can be tested. If successful, they may well be brought to enlightenment or rebirth, to triumph over obstacles, and so develop towards a maturity that is needed if the quest is to be fulfilled. Such thresholds in the Jordan texts can be divided into roads and labyrinths. In keeping with the polarity of

Light and Dark, which forms the undergirding framework of so many high fantasy texts, the reverse of this is true for the antagonists or anti-heroes. For them, such thresholds prove to be a perversion of the development associated with rites of passage and, instead, are shown to lead to a reinforcement of their enslavement of both body and mind.

Roads to adventure and growth

In his discussion of Tolkien's process of storytelling, Brian Attebery suggests that 'roads' in the metaphoric sense are constructs that take the 'unwary traveller' from 'his own doorstep into realms of fable' (1992, 41). Actual and symbolic roads and the way in which the hero chooses to travel on them play an important, and Tolkienian, role in the Jordan series. In the opening pages of the first book (*EOTW*) it is on a very ordinary road between the village of Emond's Field and the al'Thors' family farm that the Dark first shadows Rand's footsteps. This is the catalyst that forces the central hero Rand al'Thor, and his companions, to undertake ever longer and more 'worldly' road journeys that take them far from home and draw them into a cosmic conflict, which they had thought only happened to heroes in the old stories. They repeatedly remark that their lives are not like those of such heroes, yet paradoxically they too are part of a larger 'story' and gradually through their ensuing life choices and consequent deeds grow to fit the mode of the heroic (clearly a device to encourage ordinary readers to identify with them). This is especially true of Rand as he accepts his destiny and assumes the heavy mantle of the Dragon Reborn, the one prophesied to be both 'saviour' and 'destroyer' of the world. Early on he becomes aware that 'death is lighter than a feather, duty heavier than a mountain'. (*GH*, 679) Through his acceptance of the inevitability of all these contradictory demands he displays a strength and maturity that raise him in stature. At the same time, it must distance him from his companions whose own duties are those of lesser service and more personal loyalties: Rand bears the heaviest burden.

Another type of primeval road are the 'Ways', passages that exist outside the confines of accepted time and space in the imaginary world, that have been 'grown' by the One Power and long tended by the Ogier – a gentle, giant-like race of spiritual and actual carers. In the depicted

Third Age they too are contaminated by the Shadow and haunted by the Black Wind (*Machin Shin*), 'steal[er] of souls'.[2] (*EOTW*, 686) The Ways can be interpreted as an intense personal experience or test of the dangerous and the unknown. To enter them is to step into utter blackness, a realm highly suggestive of the convention of the mythic hero's descent to the 'classical'/Christian Underworld. To lose oneself in the Ways is to fall into the abyss or to be swallowed by the Black Wind – a fate to which those of the Shadow are also vulnerable as shown by the lifeless 'frozen shapes of Trollocs … forever snarling with fear,' encountered by Rand and his companions. (*EOTW*, 681) They show how safe travelling through the Ways depends on the faith and courage of the one journeying and the companionship of the 'Company'. Rand and his friends had initially entered the Ways despite their deep fears and the apparent danger, because of an overriding need to reach the Green Man's grove (in *EOTW*) in time to foil the Dark One's diabolic plans. Any subsequent journeying in the Ways is to be undertaken only in times of dire need, and when no other feasible choices remain open to the protagonists.

Portal Stones stand as spatially located gateways to alternative realities or 'mirror' worlds that might have been, but as they also provide a means of travel from one location to another without crossing the intervening space, they afford another variation on the metaphor of the necessary hard road. Travellers using Portal Stones often experience 'flashbacks' to lives that they might have led or might yet lead, visions that shed light on their own personal character weaknesses or flaws. In *GH*, the second volume, during such transportation the hero Rand relives:

> a hundred lives. More. So many he could not count them. And at the end of every life, as he lay dying, as he drew his final breath, a voice whispered in his ear. *I have won again Lews Therin.* (*GH*, 532)

For Rand this is a realisation of the eternal nature of the battle against the Dark and perhaps also a projection of his fear of making the wrong decisions in his role as Dragon Reborn. His brave refusal to give in to dark visions of defeat is evident in his denial of any connection to the defeat of the past Dragon, Lews Therin, for he declares: 'No! I am Rand al'Thor!' (*GH*, 533) Yet for the reader Rand's visions emphasise the weight of the task he has shouldered and introduce the disturbing possibility of failure. By contrast, the Shienaran soldier Ingtar, during the same transportation, was brought to face the truth of his own weak and deceptive nature, the fact that for selfish glory he was and always had been a betrayer of his people and of the Light. (*GH*, 534; 654) Ingtar's moment of revelation recalls an earlier one when Perrin had thought that 'sometimes to [his] eyes, the crescent crest on the Shienaran's helmet looked like a Trolloc's horns,' an image the reader now realises provided an externalisation of Ingtar's dark secret. (*GH*, 407) Perrin's far-sightedness is connected to his mental wolf-link, which has enhanced both his vision and his natural intuition. Thus, Jordan, through an associated layering of images, deepens the pathos of the soldier's fall.

Like Tolkien's ill-fated hero Boromir, who succumbs to the lure of the One Ring for confused reasons, Ingtar desires to use the numinous Horn of Valere for self-glory. His wish is to atone for his years of betrayal by blowing the Horn to save his nation, to 'keep the Shienar ... from being swept away and forgotten', and through this act to gain his own 'salvation'. In his visions of many lives he sometimes 'held the Horn, [but] never sounded it', and he constantly 'tried to escape what [he had] become', but 'never did'. (*GH*, 654-55) But, Jordan permits this tragic Darkfriend, like Boromir, a moment of redemption, as through accepting the truth about himself he finally gives up his life (in *GH*), so that Rand and the others can escape from the Seanchan invaders. The idea of such belated redemption in the Wheel world is apparent in the popular belief that 'no man can walk so long in the Shadow that he cannot come again to the Light'. (*GH*, 654) The restoration of Ingtar's dignity and worth as a warrior is shown when Rand accords him the Shienaran final blessing: 'The Light Shine on you, Lord Ingtar of House Shinowa, and may you shelter in the palm of the Creator's hand'. (*GH*, 655) Jordan uses Ingtar's emotional journey of self-knowledge through the Portal Stone and his subsequent act of self-sacrifice to foreground the point that the extent of the Dark One's influence in his imaginary world rests upon the choices and actions of very ordinary human characters. Further, Jordan uses Ingtar's weaker character (as demonstrated by his response in the portal vision) as a foil to Rand, to show his strength and heroic nature.

The Ways and Portal Stones are an extension of the characteristics of roads, to be seen as places of journeying into the unknown that bring danger, temptation and challenge and, for some characters, loci of self-realisation and growth. All these Jungian extensions of the notion of the road as a place of intersection with the world of the possible through imagination also encourage the reader more readily to cross strange thresholds and so to enter and accept the altered time zone and spatial constructs of the narrative, and then to mentally inhabit the Secondary World. The book itself becomes a metaphorical portal that the reader opens, and thus it provides the liminal space through which the reader is able to imaginatively enter the Secondary World of the text. Within the Secondary world as the inhabitants enter portals that provide liminal spaces of emotional testing, the reader is brought to vicariously share in their experiences and growth.

Labyrinths as thresholds of 'hope'

Jordan's Ways and Portal Stones can further be interpreted as forms of the puzzle of the ancient labyrinth – a motif traditionally symbolic of ordeals and trials, places of temptation, self-realisation through initiation, rites of passage or even death and rebirth. An illustration of this is provided by the array of puzzling symbols that are engraved on the surface of the Portal Stones, each of which offers the key to a different location in time and space. Travellers must choose which symbols to use with great care or find themselves transported to unknown realms, or lost in a space out of time. Even a successful traveller must encounter bewildering layers of previous life experiences, a mental labyrinth from which he or she may not emerge unscathed at journey's end, as shown by Ingtar's plight.

The Ways are to be traversed along narrow, spiralling ramps and bridges, that fall away to a bottomless abyss, the only glimmer of light in the surrounding 'dead black' being provided by the travellers' oil-filled lanterns. (*EOTW*, 671ff) The labyrinthine Ways bear comparison with the myth of Theseus and the Minotaur, for although there is no physical thread, the broken white line on the stone floors and the strategically placed 'Guidings' (tall slabs of stone inscribed with Ogier script) provide a kind of thread, and the Black Wind to be met therein is analogous with the ancient foe the Minotaur. (*EOTW*, 670)

In his multi-dimensional, imaginary world Jordan also uses the World of Dreams to present a repeating motif of symbolic mazes, such as reflecting mirrors, endless corridors and doors that open into the same room of horrors, or multiple staircases, in which his young male protagonists are relentlessly pursued by Ba'alzamon, mouth-piece for the Dark Lord, or others of the Forsaken. (*EOTW*) These fearful night journeys of the mind emphasise anew the gravity of the danger in which his young protagonists stand, as they struggle to contain their fears and to resist the lies, threats or temptations of the Dark Lord's minions, these conflicts heightening the suspense of the narrative.

The *ter'angreal* archways used by the Aes Sedai as part of the rites of passage to gain full sisterhood (*DR*, 245-67) and the twisted Redstone *angreal* doorframes through which various characters step into the strange realm of the *Aelfinn* or the *Eelfinn* to seek answers to the future, all provide further examples of labyrinths that Jordan's heroes must engage with or enter. A notable instance of this testing of the hero figure occurs when Mat first steps through a Redstone *angreal* doorframe to a place with no 'straight lines', and walks along 'continuously curved' hallways where even the 'tilework made spirals and sinuous lines'. (*SR*, 245) The riddling answers he receives from the alien beings he encounters give the sense of a verbal puzzle or mental labyrinth; for instance his fate being to 'give up half the light of the world to save the world'. (*SR*, 249) These cryptic words suggest that Mat will sacrifice an eye; an interpretation strengthened by Min's viewing of him with 'an eye on a balance scale', an image that resonates further with Egwene's dream of 'Mat, placing his own left eye on a balance scale'. (*EOTW*, 216; *DR*, 291) Jordan's repetitious patterning of predictions of such a gory sacrifice intensifies the significance of the act, as well as pointing to Mat's underlying moral strength of character – despite his outward devil-may-care attitude. For as the *Aelfinn* and *Eelfinn* are said to speak only the truth, and the Aes Sedai believe Min's viewings will come to pass, the reader feels that Mat will not shirk from his prophesied gruesome destiny. The higher purpose for Mat's bodily maiming resonates with Rand's wounding during his battle with Ba'alzmon. He leaves himself open to a blow in the side, purposely using a tactic known as 'Sheathing the Sword', in order to get under his enemy's guard and so to deliver a fatal strike. (*GH*, 147) Furthermore, Rand is resigned to sacrificing himself to save the world. Thus, by association, Jordan draws the life-threads of Rand and Mat – as he will Perrin – toward the same destined path, and so weaves the fabric of his story towards the construction of a triple male hero figure.

Although most characters enter the strange realms of either the *Aelfinn* or the *Eelfinn* in search of truth and knowledge, Mat's second encounter there – discussed more fully later – brings metamorphosis through a ritual of death and rebirth, a repeating motif in these texts that is also applied to Rand and to Perrin as well by means of his wolf/human transition. It seems safe to speculate that this motif will apply to Moraine as well, whose Gandalf-like disappearance has already been discussed in chapter two. Jordan's patterning of variations on the motif of death and rebirth further helps to underscore the importance of the transformative development of the protagonists.

Rand's journey into the labyrinth-like forest of 'glass' columns in the central courtyard of the hidden city of Rhuidean, provides a pivotal point in his development as a leader of the Aiel. (*SR*, 404ff) It is a place where those who would become clan chiefs of the Aiel must face the disturbing truth about their nation's past and either return marked on one forearm with the sign of the dragon, or perish. In Rand's case, he emerges marked on the forearms with twin dragons, 'sinuous golden-maned form[s] scaled in scarlet and gold', a prophetic sign and initiation that proclaim him as the long awaited messiah of the Aiel – 'He Who Comes With the Dawn'. (*SR*, 558) These glittering 'tattoos' mimic the scarlet and gold scaled creature that is woven on the ancient banner of the Dragon, and thus are symbolic of the future co-joining of the life-paths of the desert tribes with the destiny of the Dragon Reborn.

During Rand's ordeal among the glass spires each step takes him 'forward and back'; a physical journey 'forward' into the centre of the forest of glass, but mentally 'back' in time. (*SR*, 422) At one point Rand catches a glimpse of Muradin, another would-be Aiel clan chief, weeping, tearing at his face and gouging at his eyes with his nails through his inability to accept the stark truth of his visions, that his people and the despised, passivist Travelling People were originally the one race. (*SR*, 432) Consequently, Muradin had failed the test and remains lost forever in shadowy void, a space beyond that of the waking world of the Wheel, somewhere between past and present, vision and reality.

Jordan's juxtaposition of success and failure in a patterning of opposites foregrounds the hazardous nature of initiation, and suggests that, for his protagonists, personal development includes finding the courage to confront unpalatable truths and to overcome fears arising from them. Such patterns of initiation are further set against the destructive labyrinthine journeys faced by the Forsaken who, since the Age of Legends, have chosen to walk in the footsteps of the Shadow.

Labyrinths as thresholds of 'despair'

The experiences of two such antagonists, Demandred and Moghedien, reveal that their physical journeys through the labyrinth-like tunnel into the bowels of the black mountain at Shayol Ghul, where 'so long ago' they had first made 'obeisance to the Great Lord' and 'pledg[ed]' their 'souls' have led them to an ever-downward spiral into darkness, degradation and slavery. (*COS*, 456) Within the tunnel 'jagged spikes jutted from the ceiling, stony teeth ready to snap shut, the Great Lord's teeth to rend the unfaithful or the traitor'. (*LOC*, prologue, 3) For the present, Demandred will pass freely to receive orders to commit further horrors he dare not refuse. But as Moghedien has failed to please, the 'Great Lord's fangs' descend and force her to slither along the tunnel 'on her belly'. (*COS*, 456-57) Jordan's choice of serpent-like imagery resonates with the Christian portrayal of Satan and by association must suggest damnation. The tunnel leads to a cave where the 'thinness in the Pattern' allows the 'presence' of the Dark Lord to be keenly sensed, in a rapture of both 'ecstasy' and 'pain'. The location is described as a 'lake of molten stone, red-mottled with black, where man-high flames danced, died and rose again', known as the 'Pit of Doom'. (*LOC*, prologue, 4) It is a scene that vividly recalls Milton's depiction of Satan's hellish realm and, for the reader, heightens the horror of how the Forsaken One's desire for unbridled power and immortality has actually brought eternal entrapment for him and his companions. As a further punishment Moghedien's soul is caught in a 'mindtrap' (*cour'sourva*), to be worn on a cord around the neck of Moridin, the Right Hand of the Dark Lord, and if he should break it she will be severed from her soul to become a helpless, utterly obedient 'automaton'. The lightest 'caress' of his 'thumb' upon the crystal is felt 'across her mind, her soul,' a reminder of how easily he could increase the pressure and crush her core. (*COS*, 463) The image of a 'tiny, fragile cage of gold wire and crystal,' a blending of exquisite beauty with exquisite pain, becomes a cruel, symbolic micro-labyrinth, from which the victim, no matter how she may twist and turn her mind, has no means of escape. (*COS*, 458)

Jordan uses the labyrinth structurally in the hero's emotional journey as a means of bringing his main protagonists to face and overcome their greatest fears and so gain the strength to accept their fated roles in the focal quest. By contrast the antagonists' journeys into the labyrinth function to externalise graphically the ever-present fear and torment of their minds, by which means the Dark Lord keeps them in eternal servitude. Jordan thereby points to the folly of their self-seeking, as they have no option but to obey every whim of their Dark master. Through this alternating pattern of light and dark, of hope and despair, Jordan highlights the essential vulnerability of his human characters. These labyrinthic journeys can also be seen to mirror the complicated interweaving of the life-threads of the companions who surround the main heroic figure in Jordan's Wheel world. The following section extends consideration of this complex motif of the twists and turns, the emotional testing and triumphant negotiations of the labyrinth, to the way Jordan deploys his other characters throughout the narrative.

The interwoven pattern of supporting characters

In Jordan's world of the Wheel the main protagonist, Rand, is surrounded by a cluster of companions who at times follow their own paths but also have key parts to play for Rand's ultimate fulfilment of his cosmic quest. Like him, too, they must mature, both physically and metaphysically, to enable them to fit their greater roles. In some form or other Jordan's primary and secondary protagonists (female and male) face personal inner struggles as they attempt to come to terms with the emergence of superhuman or super-sensory powers that raise them above the ordinary, while at a more human level they are all brought to explore and develop their awakening sexuality – a recurring point of departure from the Tolkienian model.

Rand is strongly linked to two other *ta'veren* youths, Mat and Perrin, without whom it is prophesied he will fail at the Last Battle. Together they form the core triple hero figure – the focus of the next chapter. As one of their adversaries remarks of their interconnected status: 'Cut one leg of the tripod ... and all fall down'. (*DR*, 77) As well, Rand's destiny is further tied to his young women companions and supporters, Nynaeve, Egwene, Elayne, Aviendha and the seer Min, and they too are threaded into the heroic paradigm. Strengthening the role of the female protagonists and their ties to the main hero figure is Jordan's concept of Rand's triple mental bonding with Min, Elayne and Aviendah – a reduplication of the *ta'veren* threads that link him to Perrin and Mat. Jordan's use of the imagery of weaving, and Min's prowess as a seer, may well seem analogous to the motif of the Three Fates of ancient mythology, which he also evokes in his portrayal of Casuane and her unfinished tapestry. But in this instance Min, Elayne and Aviendah form a mental web through the weaving of intricate threads of *saidar*, 'a tracery of Spirit that made the finest lace seem drab,' and as this 'spiderweb of Spirit' settles into Rand he becomes bound to them in an intimate sharing of emotional and physical feelings. (*WH*, 291) In a later episode Rand and Nynaeve are mentally linked through a confluence of *saidin* and *saidar*, which enables him to cleanse the male side of the One Power. Thus, Jordan's repetition of the weaving metaphor works to interweave Rand's greater destiny not only with the life-threads of Mat and Perrin, but also with those of his female companions. This tactic emphasises the importance of their roles, as they provide much more than a part of the background against which he is to be viewed.

Heroic feminine journeys of growth in the *WOT*

Jordan's secondary female protagonists may not gain the same heroic status as the three main male figures, but they experience their own life-changing journeys of self-growth and have significant, at times pivotal, roles to play in the focal narrative. Thus Jordan finds ample space for them within the traditionally male-oriented heroic quest paradigm. In his portrayal of these women Jordan moves away from the stereotypical female figures of sage and temptress that informed his presentation of Moiraine and Lanfear and, in part, helped to mould Rand's character. The significant and individualistic roles that Jordan creates for these women are a distinct departure from the traditional literary assumption of the male hero figure, and befit his theory of a balance between the male and female aspects of the One Power in the Wheel world. Jordan, in a similar fashion to many women writers of modern fantasy (i.e. Ursula Le Guin, Patricia McKillip, Marion Bradley or Robin Hobb), has shifted away from the presumption that:

> female characters in the Secondary World must be restricted to the roles played by women in our primary world's medieval romances – object of the quest, mother, temptress, witch – or else absent, as in epics such as *Beowulf* or the *Song of Roland*. (Ringel 2000, 165-6)

In Jordan's *WOT* the three main hero figures (Rand, Mat and Perrin) remain traditional warrior types, but the women who surround this trio are depicted as strong-willed, vital figures, and through their own ancillary journeys assume a heroic cast. The author portrays them as women who are prepared to take their destinies into their own hands and to go in quest of self-knowledge. In line with the interlace technique of his narrative, where each strand contributes to the overall pattern, it is to be expected that their stories will become interwoven into Rand's focal quest, as do the stories of his male companions.

The women's ancillary quests place them in the heroic mode as their stories provide a mirroring of the focal quest. Jordan thus demonstrates that heroism in the *WOT* is not to be entirely focused on a singular (male) protagonist, for the heroic figure comprises a number of interlaced life-threads, including those of Rand's female companions. Jordan's splintering of the hero figure suggests that he is drawing on the concept of the hero in mediaeval romances in which it is usual (even conventional) to have more than one hero. Yet despite these helpers the final test, signifying the success or failure of the quest, is one that the central hero must confront alone. Jordan emphasises this in the *WOT,* as the Dragon Reborn remains the central heroic figure, the apex of the triangle, but his various companions are caught in the web of his destiny and their ancillary quests can influence the progression of his own journey. A comparison can be loosely drawn with the mediaeval interlaced narrative of Malory's *Morte d'Arthur,* and the company of questing knights who surround King Arthur, lynch-pin of the depicted society, as their individual quests impact on the stability of both their king and his kingdom.

Jordan's development of Rand's main female companions may be examined in terms of the initiations they face as they negotiate their own ways through a labyrinth-like series of experiences, which lead to death or rebirth and provide a counterpoint to the central heroic quest motif. But the women's journeys of self-growth, and their attainment of extra-sensory or superhuman powers, demand that they abandon either a person or a role in life that is dear to their hearts. Repeatedly, they have to walk away from people who need them and whom they love, unlike the male heroes who are tested according to abstract concepts of heroism. Thus in his testing of his female characters Jordan focuses more on their emotional responses, which for the reader adds a poignancy to their dilemmas that is not so strongly felt in regard to his male characters. This point can be demonstrated through a brief examination of the women's initiation process.

Nynaeve, Egwene and Elayne have the innate potential to become powerful channelers of *saidar*, and their initiation into the sisterhood of the Aes Sedai at the White Tower entails entering a powerful *ter'angreal* in the shape of a triple archway. They must step through each of the arches in turn and therein face their greatest fears – once 'for what was', once 'for what is' and once 'for what will be'. (*GH*, 338-49) The way back to their reality is offered, briefly, each time they enter, and if they fail to return through the archway when summoned they will be lost forever. Nynaeve initially steps through the arch into a stone-walled maze to be pursued by one of the male Forsaken. In this other-worldly dimension she gains the ability to annihilate him with the One Power, but must forego the opportunity to do so, in order to return through the archway. Before joining the White Tower Nynaeve had held the position of Wisdom, or healer, in her home village of Emond's Field, but she steps through the archway for the second time to discover she must now abandon the people she loves to the cruel bullying woman who has replaced her. In the final test she finds herself happily married to Lan, the man she loves, but must make the heart-wrenching decision to walk away from him and their children, as he begs: 'Stay with me, always'. (*GH*, 351) Jordan thus links his female protagonists to the concept of heroic sacrifice for a higher purpose.

Within the archways Egwene discovers that she must abandon Rand to madness and the Dark, 'to betray him, fail him, again and again'. (*DR*, 266) Jordan gives no details of Elayne's ordeal, but as she weeps uncontrollably and whispers, 'I could not be that awful ... I just couldn't', the reader feels she has faced a similar cruel pattern of testing. (*DR*, 273) As with his male protagonists, Jordan also foregrounds the difficulty of acquiring enhanced powers and of becoming a magus in his imaginary world, which always entails some form of sacrifice and loss. As is explained by Sheriam, one of the Aes Sedai officiating at Nynaeve's initiation:

There is always some reason not to return ... This *ter'angreal* weaves traps for you from your own mind, weaves them tight and strong, harder than steel and more deadly than poison. That is why we use it as a test. You must want to be Aes Sedai more than anything else in the whole world, enough to face anything, fight free of anything, to achieve it. (*GH*, 348)

Their friend Aviendha, an Aiel 'Maiden of the Spear', when summoned to join the Wise Ones of her tribe, must not only put aside her cherished warrior sisterhood, but in a harsh severing of her past life also personally destroy her old clothing and weapons. Aviendha's rite of passage takes her to the hidden city of Rhuidean where she must step though a similar *ter'angreal* archway, to be shown a variety of paths that her future could take. She learns the bitter lesson that some 'despised' things 'must be', while other 'cherished hopes' must not come to pass. (*SR*, 379) Like Rand, she cannot avoid her 'duty' or her 'obligation' to her people, but in futile words that echo his earlier anguished cry against the dictates of fate and so arouse our sympathy, she defies the Wise Ones': 'I am a Maiden of the Spear. I do not want to be a Wise One. I will not be!' (*SR*, 376) But, as in Jordan's world 'the Wheel weaves as the Wheel wills', both Aviendah and the reader are aware that while the threads of a destined life-path may be somewhat bent, they cannot be entirely side-stepped.

Each of these women faces painful journeys of initiation stripped of all clothing and personal possessions, much as Moiraine did when she gained permission from the Wise Ones to enter Rhuidean. For these women, as with the men, their only weapons of defence during initiation are 'a strong mind and a strong heart'. (*SR*, 379) Their nakedness is symbolic of the laying aside of their previous lives, so they emerge re-clothed in self-knowledge, and such rebirth is celebrated by the putting on of new garments that denote their enhanced status. At the White Tower successful initiates are also symbolically 'washed clean' of their past identities, 'washed clean, in heart and soul' with a chalice of water; a type of holy baptism that adds an aura of sacredness to the rituals. (*GH*, 353) Indeed, Jordan's portrayal of the White Tower and the Aes Sedai bears comparison to the influential mediaeval orders of holy women. Ritual nudity is an old motif of initiation and symbolic of a return to a state of innocence, freedom from earthly taint, or of resurrection in rebirth (Cooper 1992, 112-3) so it is intriguing that Jordan does not require his male protagonists to strip off anything, except their weapons, when faced with similar situations of testing; for instance Rand and Mat's journey to Rhuidean. The implication is, surely, that men are to be deemed naked without their weapons.

Jordan suggests that the women's personal sacrifices and painful initiations bring deeper understanding and maturity to prepare them to take on significant roles of leadership within their societies, and to engage in their own dangerous journeys of adventure that are threaded into the focal narrative. These young women are not presented as *ta'veren*, but they are drawn into Rand's orbit of influence and their ancillary quests, such as the finding of long-lost objects of power, work to favour his greater cause: for instance, their recovery and use of the long-lost 'Bowl of the Winds', a legendary *ter'angreal*, brings about a reversal of the adverse weather patterns that had been caused by the Dark Lord, thus undermining his influence in the Wheel world and implying that he can be defeated. (*COS*, chap. 38; *POD*, chap. 5) They also discover and arrange for the apparent safe disposal of a 'necklace and two bracelets of jointed black metal' that would enable any female Forsaken or women of the Black Ajah to enslave Rand and turn him to their own dark pattern. (*SR*, 882) In a further twist of Jordan's plotting, only the reader is aware that this *ter'angreal* subsequently falls into the wrong hands and so still poses a grave danger to Rand's future. (*WH*, chap. 21) By revealing this fact to the reader but keeping his characters in the dark, the author achieves an element of intrigue and suspense.

Through the cause-and-effect pattern of actions, as described above, or by narrative echoes and anticipations, Jordan continuously entangles the stories of the women with the central quest. For example, if Rand is to remain sane he must cleanse the tainted male side of the One Power, but to do so requires Nynaeve's assistance as she is the only powerful female channeller in whom he has complete trust. But in order to help him Nynaeve must gain control of her considerable talent, for at an early age, out of fear, she set up a mental block that now prevents her from channelling unless roused to anger. To be able, freely, to access her potential power she must learn to completely surrender to it, a state of mind she achieves, in another symbolic rebirth, after becoming trapped in a sunken boat. On the point of drowning she totally surrenders her mind to *saidar*, shattering her long-held block, and uses her now unfettered power to free herself from the wreck. From this point on Nynaeve is empowered to assist Rand, and her action anticipates his necessary surrender to the female side of the One Power, when they later achieve a mental bridging of *saidar* and *saidin* that enables him to achieve his goal.

Other threads of the women's stories are interwoven into that of Rand's. Elayne not only becomes an Aes Sedai but also comes into her own kingdom as the Queen of Andor. Her ability to unite the factions of her own peoples aids Rand's quest, as his success, in part, is dependent on a unification of the various peoples of the Wheel world. Egwene is appointed as the Amrylin Seat, the head priestess of a rebel group of Aes Sedai from the White Tower, and she then raises an army to over-throw the old hostile regime on the island at Tar Valon. Her friendship and support of Rand anticipates the likelihood of a union between the White Tower and Rand's Black Tower, between female and male, as symbolised by the ancient *yin/yang* symbol of the Aes Sedai. Jordan works to integrate Rand's female companions into the greater quest, but along the way he empowers them to achieve their own heroic journeys of self-growth and self-determination, and for the reader they emerge as vital, fully-rounded characters in their own right.

On the persistent use of the 'companions' or 'helpers' motif in epic-style high fantasy texts, Clute makes the following observation:

> [The] extended narrative sweep ... offers ample scope within which secondary characters may act out their destinies ... fill the scene, bolster the hero, perform feats he or she cannot, depart upon ancillary quests whose accomplishments will help trigger the climax, and die if necessary. (1999, 220)

Clute further suggests that the 'reasons for this are obvious: variety, pleasure, a reservoir of possible response when action is required' (1999, 221). Thus, the author is able to offer the reader an intricately structured and layered narrative that often unfolds through separate yet thematically interconnected storylines. Not only does such a tactic complicate and enrich the overall pattern of the story, it also widens the reader's knowledge of the various main characters and of their world, thereby enforcing a stronger sense of its authenticity that helps sustain Secondary Belief. An author such as Jordan, is able to encompass a large cast of characters and ancillary quests, and yet bring them to bear on the focal narrative of Rand's final battle.

THE METAPHOR OF A 'HEROIC LINE'

Because of Jordan's fondness for multi-stranded yet interlaced plots that at times can loop backwards and forwards across the various books, the metaphor of a 'heroic line', loosely centred on Rand, that runs throughout the narrative, with the three *ta'veren* and at times the women, orbiting and moving across it, seems most appropriate. It is a metaphor that represents the heroic figure textually as well as narratively. As these characters circle in and out of the main narrative, but continuously add threads to it from their own stories, they are all being woven in some fashion into Rand's quest and placed along the 'heroic line' as the narrative progresses. It seems likely that by the time of Rand's prophesied final confrontation with the Dark Lord, the life-threads of the three *ta'veren* youths, in particular, will have become braided together to form a tight weave that enables them to act in unison and thus to form a type of triple hero. Such a union is symbolically suggested by the three ancient war banners that they resurrect: Rand has the banner of the Dragon; Perrin, the Red Eagle banner of Manetheren; and Mat, the banner of the Band of the Red Hand, a legendary warrior troop. Jordan's interlacing of these three main male protagonists allows him to explore different aspects of the hero figure, and it is an exposition of each of these figures that follows now.

4 HEROIC INTERLACE: THE JORDAN HERO AS DESTROYER, BUILDER AND PRESERVER

Men of Manetheren ... thorn to the Dark One's Foot and a bramble to his hand.
(*EOTW*, 132)

THE POWER OF 'THREE'

Jordan's use of the triple hero figure draws on the long symbolic power of the number three. Across a diversity of cultures, myths, legends, folklores and religions feature 'innumerable trinities of gods and powers' or 'threefold goddesses', that can represent 'different aspects or potencies, of one deity' (Cooper 1992, 114). Consider, for example, the Christian Trinity of Father, Son and Holy Ghost, or the Hindu Trinity of Brahma, Vsihnu and Shiva. Other well-known triple figures include the Parcae, the Three Fates who spin, measure, and cut the life-threads of humankind; the three Graces who bring beauty to the world to lift the hearts of both gods and mortals; and the three-faced figure of the goddess Hecate, whose association with witchcraft sees her reflected much later in the three witches of Shakespeare's *Macbeth*. Monsters in classical myth are frequently three-bodied or triple-headed, such as Geryones, the three-headed giant fought by Hercules; the three Gorgons, of whom the most feared is Medusa; and Cerberus, the three-headed dog who is said to guard the entrance to the underworld. Traditionally in European thought the number three is symbolic of 'infinity, perfection, power and greatness' (Trickova-Flamee 2004). It can also be representative of 'past, present and future' (Cooper 1992, 114), and this is particularly interesting in Jordan's Secondary World as each of the three *ta'veren* youths, in different ways, brings the past into the present and uses ancient talents or knowledge thus gained to weave towards the future. For as the Ogier, Loial, explains to them: '*Ta'veren* pull history along behind them and shape the Pattern just by being'. (*GH*, 35) Therefore, in some ways they are poised on the threshold between what was and what is to be, a critical point of change (the 'Crossroads of Twilight', as suggested by the title of the tenth volume) and Janus-like they can look both ways.

It is a convention of heroic or epic high fantasy that the past may be brought to bear on the present – in the sense that in past actions lie the seeds for the current disruption to the imaginary worlds. For instance, in Tolkien's *LOTR* the background story reveals how Sauron's obsession for control and power brought about the forging of the destructive One Ring, while in Le Guin's *Earthsea* series it is Ged's arrogant actions that lead to the wizard Cob turning to the black arts and rupturing the delicate barrier between the living and the dead. Similarly, in Jordan's world of the Wheel it was human over-reaching, the lust for unbridled power and immortality that allowed the Dark Lord to lay his touch on the world, and led to the destruction of the Golden Age. Nevertheless, in all such texts the past can also have positive influence on the present and add a further dimension to the narrative. Thus, in the *WOT* the past enters the present through the resurgence of old heroic bloodlines, as with Jordan's simple country folk of the Two Rivers who had long forgotten their distinguished ancestry, or primaeval talents such as Perrin's ability to link with the minds of wolves, or Mat's memories of past battle strategies and of the Old Tongue. In fantasy the disruption of linear time allows room for elements from the past to be activated in the present in order to provide invaluable assistance in times of great need. In Tolkien's Middle-earth, Aragorn's summoning of the dead to fulfil a dishonoured pledge of the past turns the tide in the battle and, similarly, in the world of the Wheel, Mat's sounding of the Horn of Valere compels the dead heroes of the past to assist in his bid to vanquish the forces of the Seanchan invaders. The ability of Rand and his companions to locate the legendary Green Man's grove and the items it holds that are needed to forward the quest, also falls into this category. Indeed, in respect of Jordan's portrayal of a linked three-figure hero, the fluidity between past and present is vital to their make-up and to the fulfilment of the fated roles they must enact. As it is through the minds of Rand, Perrin and Mat that aspects of a previous Age of the world of the Wheel are imposed on their present day so they, too, reflect the repeating Pattern of Ages that makes up the world of the Wheel.

The depiction of the triple hero figure allows Jordan to present an integrated, multi-faceted, multi-talented hero figure, yet to retain believably human characters that the reader can relate to. Perhaps, through the interdependent actions of the triple figure, and those of the lesser characters who are drawn into the heroic line, such complication of the conventional quest paradigm underscores the concept of universal unity, one which is needed to restore and preserve the integrity of the invented world. In his portrayal of a multiple hero figure Jordan is drawing on a convention in epic or romance to assign specific tasks in the quest to a number of heroic figures. But Jordan's concept of his characters Rand, Mat and Perrin as a form of heroic triad is an interesting adaptation of the convention of the motif of the hero and his companions. In this regard he may well have been influenced by Icelandic sagas, especially as the mythological ancestry of Perrin and Mat is drawn from the Northern gods, Thor and Othin. For in some saga sources, as Dean Miller notes:

> [the] permutation of the motif of the hero and helpers presents the following shape or pattern: a pair of heroic figures, each with a specific valence or talent, is joined by a third figure whose powers are drawn from a manifestly different, usually supernatural source. The Icelandic *þáttr* 'Bósa or Herrauðr' for example, is best described as a breezy adventure tale of warriors and warlocks, one in which Herrauðr has the role of the normative or 'straight' actor while Bósi is a freer spirit, a bit of a trickster, and an uninhibited sexual adventurer. The *tertium quid* is Bósi's brother Smidr, who possesses all the tricks of the magician with all the associated gifts of shape changing and sorcery. (2000, 106-7)

Jordan's reworking of this motif presents a similar pattern: Rand, the Dragon Reborn as the magician; Mat, as a type of trickster/gambler and sexual adventurer; and Perrin, through his mental wolf-link, as a shape-changer who adopts the form of a wolf when he runs with his wolf brothers while in the World of Dreams.

In Jordan's imaginary world these three male figures all follow the conventional stages of the heroic quest: separation as youths from their known world, and personal growth effected through both physical and metaphysical journeys. In different forms each plays a crucial role in the overall cosmic quest, although Rand, as the reincarnation of the Dragon, stands firmly at the apex of this human triangle. He is set apart as well by his ability to wield the One Power, and by the Christ-like imagery that surrounds and, by association, elevates him further in stature. In another configuration of three, he is a triple messiah known in his own land as the 'Dragon Reborn'; to the Aiel of the desert as 'He Who Comes with the Dawn'; and to the Sea Folk as 'The Coramoor', and all these peoples have their own beliefs and prophecies in regard to him. Through this rhetoric of repetition, the concept of a thrice-named messiah, Jordan is playing on the Eastern notion that there are many diverse paths to the one cosmic Truth and, by implication, making a call for a universal tolerance of the disparate spiritual beliefs in our own world.

In *LOTR*, through his use of the romance convention of a number of heroic figures, Tolkien also advocates the merits of the 'heroic Company', where each member plays a specific part. Thus, at Rivendell, Gandalf reminds Bilbo that 'only a small part is played in great deeds by any hero'. (*Fellowship*, 263) However, in Jordan's Secondary World the fate of the three *ta'veren* youths is presented as being more tightly interwoven than that of, say, Aragorn, Frodo and Sam, for without Mat and Perrin it is clearly foretold that Rand not *might*, but *must* fail. Because of their physical and metaphysical links the three Emond's Fielders constitute a composite secular personality, offering various psychological perspectives on the ancient notion of trinity. In addition as hypothesised by Karl-Johan Norén(2003), within the Pattern as they perform certain roles and tasks, they can be seen to form a secular variation on the classical Hindu trinity of gods, to present a theme of Destroyer–Builder–Preserver, with Rand as the Destroyer (Saviour),

Perrin as the Builder, and Mat as the Preserver, a theory which sits well with the Hindu-influenced cosmology of Jordan's Secondary World. However, there is no suggestion that Jordan is drawing on more than the concept of three god-like figures that together work to one end.[1]

DESTROYER—BUILDER—PRESERVER

The concept of a secular model of Destroyer–Builder–Preserver is the one I use to 'unpack' the way in which each of the three *ta'veren*, through their parallel existences, offers different perspectives on the function of the Jordan triple heroic figure. Each figure is also examined in terms of how his development is enhanced through a fusion of past and present, while the Great Pattern relentlessly weaves the strands of their life experiences towards a catastrophic event in the future. For instance, Rand as Dragon Reborn is presented as the current embodiment of the past Dragon, whose voice he hears in his head, while Perrin develops the ancient talent of linking with the collective, timeless minds of wolves. Through painful initiation Mat gains memories of past lives that provide prowess in battle tactics, along with the ability to speak in the Old Tongue, and so he becomes the 'sounder' of the legendary Horn of Valere that summons the crucial aid of heroes from the past. Furthermore, in all three youths the 'old blood' of the long forgotten heroes of Manetheren still 'sings' in their veins, another linking of past to present, and to their ties as blood-brothers. (*EOTW*, 170) Yet Rand's mind can be taken over by the former Dragon, and the taint on *saidin* can bring insanity; Perrin faces the danger of becoming more wolf than human or of being trapped in the wolf dreaming; and Mat faces being consumed by the evil in the tainted dagger, or by the memories of past lives that continuously assert themselves in his mind. Jordan thus presents each of them with a personal crisis of identity, which must be resolved if they are to develop and to advance along the heroic line of the narrative.

The struggle for identity faced by these protagonists equates well with the Jungian thought of the 'hero in all its archetypal forms' as being the 'most important figure' in the 'quest', because it 'represents the struggles of the Self for individuation, growth, and centring'. Through 'identifying with the hero' the reader 'travels with him in quest of the *numen* ... the universal truth at the center of one's own soul' (Potts 1991, 4). In other words, the quest of the hero to self-realisation can provide the catalyst for personal growth in the reader. But adding to the conundrum of identity faced by Jordan's three protagonists is the paradoxical idea that, while the three *ta'veren* have separate psyches, they are still one, 'three ... centrepoints of the weaving' that will shape the Pattern of the Age Lace. (*GH*, 35) It is only by means of their entwined and fated paths that the Dragon Reborn has any hope of victory at *Tarmon Gai'don*. Further, Rand knows well that, even if they are set separate tasks along the way, the 'three *ta'veren* who had been tied together since infancy' at the end would become 'tied together once more'. (*FOH*, 614) Thus, through the interwoven life-threads of Rand, Perrin and Mat, Jordan presents different guises of the hero figure who can be seen to reflect each other and in turn to reflect and embody what is at stake in the world, a narrative technique of reduplication that intensifies the urgency of events in the depicted Age, and through which means the author works to convince the reader of this fact. A detailed exposition of each of these figures may now be made, beginning with Rand, and then turning to Perrin and Mat.

THE TRIPLE HERO

Three threads woven together share one another's doom. When one is cut all are.
(*DR*, 67)

Rand al'thor: The Dragon Reborn

'Death is lighter than a feather, duty heavier than a mountain'.
(*GH*, 679)

Rand as the Dragon Reborn stands at the apex of Jordan's triangle of male heroes. There are many textual references to Rand as the 'breaker of the world' and it is prophesied that he will be both 'Destroyer' and 'Saviour', and so a seemingly secular Christ figure. In the design of the

Great Pattern Rand's central *raison d'être* is to overcome the Dark Lord at *Tarmon Gai'don*. Thus Jordan suggests that, despite the interlacing of Rand's life-path with those of Perrin and Mat, and the importance of their roles, the final confrontation with his nemesis will be his alone. All Rand's actions and tasks are designed by the author to strengthen and prepare him for this climactic event, as in his metaphysical battle with one of the Forsaken at Falme in the second book where he is first publicly proclaimed as the Dragon Reborn. (*GH*, 676) The Dragon Reborn is predicted to be 'born of *Far Dareis Mai*' (a Maiden of the Spear) on the 'slopes of Dragonmount', and the Aiel say he will be 'blood of our blood mixed with the old blood, raised by an ancient blood not ours'. (*DR*, 443-45) These prophetic details, surrounding the rebirth of the Dragon, finally force Rand to accept the unpalatable fact that he is a fosterling, and not native to the pastoral county of the Two Rivers. He learns from the Wise Ones of the Aiel that although his mother had been a Maiden of the Spear, she was not one of their people, and had come to them as a stranger seeking refuge. Later, she had died in the midst of battle after giving birth to him on Dragonmount, where he was found in the snow by Tam al'Thor of the Two Rivers, who then raised him as his own.[2] Thus, Jordan is utilising a common convention from both myth and fairy tale where the hero is an orphan child of mysterious birth, one traditionally associated with water, whose birthright is hidden but who is destined to bring extraordinary benefits to society. Well-known examples of this motif include the biblical myth of Moses, the castaway child in *Beowulf* who becomes king of the Scyldings, or Oscar Wilde's *Star Child*. In regard to this motif Pierre Brunel suggests that:

> surrounded by death, threatened from his glorious birth by a hostile universe, given up to the caprices of the waters (as were the Assyrian king Sargon and the founders of Rome, Romulus and Remus), the child is saved by fishermen (Perseus), shepherds (Oedipus), a herdsman (Cyrus) or indeed looked after by kind animals (Romulus and Remus). He then lives an obscure life, very different

from the one for which his birth should have destined him. This is the period of hidden life, of apparent death. (1992, 558)

In the *WOT* Rand's foster father is presented as a widowed shepherd, and Rand is raised by him in an obscure corner of the country, in ignorance of his true destiny or of the dangerous forces, Light and Dark, that will seek him out and so provide the catalyst for his dramatic rebirth.

When Rand is eventually forced to leave his home he carries with him a heron-marked sword that serves as a bond to his father Tam, for it had once been his weapon. Later, when the precious sword is broken during his battle against Ba'alzamon, at which point he is hailed as the Dragon Reborn, the broken blade becomes a poignant metaphor for his disturbing realisation that he cannot be Tam's blood son, and instead has a fearful heritage that has cast him onto the world stage. His subsequent actions, in fulfilment of old prophecy, such as the taking of the Crystal Sword, 'that no hand but his should wield' make it impossible for him to deny his birthright, as do the prophetic twin heron marks on his palms (akin to the stigmata of Christ) and the Dragon markings that appear on his forearms during his initiation in the hidden city of Rhuidean. (*DR*, 675) As well as this, he faces the fact that he is able to channel the One Power, and must wield it, despite the risk of insanity, for there is no 'unstilled' male Aes Sedai of the Light living to teach him to control his talent. Rand thus emerges as a reluctant hero who out of a strong sense of duty assumes the mantle of Dragon Reborn, and who ruefully thinks that his life 'would be easier if this was a story'. (*FOH*, 671) He believes that 'in stories things always happened as the hero planned, seemingly when he wanted them to happen'. (*SR*, 827) Ironically, for the reader, Rand's life *is* a story, and one controlled by a pattern created by the author, which adds to the pathos of his dilemma. The burden of his task is summed up by his resignation to the fact that 'duty is heavier than a mountain, death lighter than a feather'.[3] (*GH*, 679)

Yet, as the narrative progresses and Rand's leadership qualities are brought to the fore, he becomes colder, more arrogant, aloof and manipulative. His process of isolation is metaphorically expressed in one of Egwene's prophetic dreams in which Rand is 'building a wall' of 'stones' to separate him from his friends and allies, and saying: 'It has to be done ... I'll not let you stop me now'. (*SR*, 200) To balance this dangerous pattern of behaviour Jordan introduces several women companions into Rand's life to help to humanise him. And, as discussed in the previous chapter, both Cadsuane and Bair, the Aiel Wise One, believe it to be crucial that he remember how to 'laugh again, and cry', and to be human. (*WH*, 508)

By this means Jordan suggests that 'power', too far removed from any sense of compassion and human warmth, can easily perform evil in the name of good so that his protagonists, unwittingly, could become party to the tenets of the dark impulse that they fight against. Warnings of power as a double-edged sword are clearly signalled in the text by the cruel excesses of the fanatical Whitecloaks, supposedly moral warriors of the Light, or by the cold righteousness of Elayne's half-brother, Galad, of whom she says: He takes right above mercy, or pity ... [h]e's no more human than a Trolloc'. (*GH*, 363) Such warning is reinforced by the background story, for, as mentioned in chapter two, in the past it was hunger for personal power that brought a group of thirteen Aes Sedai to negate any vestige of human decency and so to embrace the Dark. These Forsaken Ones are even prepared to accept the end of Time itself, and the horror of eternity in a Shadow world, as long as they can be figures of power in it. Thus, on one hand Jordan presents Rand as an elevated figure, but on the other insists that if he is to succeed in his quest he must remember he is a mere mortal. As a consequence there is much tension between the Rand of the past, the naïve shepherd, and Rand the world figure, one marked out by destiny to adopt the overwhelming role of the Dragon Reborn, a dilemma which evokes reader sympathy for his plight. In his depiction of an ordinary, country youth who is fated to take up an extraordinary life-journey of cosmic significance, Jordan's utilisation of Christian parallelism is telling.

In relation to Rand as Dragon Reborn, typology and the prefiguring of Jesus are of special interest, not only because of the many parallels to the Christian myth in the texts, but also because of Jordan's repeated statement that he is an 'Old Testament God with [his fist] in the middle of their lives' (CNN 2000). The Wheel weaves as Jordan wills and he constantly reshapes a wealth of traditional material to his own needs, so that although his imaginary world is not presented as overtly Christian, Rand is, in part, a secularised Christ figure, and the enduring power of the underlying Christian mythic material helps to make him much larger than life. A few examples will suffice. The Dragon is prophesied to be reborn as he has been in the past and to bring both destruction and salvation. False Dragons (i.e. false saviours) are also spun out by the (Jordan) Pattern. The mad prophet Masema believes Rand, 'The Lord Dragon' to be the 'source of the Light', while ancient prophecy decrees that Rand's blood is to be shed on the black 'rock of Shayol Ghul', the place of the Dark One's prison, in order to save the world: 'Twice dawns the day when his blood is shed. Once for mourning, once for birth. (*FOH*, 562; *SR*, 387) This brings to mind the darkening of the sun when Christ is crucified. And, as for Jesus, his peace will be 'the peace … of the sword' that will split 'all in twain'. (*FOH*, epilogue) Rand is also referred to as 'lord of the dawn', and 'prince of the morning' suggestive that, like the Saviour of Christianity, he too will bring Light to the world.[4]

Rand carries a wound in the left side, inflicted by Ba'alzamon during the battle at Falme, which cannot be fully healed. This must suggest the legend of the Fisher King, one symbolic of Christ, with the wound representative of His suffering on the Cross. The Fisher King is traditionally tied directly to the land, which cannot be healthy as long as he is wounded. The world of the Wheel is being torn apart by civil unrest, and the prolonged drought and encroachment of the Blighted Lands are a metaphor for the insidious spread of the Shadow. It is prophesied that 'there can be no health in us, nor any good thing grow, for the land is one with the Dragon Reborn, and he one with the land'. (*COS*, epigraph) The Welsh people have a notion of the Dragon as a divine symbol in life and traditionally the Dragon is to be both feared and revered, so Jordan may be said to be alluding to this concept as well. Rand's unearthly sword of fire, formed of *saidin* when he embraces the One Power, is metaphoric for the destructive and fiery breath of a Dragon and perhaps makes it a fiery sword of retribution, especially as he wields it to dread effect against the emissaries of the Dark Lord. Jordan's use of such resonating imagery is designed to strengthen the reader's concept of Rand, the Dragon Reborn, as being an apocalyptic figure.

Jordan deliberately employs a prophetic/oratorical style in the texts in relation to the Dragon figure, these often occurring in a Biblical phraseology, as in this Old Testament-sounding passage:

> And it came to pass in those days, as it had come before and would come again, that the Dark lay heavy on the land and weighed down the hearts of men, and the green things failed, and hope died. And men cried out to the Creator, saying, O Light of the Heavens, Light of the World, let the Promised One be born of the mountain, according to the prophecies, as he was in ages past and will be in ages to come. Let the Prince of the Morning sing to the land that the green things will grow and the valleys give forth lambs. Let the arm of the arm of the Lord of the Dawn shelter us from the Dark and the great sword of justice defend us. Let the Dragon ride again on the winds of time. (*EOTW*, prologue, xv)

Other visionary passages are of a later style, with both the New Testament – and Bunyan – seemingly echoed:

> And his paths shall be many, and who shall know his name, for he shall be born among us many times, in many guises, as he has been and ever will be, time without end. His coming shall be like the sharp edge of the plow, turning our lives in furrows from out of the places where we lie in our silence. The breaker of bonds; the forger of

chains. The maker of futures; the unshaper of destiny.
(*DR*, epigraph)

Despite its ambiguity, there is a sense that 'unshaper of destiny' here is meant in a positive light, perhaps referring to the way in which a *ta'veren* brings necessary changes to the pattern of the Age Lace, which are not wholly pre-determined by the Great Cosmic Pattern. By contrast, it is also said of the Shadow: 'The Dark One is the embodiment of paradox and chaos, the destroyer of reason and logic, the breaker of balance, the unmaker of order. (*DR*, 239) This sentiment is parallel to that of Le Guin's in her *Earthsea* series and is clearly meant in a negative light.

Jordan presents these and similar visionary passages as prologues or epilogues, thus set outside of the action of the novels. These writings are offered to the reader as excerpts from a variety of historical sources in the imaginary world, some pre-dating the 'Breaking' that ended the Age of Legends, but all deal with prophetic writings concerning the Dragon. The material includes various translations taken from the Karaethon cycle (the 'Prophecies of the Dragon'), along with pieces of poetry, folk sayings, and even a few lines of a chant from a children's game. The authors of these works are purported to be Aes Sedai of notable rank, historical librarians and other employees of royal households, such as the court of the famed Artur Hawkwing or that of the queen of Andor. One is said to be the legendary hero Jain Farstrider, while yet others remain anonymous.

This device of giving the imaginary world a long documented history relating to the deeds of the former Dragon, and to the coming of the Dragon Reborn, deepens the reader's sense of this figure's authenticity and grandeur. The use of such prophetic writings, at the start or finish (sometimes both) of each successive volume, builds narrative tension since for the reader they reinforce the apocalyptic nature of Rand's destiny in the imaginary world. Jordan also intersperses other pieces of prophetic material into the main body of the texts, these being revealed through the knowledge of wise characters such as Moiraine, Lan, Thom, and the Ogier, Loial, or from hearsay among the common people. Thus, he shows the suspense and fear shown by the inhabitants of the Wheel world, especially as they are witness to Rand's fulfilment of some of the prophecies of the Dragon and so cannot deny his heritage. The reactions of the characters in turn evoke an emotional response in the reader, who is also bought to be fearful of the outcome of Rand's actions. Furthermore, the importance Jordan gives to historical documentation among the various peoples of the Wheel world – that is, the archives of the White Tower, private libraries, the memories and writings of the long-lived Ogier, and the gleeman's bottomless bag of stories – helps to foster the reader's sense of the credibility of this extensive and detailed store-house of history, and so invites a belief in the prophecies of the Dragon that it contains.

It is not only through the use of the Christ myth that Jordan adds stature to his hero Rand. He also borrows elements of the Arthurian material, a rich, repeatedly mined source for fantasists, the most obvious of these being Rand's taking of the numinous *sa'angreal*, the crystal sword. Jordan's coinage of the word *sa'angreal*, that is analogous with *sangreal* – 'holy grail', adds to the impressiveness of the glittering sword that Excalibur-like 'flare[s] as if with a light of its own', and of the hero who displays the ability to grasp and to wield it. (*DR*, 648) A further example is evident during Rand's metaphysical battle against Ba'alzamon in the skies above the city of Falme, where the ancient Dragon Banner ripples behind them, and from then on becomes the standard the followers of the Dragon fight under. (*GH*, 676) Woven into the white banner was a 'figure like a serpent, scaled in scarlet and gold' but with 'scaled legs' and a 'great head with a golden mane and eyes like the sun'. The 'stirring of the banner made it seem to move, scales glittering like precious metals and gems' so that it seemed 'alive'; a symbol that the legendary Dragon (i.e. Rand) now lives again. (*EOTW*, 773) For some readers, the dragon banner in the sky would further resonate with the vision of a flaming dragon in the sky that allegedly came to Uther Pendragon, father of the legendary King Arthur (compare Jordan's 'Artur Paendrag'), and who thereafter carried the emblem of a golden dragon into battle, as did later Anglo-Saxon kings. 'In England before the Norman conquest, the dragon was chief among the royal ensigns in war, having been instituted by such by Uther Pendragon, father of King Arthur' (*The New Encyclopaedia Britannica*, vol.4, 209). The idea of Uther Pendragon has extended into popular lore and Jordan's mediaevalist sensibilities mean this resonance is not lost on him or his readers.

As the dragon beast has been believed to have qualities of being both 'protective and terror-inspiring', dragon effigies in one form or another have been used on the shields of legendary warriors (e.g. Homer's Agamemnon, in the form of a blue three-headed snake), and by the Vikings on their shields and the prows of their ships (*The New Encyclopaedia Britannica*, vol.4, 209). Thus, Jordan is reworking a long, varied tradition, both mythical and historical, of applying the dragon motif in relation to heroic warriors and kings, which, by association, accrues similar qualities of both might and fearfulness to his own protagonist, despite his youth.

Traditionally the motif of the dragon is also ascribed to some form of scaled, wily, avaricious beast, as faced by a multitude of mythic or literary heroic figures, from Siegfried, the slayer of Fafnir; and Beowulf, the mighty king of the Geats; to the humble hobbit, Bilbo Baggins; and Ged, Archmage and Dragon Lord of *Earthsea*. Dragons, it is well-known, are both terrifying and awe-inspiring: Jordan twists these traits to create the sense of an apocalyptic human figure known as the Dragon. In the Wheel world the Dragon Reborn is feared for, in a past incarnation, in saving the world from the Dark Lord he had then brought about its destruction after losing his sanity through the taint in *saidin.* In keeping with Jordan's ontology for his imaginary world of an eternal circling of time and lives, apocalyptic prophecy must suggest this cosmic destruction and resurrection by the Dragon to be a repeating pattern, to be faced by each successive turning of the Wheel of Time, for it is written:

> Yet one shall be born to face the Shadow, born once more as he was born before and shall be born again, time without end. The Dragon shall be Reborn ... and he shall break the world again by his coming, tearing apart all ties

that bind. Like the unfettered dawn shall he blind us, and burn us, yet shall the Dragon Reborn confront the Shadow at the Last Battle, and his blood shall give us the Light. Let tears flow … people of the world. Weep for your salvation. (*GH*, epigraph)

The notion of such an eternal return is clearly symbolised by Jordan's incorporation of the uroboros motif into the official logo for the Wheel of Time series. This ancient motif of the serpent biting its own tail symbolises the infinite renewal of the universe. Yet, paradoxically, Jordan also stresses that a danger to the continuation of the pattern exists, for if the Dragon dies, there can be no hope of resurrection. Ba'alzamon appears to Rand one night and warns that this time at the Last Battle 'the cycle will not begin anew with your death' and that the 'Wheel will be broken … and the world remade to a new mold', one of the Dark Lord's choosing. (*GH*, 243) Jordan thus implies the uneasy possibility that this time the Wheel of Time may be destroyed and that the Dark will triumph, for neither the characters nor the reader can be sure if the Forsaken One's prophetic words are a possible truth or a total fabrication.

THREE METAPHYSICAL DRAGONS

Jordan adds to the complexity of Rand's character through a repetition of the dragon motif that provides an externalisation of the triple monsters Rand grapples with in his mind. On a personal level Jordan's protagonist presents a paradox as he represents both Dragon and Dragon-slayer, although the three monsters he faces are incorporeal, and to be conquered on an inner, metaphysical level, and all of them contribute to his development. Jordan sets up each of these metaphoric dragons to test Rand's resilience in different ways: through the temptations, threats and lies of the Dark; through the despair and madness of the past manifested in his mind in the voice of the previous Dragon; and through the potential destruction of self-contained in the tainted male side of the One Power.

The first of these monsters Rand faces is the Dark Lord who, in the metaphysical dream realm of *Tel'aran'rhoid,* uses surrogate figures, human puppets manipulated by 'black lines like steel wires' that in the dark stretch back into 'unimaginable heights and distances' to give himself form and a voice. (*DR,* 665) Through the body of his puppet, Ba'alzamon, the Dark Lord searches for the one who is the Dragon Reborn. Jordan shows the close ties between the destinies of the three *ta'veren* youths as Rand, Perrin and Mat experience a series of identical nightmarish dreams of pursuit, wherein they must deny the Dark Lord, for at first he is unsure which youth is the one he seeks. This reduplication of dream sequences suggests that each of the *ta'veren* is to be viewed as a potentially powerful figure.

In *Tel'aran'rhoid* during a series of maze-like dream sequences, Rand is pursued by Ba'alzamon down spiralling stairs, along endless corridors with doors that all lead to the same room, or faces multiple reflections of Ba'alzamon and himself, 'staring wide-eyed and frightened', into an endless array of mirrors:

> In every mirror, the flames of Ba'alzamon's face raged behind him, enveloping, consuming, merging. He wanted to scream, but his throat was frozen. There was only one face in those endless mirrors. His own face. Ba'alzamon's face. One face. (*EOTW,* 351-2)

On a psychic level this dream sequence is a projection of Rand's fear of a loss of his own identity, the possibility that he may not be able to stand firm against the Dark, and that the very monster of his worst nightmares exists within the recesses of his own mind and could sweep him away. In an earlier visitation the Dark Lord, angered by Rand's refusal to accept him as his master, asserts that the 'death of time' will return him 'power' such as a 'worm' like Rand 'could not dream of'. (*EOTW,* 204) He later threateningly warns Rand: 'Serve me and I will give you the world. Resist, and I will destroy you, as I have so often before'. (*GH,* 665) The power and immortality offered by this persona of the Dark is constantly undercut by the inferno glimpsed when Ba'alzamon's 'mouth and eyes became openings into endless caverns of flame ... peepholes into a furnace that seemed to stretch forever', and suggestive of a horrendous eternity of agony and damnation. (*EOTW*, 202-03) This fearful image is made doubly so by Jordan's mixing of the sacred and the profane – the inferno of the Hell of Christian theology with the destructive, pagan fire of a dragon.

It is Rand's inner core, his connection to 'the soil of his home', which has produced a people as 'strong' and 'hard as the mountains' that finally sustains him, too. Min jokes that, underneath, 'Two Rivers folk' are 'as tough as old oak roots' and if you 'prod too hard' you 'dig up stone'. (*EOTW*, 759; 214) This centre of resilience enables Rand to withstand the onslaught of the lies of the Dark One, and to declare: 'I will never serve you, Father of Lies. In a thousand lives I never have ... I'm sure of it'. (*GH*, 666) A prominent theme in Jordan's narrative, as shared with many other high fantasy texts, is this need for individuals to find the inner strength to face and overcome all doubts, fears, and temptations, and so have the courage of their convictions to make difficult, but morally based and selfless choices.

The second monster is the insistent voice, and invasive memories of the violently insane dead hero Lews Therin, the ur-Dragon, who manifests himself in Rand's mind once the young champion gains some measure of control over the One Power. Therin constantly urges Rand to 'kill them all' and moans of 'death' and the 'pit of doom'. (*LOC*, 783; *WH*, 249) On a metaphysical level this double personality accords with the general Jungian principle that 'every psychological extreme secretly contains its own opposite' (Jung 1956, par. 581): in this case, the destructive principle of the unhinged mind of the past Dragon and the constructive principle of Rand, his current reincarnation, the Dragon Reborn whose destiny it is to once again save the world.

Rand has to struggle to bring salvation to a falling world from a masculine inheritance of power linked with mayhem and destruction. In relation to this, Jordan's use of the dragon motif shows the apt influence of Chinese thought where the Dragon is believed to have 117 scales, 'of which 81 are imbued with Yang and 36 with Yin, because the dragon is partly a preserver and partly a destroyer' (Cavendish 1995, 633-4). In

Chinese philosophy it is this principle of *yang* and *yin* that enables the dragon to be transformed into a beneficent being for, unlike in the West, this creature is not seen as the symbol of evil. In relation to such balance Jordan shows that one of Rand's tasks is to redress the imbalance between the masculine and feminine aspects of the One Power (the governing principles that sustain the world of the Wheel), one inadvertently caused by his predecessor Lew Therin. It was through Therin's well-intentioned actions in protecting the world from the 'Father of Lies', during the Age of Legends, that the male side of the One Power became tainted and linked with madness, and if Rand is to remain sane he must achieve the cleansing of *saidin*. His subsequent success of this task through a melding of the two sides of the power will be discussed further on.

In Rand's head the past Dragon becomes increasingly enmeshed with his own personality. He thus catches himself using Therin's 'turns of phrase', or mannerisms, such as 'thumbing his earlobe', and finds the other man's 'memories mingling with his' own. (*COT*, 550; *COS*, 358) He also discovers the name of Therin's dead wife, Ilyena, involuntarily added to his own mental list of women for whose deaths he holds himself responsible, and for whom he now mourns. He also has to fight, consciously, to retain control of his mind, and of the One Power which, increasingly, Therin attempts to wrest from him. Of the voice in his head Rand thinks: 'Are you really there?' (*LOC*, 397) He reasons that he is 'Lews Therin reborn' and that 'everybody was someone reborn' as that was how the 'Pattern worked', but surely only 'madmen' spoke with 'who they used to be'. (*COS*, 146) As Jordan gives no external perspective on Lews Therin neither Rand nor the reader is sure if the voice is real, or a signal that the hero is succumbing to madness as a result of the taint in *saidin*, a narrative device that adds a further element of tension.

Jordan's portrayal of a past personality attempting to assert itself in the present bears a striking similarity to Victorian supernatural writing, as well as to Raymond Feist's fantasy text *Magician* (2002). In Feist's narrative a young and naïve protagonist, Tomas, receives a gift from a dying dragon beast, the armaments of an ancient Dragon Lord, including a magical golden coat of chain mail. Through wearing it Tomas begins to take on the physical and mental attributes of the long dead, non-human and merciless warrior named Ashen-Shugar. In the final battle for control of his mind Tomas emerges as the victor:

> I *am Ashen-Shugar!* I *am Valheru!* Sang a voice within, in
> a torrent of anger, battle madness, and bloodlust.
> Against this sea of rage stood a single rock, a calm, small
> voice within that said, simply, I *am Tomas.*(540)

In the end, Tomas remains human, but must bear the weight of guilt over the slaughter (and joy in it) performed by him during times of blood lust, when the will of the Valheru had held sway in his mind. Yet he is now neither the boy of the past nor the ancient Dragon Lord, having gained attributes of them both that set him apart:

> Gone was the alien cast to his features ... Again he was
> Tomas, though there were legacies of his experience that
> would forever proclaim him something more than a man:
> the elven ears, the pale eyes. Gone was the Lord of Power,
> the Old One, the Valheru. Where before a Dragon Lord
> had stood now crouched a troubled, sick man in torment
> over what he had done. (541)

Feist, like Jordan, uses the concept of a double personality as a means of testing the protagonist, a painful rite of passage to adulthood that his hero eventually survives, although not without psychological scars. It is yet to be seen if Jordan's hero will remain untouched after grappling with 'two men inside one skull'. (*COS*, 158) As the narrative progresses Rand and Lews Therin begin to have interactive conversations, as when Therin suggests that Rand should 'work' with him. (*LOC*, 958) As well as this, Rand sometimes glimpses a 'murky' face of a third person in his head, while Therin whispers in his mind: 'How many will we three kill before the end'. (*WH*, 447) It is uncertain whether Jordan intends there to be some merging of a triple personality at the Last Battle, or if the shadowy 'man's face' in his mind that Rand finds 'almost recognizable', is his complete psychological self, to be produced by a blending of his mind and that of Lews Therin. (*WH*, 657)

Such a concept is supported by Egwene's prophetic dream in which 'Rand' wears 'different masks, until suddenly one of those false faces was no longer a mask, but him'. (*POD*, 328) And Sammael, one of the Forsaken, believes: 'Al'Thor was not Lews Therin, but al'Thor was Lews Therin's soul reborn, as Lews Therin himself had been the rebirth of that soul', thus reinforcing the concept of a champion of the Light, one whose spirit has been reincarnated down through the ages to engage in the eternal battle against the encroachment of the Shadow. (*LOC*, 179) This image is also suggestive of the notion that evil in the imaginary but flawed world, for the Pattern contains good and evil, is capable of being beaten back but never totally vanquished, and so may have to be faced again at a future time. The words of writer and critic Hal Colebatch, who believes Tolkien's intent in *LOTR* was to show that 'the human race lives in a hard but not desperate and not hopeless situation', would seem relevant to Jordan's themes and common to a number of other writers of heroic modern fantasy (Colebatch 2004).

Another contemporary fantasist, Robin Hobb, offers a different interpretation of the dragon motif in her popular *Farseer* trilogy: that of a voluntary forging of man and beast. King Verity, with the aid of his magical power known as 'The Skill' puts his whole essence into carving a stone dragon, and so brings it to life. (This is similar to Jordan's *Aelfinn* and *Eelfinn*, alien beings who feed on human 'sensations', 'emotions' and 'experiences' [*SR*, 252]). It is through this strange melding of stone with human flesh and spirit that a special creature can be created in order to save his land and his people. As the last of the king's being 'flowed into the [carved] dragon' (1998, 802) his bastard nephew, FitzChivalry, stands witness to his metamorphosis into 'Verity-as-Dragon':

> His eyes when he opened them, were black and shining, the eyes of a Farseer, and I knew Verity looked out of them ... He stretched like a cat, bowing and rolling

reptilian shoulders and spreading claws... his immense
wings unfurled ... His tail gave a single lash, stirring rock
dust and grit into the air. The great head turned, his eyes
demanding we be as pleased with this new self as he was.
Verity-as-Dragon strode forward to present himself to his
queen.(1998, 802)

King Verity, through his integration with the very stone of the land,
becomes its saviour. Hobb, like Jordan, is utilising a variation on the
myth of the Fisher King. As noted by Stephen Potts in his discussion on
Tolkien's notion of the hero in *LOTR*, this particular myth is
represented in figures as 'widely disparate as Osiris, Adonis, Oedipus
and Christ'. Potts further contends that such a figure can be described as
being:

the hero whose spiritual and physical health determines
that of his followers, who must allow himself to be
sacrificed if necessary to permit his community to live, and
who thus embodies in his own person the life-force of his
people and their bond with nature and the cosmos. (1991,
4)

The actions of King Verity fit this sacrificial paradigm. With other
dragon statues from the ancient 'Stone Garden' in the mountains,
brought to life by human 'blood' and the lesser magic known as the
'wit', Verity-as-Dragon destroys the invaders of the Red Ships and
reunites his beloved Six Duchies. But his metamorphosis cannot be
reversed so his humanity is forsaken forever. Once the battle is
completed he reverts to statue form, and will 'sleep well in the Stone
Garden' unless called into life again by a future world need. (Hobb
1998, 829) Yet, the regeneration of his society is ensured by his wife's
conception, as the night before he puts the last of himself into the stone
dragon, his brother's bastard son, FitzChivalry, permits the king,
through a transfer of minds, to borrow his body, so Verity spends one
last night with his queen.

Like other heroic figures such as Frodo, Ged, or Rand, Verity takes up the quest needed to save his world with no thought of self-survival. But, as the necessary sacrificial king, he then becomes the rejuvenator of his world. From the above examples it is apparent that Jordan, Feist and Hobb draw on similar themes from the traditional story-hoard in their use of the dragon motif. They succeed in reworking them in an individualised fashion, yet all of these narratives are concerned with the making of ethical, moral choices that are key hallmarks of heroic fantasy.

The third internal dragon to be faced by Rand is the monstrous One Power itself, which is not only tainted but, because of Rand's inexperience, is a force that threatens to sweep away his mind, to erase his essence of self. Hence it must be conquered if he is to qualify as a magus:

> The Power felt like life itself swelling inside him ... the Dark One's taint filled him, too, death and corruption, like maggots crawling in his mouth. It was a torrent that threatened to sweep him away, a raging flood he had to fight every moment ... And all the while the deluge tried to scour him to the bone and burn his bones to ash. (*FOH*, 71)

Jordan's depiction of the dangers inherent in *saidin* helps to reinforce his theme of the destructive potential of power itself, and the ambiguity that exists between the impulses of good and evil, as it can become a weapon for either. (In an ironic twist it is Asmodean, a leading servant of the Dark, who is coerced into teaching Rand to use and control *saidin*. But this figure, unlike the soldier Ingtar, does not seek redemption, and for his unwilling betrayal of the Dark Lord is callously murdered.)

The danger associated with power is equally apparent in the female half of the One Power. In a Secondary World where the governing paradigm is presented as a duality of opposites, Jordan equates male power with aggression and female power with passivity, a philosophy of life embedded in the folk wisdom of the Two Rivers where it is spoken that 'a man is an oak, a woman a willow ... [t]he oak fought the wind and was broken, while the willow bent when it must and survived'. (*FOH*, 565) As it is the female side of the One Power that survived the former 'Breaking of the World' without taint, these words become a metaphor for the resilience of women, and are also suggestive of the greater strength to be gained by a tempering of heedless masculine might with the enduring, and more subtle strength of feminine passive resistance.

Masculine control of *saidin* is only to be maintained by dogged mental force, whereas females effect control through willing surrender to *saidar*. Rand's cleansing of *saidin* is brought about through a metaphysical linking with Nynaeve, one of his companions from the Two Rivers. To achieve the link Rand has to 'fight' *saidin* to master it in the 'deadly dance he knew so well', whilst simultaneously 'surrendering' to the 'tranquil' flow of the smooth 'river' of *saidar*, a contradiction of terms that forms a delicately held balancing of the male and female principles of *yang* and *yin*. This action in turn reflects the patterning of the two halves of the True Source, 'male and female ... alike and unalike', 'fighting against each other even as they worked together to drive the Wheel of Time'. (*WH*, 658-9) Rand's personal, metaphysical union of masculine and feminine powers is mirrored in his formation of a 'Black Tower', where he gathers men who have the inborn 'spark' to channel the One Power. Defined by Jordan as Ash'aman, in the 'Old Tongue' one who 'defended truth and justice for everyone, a guardian who would not yield even when all hope was gone', these men of the 'Black Tower' will surely be used to form a union with their female counterparts, the Aes Sedai of the 'White Tower'. (*Companion*, 417) For it has been foretold that at the Last Battle the Dragon will 'conquer' under the old sign of the Aes Sedai the 'black teardrop' and the 'white ... flame of Tar Valon'. (*FOH*, 134) Thus Jordan uses this interconnected narrative patterning to highlight the importance of regaining balance if the Wheel world is to be healed.

Through a combination of associations with the Christ figure, the Arthurian cycle, and the motif of the dragon, Jordan lifts Rand, the naïve farm boy, to the status of a world figure, one that is to be both revered and feared. Jordan's repetition of the motif of triples in relation to Rand, that is, three titles, three internal monsters, bonding with three women, three women mentor figures, and his testing in the triple-arched *ter'angreal*, all reveal and enhance the different facets of his personality as well as contributing to his growth. The motif of triples mirrors the patterning of Rand's life-threads with those of the other two *ta'veren* youths, thus suggesting that their own journeys will both reflect and advance his cause.

From the apocalyptic figure of Rand I now turn to Perrin, whose axe/hammer dualism is suggestive of him too being a type of destroyer/saviour figure, and it is through his acceptance of both the destructive and creative aspects of his nature that he also emerges as a constructive force in his world, and becomes the saviour of his home village.

Perrin 'Goldeneyes'

'Your hands were made for a hammer, not an axe.
Made to make things, not to kill'. (*DR*, 66)

Perrin, a former blacksmith's apprentice, is characterised as humble, kind, a deep thinker who does not act in haste, is physically strong but gentle, honest and reliable, slow to anger yet terrible when aroused, and essentially a craftsman. But as noted by Karl-Johan Norén, his great physical strength, his beard, his hammer and aspects of his personality draw on the association of the god Thor of Norse mythology, whose hammer Mjollnir was symbolic of both destruction and creation (1995).[5] This link not only makes Perrin a larger figure, but also a man of the people, as Thor was the god of the common, free man. The latter certainly accords with Perrin's egalitarian thoughts that in the Two Rivers there is no need for 'lords' or 'kings or queens', because they are all 'free men'. (*SR*, 741) Perrin's initial naivety and innate goodness are apparent when Moiraine warns that the Pattern of an Age is neither good nor evil but woven from both, a 'warp and woof of good and ill'. (*DR*, 378) To him the Creator of the Pattern must surely be a master artisan, and any flaw in the Age Lace must lie solely within humankind itself, for:

> he wanted to believe the Pattern was good. He wanted to believe that when men did evil things, they were going against the Pattern, distorting it. To him the Pattern was a fine and intricate creation made by a master smith. That it mixed pot metal and worse in with good steel with never a care was a cold thought. (*DR*, 378)

Such imagery of blacksmithing and metallurgy runs through the series in relation to Perrin. Through the associations of magic that have accrued to the work of the blacksmith – for instance, the legendary smith, Weland, and the making of spell-wrought swords and armour – Perrin's art with metal suggests that, like Rand, he is a type of powerful, magical figure.

Jordan presents Perrin as the most idealistically minded of the three *ta'veren* youths and perhaps the strongest moral voice of this triumvirate. Yet Perrin's strong axe/hammer dualism reflects the potential for acts of violence in the gentlest of souls, and the anguish of having to resort to such dark means in the pursuit of good:

> The axe was a wicked half-moon blade balanced by a thick spike, meant for violence. With the hammer he could make things, had made things at a forge. The hammerhead weighed more than twice as much as the axe blade, but it was the axe that felt heavier, every time he picked it up. (*SR*, 46)

Jordan uses the tension caused by Perrin's Axe (destruction)/Hammer (creation) dilemma, and the moral ambiguity it generates, as an anvil to strengthen and temper him for his true constructive role in life. Perrin's underlying decency is shown by the prediction of his fellow wolfbrother, Elyas, that as long as he 'hate[s] using' the axe, he will 'use it more wisely than most men would', and that the time to give it up is when this is no longer the case. (*EOTW*, 440) These prophetic words are borne out when his wife Faile is kidnapped by the Shaido, at which point, Perrin, driven by the need to rescue her, resorts to cruelly chopping off the left hand of a Shaido prisoner, then throws the axe away. To him the 'blood' on his axe 'had never looked so black', a metaphor for his self-loathing at what he is capable of when the life of the woman he loves is at stake, and fear, that as in battle, he will come to 'feel alive' through such deeds. (*COT*, 597; 600) Faile, in a sense, is presented by Jordan as Perrin's fatal flaw, his Achilles heel, as love for her can drive him to override his cautious nature and to act imprudently, much as Rand's inability to harm a woman led to his refusal to kill Lanfear, and so to the apparent death of Moiraine.

All of the *ta'veren* are protectors of women: for instance, Rand confesses to Sulin, a Maiden of the Spear, 'I could not kill a woman if my life hung on it'. (*FOH*, 833) And Mat is devastated when he is forced to kill his lover Melindhra, when she reveals herself as a Darkfriend and tries to stab him. 'He had killed men, and Trollocs, but never a woman. Never a woman until now'. (*FOH*, 804) Perrin's Axe/Hammer dilemma parallels Rand's anxiety about his fearsome nature as he struggles to hang on to the true kernel of his being: 'a shepherd named Rand al'Thor'. (*SR*, 76) But Perrin's decision to throw away the bloodied axe suggests that Rand will learn to temper his power and so avoid the wanton destruction of which he is capable. In regard to the mode of quest fantasy Jane Mobley has observed that:

> The sub-plots ... always serve to accentuate the main plot. Either a lesser hero-figure acts out a quest parallel to the main hero's, or the sub-plots provide further adventures or trials for the hero. (1974, 189)

In the *WOT* the sub plots of Perrin and Mat provide Jordan with a means of developing their individual personalities, enabling them to develop the strengths and talents that are needed to fulfil their roles as part of the triple hero figure. Thus, the journeys they take, both inner and outer, can be seen to reflect those of Rand.

Perrin's ancillary heroic quest is to save his home village from an overwhelming Trolloc attack, an episode Jordan uses to forge Perrin's leadership skills and so to raise him in stature. Perrin's battle against the Dark forces at Emond's Field can also be seen as a parallel to Rand's greater quest. Thus, Perrin's victory is suggestive of a positive outcome for Rand when he faces the Dark Lord.

Perrin's ordeals or 'rites of passage' include facing the murder of his family; the death of many old friends because they rally to his cause against the invading Trollocs; and the grim reality that, despite the heavy losses of his companions, he must continue to 'care for the living' and 'later' find the time to 'weep for the dead'. (SR, 709) His words echo those of Rand, following heavy losses in a battle to rid the city of Caemlyn of Rahvin, one of the Forsaken: 'Rejoice in what you can save, and do not mourn your losses too long'. (FOH, 881) Perrin's self-development is furthered by his acceptance that despite his longing for his former peaceful life as a blacksmith, the passivity practised by the Travelling People cannot hold back the present Dark:

> The way of the leaf was a fine belief, like a dream of peace, but like the dream it could not last where there was violence. He did not know of a place without that. A dream for some other man, some other time. Some other Age perhaps. (SR, 743)

Like the other two ta'veren youths, Perrin accepts that his understanding of the world has changed since he first left the Two Rivers, although 'he just never thought that he would have to change, too'. (POG, 255) By exposure to the reality of life in the wider world he learns that, for him, it is only through violence (the axe) that a return to the hammer (creation) may become possible. Thus Jordan creates a moral ambiguity that accentuates Perrin's dilemma, and, by inference Rand's as well, for it is only through acts of darkness and death that his people are able once more to walk in the Light.

Perrin's quest to rescue the Two Rivers includes elements of the paradigm of the epic hero, for as noted by John Leyerle, in the epic mode the character 'holds to his commitment and keeps to what he regards as his high destiny' and plays for high stakes, such as the defence of a nation. (1975, 71) Jordan uses Perrin's strong impulse to save his home village from the Dark, as a reflection of Rand's determination to save the wider world. But Leyerle further suggests that the epic hero's unswerving devotion to the quest can bring about his own death and cause 'the destruction of his followers, or even of his society' (1975, 71). A good example from earlier literature is the predicted fall of the Geats following the death of Beowulf, for it was brought about by his brave but foolhardy battle with the dragon. However, this typical tragic scenario is overturned by Jordan. Perrin freely offers to give himself up to the Whitecloaks, to be wrongly hanged as a Darkfriend, once the battle against the Trollocs is won, if they help in the 'defence, where and when' they are 'asked'. (*SR*, 750) His willingness to forfeit his life in order to save the village, and the fact that he is spared such a fate, anticipates that the much prophesied spilling of the 'Dragon's blood' on the 'black rock of Shayol Ghul', may not be a sacrifice of Rand's life. (*GH*, 387) As a self-effacing hero figure Perrin seeks neither fame nor reward for his efforts yet he receives both, becoming a celebrated, local hero, lauded as 'Lord Perrin', and gaining the hand in marriage of Faile, the woman he loves. A clear sign of Perrin's change of status is reflected by Faile's remarks that 'there will be stories about you in the Two Rivers for the next thousand years. Perrin Goldeneyes, hunter of Trollocs'. (*SR*, 670) The sheer strength of his will was already evident in his determination to defy the pull of *ta'veren* that ties him to Rand, once he knew of the plight of their home village. Although he knows that he and Mat are an inseparable 'part of Rand's destiny', he also believes that at times the Pattern can send them down 'different paths'. (*SR*, 45; 230)

Rand's belief that it is Perrin's task to 'save Emond's Field', and his tacit consent to his departure confirms this. He hopes that for a time Perrin can escape the sphere of his influence and prays: 'Help them Perrin … because I can't' as, at this point, his own life-thread weaves in another direction. (*SR*, 253; 357) But Loial, the Ogier, reminds them that 'go or stay … together or apart … for a time, the Wheel will bend the Pattern around [them]' as 'whatever' happens is 'more likely to be

chosen by the Wheel' than by the protagonists themselves. (*GH*, 35)
Later, Rand observes that:

> The Wheel wove happenstance and coincidence into the
> Pattern, but it did not lay down the likes of the three of
> them for no reason. Eventually he would pull his friends
> back to him, however far they went, and when they came,
> he would use them, however he could. However he had
> to. Because whatever the Prophecy of the Dragon said, he
> was sure the only chance he had of winning Tarmon
> Gai'don lay in having the three of them, three *ta'veren*
> who had been tied together since infancy, tied together
> once more. (*FOH*, 614)

Thus, Jordan stresses the strength of the ties that bind them and that
will pull them together again when needed.

Perrin's ability to rally the people of the Two Rivers against all odds,
and his subsequent rebuilding of Emond's Field, along with the respect
and love he engenders among the people, show a strange harmonising
of the axe and hammer, the creative continuity of village life re-gained
through the bloody violence of battle, which suggests that any
destruction wrought by Rand will ultimately be for the good of the
Wheel world. Perrin's success in the Two Rivers seems symbolic of a
more universal task to come – a rebuilding of the world following the
Last Battle, especially as Jordan has hinted that after *Tarmon Gai'don*
the 'surviving characters would still have lives to go on with, even if
more "boring" ones'. (Noren 2003)

Furthermore, as the narrative progresses Perrin, who gathers a loyal
army under the old Banner of Manetheren, continues to emerge as a
competent soldier/leader and one most willingly trust. His campaign
secretary, Balwer, a former spy for the commander of the Whitecloaks,
is an astute judge of character and he praises Perrin:

> You are what you seem, my Lord, with no poisoned
> needles hidden away to catch the unwary. My previous

employer was known widely for cleverness, but I believe you are equally clever, in a different way. I believe I would regret leaving your services. (*COT*, 188)

Despite his axe/hammer duality Perrin emerges as a simple man, a strong advocate for human justice, a person of honesty and open-mindedness, one whom Jordan uses to balance Rand's almost god-like status and the recklessness of Mat, whom I discuss later in this chapter.

Perrin's Wolf-Link

Perrin, in a further complication to his personal development and a repetition of the pattern of Rand's development, also faces an inner identity crisis as he involuntarily develops the ancient talent of mental communication with wolves. The she-wolf Dapple says that he lives 'between the human world' and their world, giving him a human/wolf duality. By this means Jordan links Perrin to the natural, primaeval world of nature, for his latent talent (a melding of past and present) is 'older than humans using the One Power … something from the birth of Time … something long vanished, now come again'. (*GH*, 226) As a 'wolfbrother', Perrin's mind is linked to the collective 'shape' of the 'history of all wolves' including 'a faded image, dim with time, old beyond old, of men running with wolves, two packs hunting together', and the wolves say 'this time comes again'. (*EOTW*, 342; *GH*, 226) This image reflects an age when humans lived more harmoniously with the natural world, and also points to the approaching battle against the Dark Lord as being one encompassing all living creatures, not just humans. For the reader, this yet again reinforces the magnitude of the imminent catastrophe facing the inhabitants of Jordan's world. Egwene's visionary dream of a bearded 'Perrin … leading a huge pack of wolves that stretched as far as the eyes could see', resonates with Hopper's words to him that in the 'Last Hunt' they will 'run together', which strongly suggests the wolves, through Perrin, are also being woven along the heroic line and have a vital role to play in the fulfilment of the narrative's focal quest. (*DR*, 290; *SR*, 467)

The convention of a mutually beneficial mind link between humans and other species is a common trope to writers of both fantasy and science fiction: for instance, the honoured telepathic communication between dragon and human 'dragonrider' in the Dragon books of Anne McCaffrey, or Ged's ability to converse with such creatures, in the speech of Creation (the 'Making') in Le Guin's *Earthsea* series. Le Guin depicts these creatures as being both majestic and terrible, but not evil. In Jordan's case, as in Hobb's *Farseer* series (to be discussed later), the use of wolves shows the positive influence of traditional American Indian lore, and these authors do not cast wolves as beasts of darkness, in contrast to Tolkien's *The Hobbit*, in which, as Margery Hourihan points out, 'wolves and Wargs, a large and evil variety of wolf,' are allied to the 'wicked goblins' (1997, 124). Hourihan further comments that 'while the totemic beliefs of tribal peoples stress their sense of human contiguity with animals, in the Western tradition, at least since Plato, human beings have consistently defined themselves in contradistinction to nature' (1997, 113).

In American Indian culture the wolf is regarded as a teacher and pathfinder, and an animal whose skills and sense of community make it an example from nature to be followed. In the Secondary Worlds of both Jordan and Hobb, their protagonists, through mental bonding, receive acceptance, loyalty and love from these so-called 'savage' beasts. Perrin is thus regarded as a brother by the wolves and they come to his aid simply because he calls. Similarly, for FitzChivalry, the hero of Hobb's *Farseer* trilogy, the wolf Nighteyes sees him as 'pack', as a brother. For both these protagonists the wolf, as in American Indian lore, can be regarded as a personal totem animal, and therefore an integral part of self.

In the Jordan books wolves are respected because they fight the Dark, and they are regarded by the people of the 'borderlands' as 'creatures of good luck'. (*GH*, 229) Once Perrin stops struggling against his talent, and accepts with 'full heart' and 'full mind' that he is a wolfbrother, he gains a spirit wolf-guide, Hopper, who guards his dreams and warns of impending dangers in the waking world. (*EOTW*, 412) Perrin's only physical sign of the wolf link is the golden colour of his eyes – a wolf's eyes – but he also gains the heightened senses (sight, hearing, smell) akin to those of a predatory animal. It is in the inner spirit realm of the wolf dream that Perrin sometimes shape-changes to a wolf and runs with Hopper – a shaman-like ability recognised in many cultures, including those of the indigenous Americans. At such times 'he felt a shifting inside him, something changing. He looked down at his curly-haired legs, his wide paws', and became aware that he was 'an even larger wolf than Hopper', and in the waking world, he sometimes feels he is 'half wolf already'. (*DR*, 628; *SR*, 467) With the wolves he can forget about his size, and there was no-one to think him 'slow witted' because he 'tried to be careful' and took his time over making decisions. Wolves knew each other even if they had never met before, and 'with them he was just another wolf', thoughts which not only speak of his acceptance of them, but that also reveal his very human insecurities. (*DR*, 81)

Perrin's emerging dual identity is clearly shown through the collective thought pictures which he receives from the wolves, for his image as a man is overlaid with the stronger image of a 'massive, wild bull with curved horns of shining metal ... curly-haired coat gleaming in the moonlight', and to them he is spoken of as the mighty fighter, 'Young Bull'. (*GH*, 227) In the frenzy of battle the narrating voice says he was 'Young Bull-Perrin' and only 'a buried fragment' of him was still human for 'wolves filled him till he could barely remember being a man'. Like a predatory animal he went for the 'hamstring and throat' of his enemy, 'snarled with his brothers', and 'felt the urge to hurl his axe aside and use his teeth, to run on all fours'. Further, he 'threw back his head and howled' in mourning for the wolves that had died. (DR, 77-79) These images of Perrin in his ecstasy, fierceness, and imperviousness to his wounds in battle, and of his 'howling with rage that filmed his eyes red' create metaphorical associations not only with a wolf but also the battle rage of a Viking Beserk, follower of Odin; a fearful combination that Jordan utilises in order to enhance Perrin's ferociousness and stance as a warrior. (*SR*, 676)

However, like Rand, Perrin faces the possibility of a total loss of identity. The great danger for Perrin is that he may become totally consumed by his wolf identity and lose all humanity, a lesson Jordan graphically enforces on his protagonist and the reader through the depiction of the wretched, caged man Noal, whose 'mind has nothing that remembers being a man' and who Perrin realises 'may not have fur, but [is] a wolf'. (*DR*, 119-120) With his wolf mind trapped in a human body, Noal is perhaps a variation on the traditional werewolf. Such a shifting between man and wolf, a pitiful creature totally alienated from both, is a motif more closely associated with the genre of horror, both literary and cinematic.[6] Hourihan's research on this topic shows that in Western culture the werewolf came to symbolise the violence of the 'beast within' an externalisation of 'the human capacity for violence, cruelty and slaughter'. Such an image has been perpetuated in a long succession of horror films, including *The Wolf Man* (1941), *I Was a Teenage Werewolf* (1957), and *The Curse of the Werewolf* (1961), *An American Werewolf in London* (1981), *The Howling* (1981), *The Company of Wolves* (1984) and the remake of the 1941 film, *The Wolfman* (2010). Hobb too, despite her positive portrayal of the human/wolf link, also deals with this theme of a human fear of succumbing to some form of bestiality that lurks within.

Furthermore, Hobb's use of the wolf/human duality shows some striking similarities to that of Jordan. In her Secondary World she posits a hierarchical order of 'magics' known as the Skill, the Wit, and the Hedge. The Skill gives the ability to link with human minds, while the Hedge refers to all forms of fortune telling such as crystal gazing or palm reading. But it is the Wit, the ability for a human to link with a non-human animal that parallels the old talent of Jordan's protagonist Perrin. In Hobb's world the Wit is regarded as a perversion, and much despised for it is feared that it can make a human a beast. Burrich warns FitzChivalry that a Witted one can lose all trace of humanity and will 'run and give tongue and taste blood, as if the pack were all [they had] ever known' (1996, 44). Yet, as in Jordan, the life of a wild wolf is depicted as a clean and wholesome way of being and some believe it was 'once the natural magic of those who lived on the land as hunters ... a magic for those who felt kinship with the wild beast of the woods'. Such a notion is strengthened by the ability of Queen Kettricken who, through her weak sendings of the Wit, immerses herself in simply 'being', becoming part of the 'great web' of life that 'touched her' and in which 'nothing [is] alone, nothing [is] forsaken', a world where all things are interconnected, a thought analogous with Jordan's Great Pattern of the world of the Wheel (Hobb 1997, 1, 231-2). The narrator further suggests that 'the Wit may be a man's acceptance of the beast nature within himself, and hence an awareness of the element of humanity that every animal carries within it as well (Hobb 1998, 88). Thus the 'Wit' becomes a two way understanding between a human and another animal of shared thoughts and emotions and a return to a primaeval and more natural state of being, one that Hobb implies could lie just beneath the veneer of human civilisation. FitzChivalry insists that he and Nighteyes must not bond and tries to deny his 'true nature' by declaring: 'I am human. You are wolf'. Nighteyes wisely replies: 'Outwardly' but 'inside we are pack'. It is through an acceptance of the wolf within that connects him more fully to the complex 'web of life' that FitzChivalry feels a complete person (1997, 148).

The bond between human and wolf is one of equality and this is continuously highlighted by the spirited, interactive thoughts between FitzChivalry and Nighteyes. The wolf's personality is also highly developed and through his dialogue he exhibits an extraordinarily human range of emotions, including rage, arrogance, sly humour, and sorrow and he can be sulky, teasing, and playful, all of which Hobb successfully uses to endear him to the reader. The wolf certainly sees himself as an equal for he tells his human-witted 'brother': 'I will be to you what you are to me. Bond brother and pack' (1997, 265). In Hobb's world the narrator makes it clear that:

> the legendary loyalty that a bonded animal feels for his Witted one is not at all the same as what a loyal beast gives its master. Rather it is a reflection of the loyalty that the Witted one has pledged to his animal companion, like for like. (1998, 99)

The telepathic link between FitzChivalry and Nighteyes is a far more personally integrated one than that experienced by Jordan's protagonist Perrin whose link is a collective one to the minds of all wolves, although he does form a closer bond with the spirit of the dead wolf, Hopper. However, both Hobb and Jordan present their wolves as noble, intelligent, communally minded creatures and, despite their savagery, the wolf way of life as being clean and free by associating it with images of vast tracts of pristine wilderness and an acceptance of the natural cycle of the seasons.

Jordan's plotted actions for Perrin, as he matures from an inexperienced country youth and earns both the title of Lord Perrin Goldeneyes, and respect as a warrior and leader, as well as coming to terms with a superhuman talent that has the potential to destroy his identity, can be seen to follow a similar psychological story arc as that of Rand. Thus, Jordan draws them together along the heroic line, and he entangles Mat's life with theirs in a similar manner.

Mat: 'Son of Battles'

'When fate gripped you by the throat,
there was nothing to do but grin'. (*COT*, 631)

Mat is presented to the reader as a gambler, a person of chance, a risk-taker, and the recurring motif of the dice spinning in his head at times of danger or significant change is a very apt one. Thus, within the trio, he provides a counterpoint to the more measured, cautious personality of Perrin. Mat's love of gambling, especially the alluring 'chance' of dicing, is used by Jordan as a recurring metaphor for the randomness of Fate, and for the pull of the Pattern that surrounds Mat and the other *ta'veren*, from which he cannot entirely escape despite his protests. He knows that when he gets too far from Rand, he can be 'drawn back like a hooked fish on an invisible line', as in 'some strange way' he and Perrin are 'tied to Rand's success or failure in *Tarmon Gai'don* ... three *ta'veren* all tangled together'. (*FOH*, 604) Like Rand and Perrin he brings the past to life in the present in a way that is vital to the outcome of the future.

In a mirroring of the pattern of the other *ta'veren,* Mat also faces an inner conflict that triggers his personal development and advances the weaving of the Pattern of the future. Once he has hung, Othin-like, on the Tree of Life at Rhuidean, 'to die and live again, and live once more a part of what was', he gains knowledge of the Old Tongue and of past battles and complex battle strategies through remembrance of his past lives. (*SR,* 249) Mat enters Rhuidean with Rand, and his remembrance of the past is juxtaposed to Rand's experiences in this hidden city where his knowledge is gained by reliving the history of the Aiel people. Mat's initial denial of the memories points to the dilemma he faces between the adult maturity of duty and responsibility, and the feckless freedom of youth – a dilemma similarly faced by Rand and Perrin. As Mat pushes down memories of past military campaigns he thinks:

> '*I am no bloody hero* … *and I'm no bloody soldier* … *that was* not *me'*… He did not know what he was – a sour thought – but … it involved gambling and taverns, women and dancing … It involved a good horse and every road in the world to choose from. (*FOH,* 603)

The phrase 'a sour thought' is indicative of the way the narrator indicates that although Mat stubbornly rails against his fate, he knows he cannot continue to sidestep it. Mat later finds himself thinking that 'battle was a gamble to make dicing in taverns a thing for children and toothless invalids', and a 'game that set the blood racing', which points to his acceptance of a melding of past and present personalities, and is a step forward in his development. (*FOH,* 609-10) The fact that Mat's utilisation of 'what[ever] got shoved' into his 'head' in Rhuidean must be woven into the Age Lace, in favour of the quest, is stressed when Rand tells Mat he 'needs' what is in his 'head', for he is not a battle strategist. (*FOH,* 800) Mat's uncanny ability to engage in 'three battles, and three victories,' to 'dance with Jak o' the Shadows' with 'small loss' to his 'own men' gains him heroic status. (*FOH,* 795; 664) He draws men to him to fight under the resurrected banner of the long dead warriors of the Band of the Red Hand, in the Old Tongue *Shen an Calhar*. (*FOH*, 794) Ironically, he wonders how they would react if they knew he was just a 'gambler following bits of memory from men dead a thousand years and more', a self-perception which, for the reader, undercuts the soldiers' idealised picture of him, and serves as a reminder that he is only mortal. (*FOH*, 649)

Mat's success as a battle leader suggests that in the triple hero figure his future role must be to win the coming Second Trolloc war, as he has been given the experience and knowledge to do this. Mat has the ancient 'foxhead' medallion that protects him from the One Power, and as long as he is wearing it he cannot be controlled by those with the ability to channel. Such immunity suggests that to him, also, will fall the task of uniting the forces of the Asha'man and the Aes Sedai. Furthermore, as the *Aelfinn* have prophesied his marriage to the Seanchan princess, Daughter of the Nine Moons, surely this influential link with the invaders from across the Aryth Ocean will give him the clout to utilise the might of their armed forces as well. Mat has a further link to the past as he has sounded the mythic Horn of Valere, which summoned the legendary heroes of the past to assist at the battle at Falme against the invading Seanchan. (*GH*, 659ff) As long as he lives, Aragorn-like, he is the only one who has the power to again call upon them to fight for the cause of the Light at the Last Battle. Thus, through his extraordinary ability as a battle leader, as well as his tie to the Horn of Valere, Mat's role in the *ta'veren* trinity seems to fit that of a Preserver.

ASSOCIATIONS WITH THE NORTHERN GOD, OTHIN

As with Perrin, in his characterisation of Mat, Jordan again encompasses aspects of a Northern god, and uses this to enhance the stature of his protagonist, and to build his character traits. It is obvious that Mat shares many attributes with Othin. For instance, like Othin, he is a master tactician and general; his knowledge gained by hanging on 'Avendesora', the Tree of Life, in the hidden city of Rhuidean equates with Othin hanging in Yggdrasil. (*SR*, 439) The two ravens, Hugin and Munin (loosely, 'thought' and 'memory') seated on Othin's shoulders, equate well with Egwene's prophetic dream where 'two ravens alighted' on Mat's 'shoulders' their 'claws sinking' into his 'flesh'. (*LOC*, 368) The numinous, unbreakable black spear Mat acquires in Rhuidean parallels Othin's own spear, Gungner, which can penetrate anything. Mat's spear also tightens the parallel to Othin as it is engraved with two ravens and a verse which includes the actual words 'thought' and 'memory'.

> Thus is our treaty written; thus is agreement made.
> Thought is the arrow of time; memory never fades.
> What was asked is given. The price is paid. (*SR*, 440)

Furthermore, as 'thought' is the 'arrow of time', the suggestion seems to be that memory creates a conflation of past and present, which in turn is constantly evolving into the future, a theory that accords with Jordan's concept of time in his Secondary World as an endless cycle of seven repeating Ages.

Other strong parallels to Othin include Mat's ability to move easily among both nobles and warriors (he gambles with the nobles in the cities), much as Othin was worshipped by the nobles and those associated with them — the warriors and skalds. The prophecy that he 'will give up half the light of the world to save the world' is a hint that Othin-like he may lose an eye. (*SR*, 249) In gambling Mat has the 'Dark One's own luck', and the way gold and silver coin endlessly pour into his purse is suggestive of Othin's gold ring, Draupnir, from which other gold rings drop every ninth night. (*DR*, 345) Yet Mat's connection to gold also manifests in a far more sinister way, adding another facet to the development of his personality.

FOOL'S GOLD: OBJECTS OF BEAUTY AND DESTRUCTION

Jordan's concept of a richly ornamented golden dagger with the power to totally corrupt both mind and body is analogous with Tolkien's golden One Ring. The evil essence of the dagger, as with the One Ring, is suggestive of enormous power but this is an illusion as in reality both objects can lead to misery and human destruction. Mat takes the dagger from the evil city of Shadar Logoth, a place where 'there is not a pebble' that is 'not tainted'. The city's ruins are haunted by an unspeakable evil, known as 'Mashadar', that long ago destroyed the inhabitants, yet it was an evil force, originally born out of human 'suspicion and hatred'. (*EOTW*, 633) Under its influence Mat quickly becomes suspicious, spiteful and his eyes 'burned with hate'.[7] (EOTW, 629-30) Moiraine says of the evil contained in the dagger:

> It will have waxed and waned in him, what he is in the heart of him fighting what the contagion of Mashadar sought to make him, but now the battle inside him is almost done, and he is almost defeated. Soon, if it does not kill him first, he will spread that evil like a plague wherever he goes. (*EOTW*, 633)

It is only through the healing properties of *saidar* (perhaps, a type of grace) applied by Moiraine and her Aes Sedai colleagues that Mat regains his identity, although his memory is left with holes, later to be filled with snatches of past lives. His contamination is analogous to the two evils that pulse in the unhealable wound in Rand's side, especially as one of them comes from the contaminated dagger, stolen by Padan Fain, who later slashes it across Rand's original wound. (*COS*, 628) Mat's recovery anticipates that a way will be found to heal Rand. Mat's corruption from the dagger also resonates with the taint on *saidin* that can destroy Rand's mind. The power of the dagger to corrupt is shown by Rand's brief contact with it, for to him it felt like 'a weight pulling him down', words which echo those of Frodo in relation to his own heavy burden, the One Ring. (*GH*, 292)

The horror of what Mat could have become (and of what Rand is still in danger of becoming) is seen through the transfiguration of the pedlar Padan Fain into something Moiraine describes as being 'less than human, worse than vile', and although, Gollum-like, he grovels and weeps to Moiraine that he wants to 'walk in the Light again' she senses this wish for redemption will always be overridden by his 'greed for his promised rewards'. (*EOTW*, 706; 715) He had exercised his freewill and chosen the Dark forty years ago thus setting his own fate, for it is stressed that the Dark cannot take you unless you are willing. Jordan suggests that within the overall Pattern a character's choices (good or evil) can to some extent determine the course of their lives. But in Shadar Logoth, Fain's already degraded soul is merged with that of the evil spirit Mordeth, so that sometimes he was not sure 'who he really was', except that he had become a 'force unto himself, and beyond any other power'. (*FOH*, 14)

Fain's ultimate plight serves as a warning of how evil draws more evil to it, creating a downward spiralling into a deeper darkness that nullifies any kernel of repentance. Gollum-like, he is drawn to seek the dagger, an artefact worked in gold and set with a large ruby that personifies the deceptive face of the evil that has consumed him. (*EOTW*, 359) Its exquisite beauty is juxtaposed with Fain's physical appearance, his 'grime layered … face', his 'matted … scraggly, uncut hair and beard', his 'hunched' posture and 'sunken eyes', and the 'rancid smell' of his body, which undercuts the power he hungers after and intensifies the darkness of his fall. (*EOTW*, 703) Without the dagger Fain constantly experiences a sharp 'desire', a 'hunger to be whole'. And with the dagger in his hand he felt he 'was whole again … one with what had bound him so long ago …given him life', although his rebirth is an abomination. (*FOH*, 326-27)

Fain's taking of the dagger that changes his life forever is parodic of Rand's taking of the crystal sword, and thus, Jordan emphasises the horror of Fain's predicament. In a further braiding of the *ta'veren* life-threads, Jordan ties this pitiful creature's destiny to that of Rand as the Dark Lord has made Fain 'his hound to hunt and follow' Rand 'with never a bit of rest' and, ironically, he seeks to kill him with the deadly weapon that Mat is responsible for releasing into the wider world. (*EOTW*, 704)

Thus, in a further configuration of the pattern of Rand's journey to maturity, Jordan shows that Mat's dilemma is between the need to act responsibly and the desire to remain feckless and fancy free. (The evil to which he almost loses his life is the result of him ignoring Moiraine's advice not to touch, or remove anything from the city of Shadar

Logoth.) But, as with Perrin, the talents he gains draw him into Rand's fate as a clever battle tactician and as sounder of the fabled Horn of Valere. Mat's blowing of the Horn, which summoned the legendary heroes of the past to aid the Dragon Reborn's victory at Falme, anticipates that he will summon them again at the Last Battle. Similarly, in book six (*LOC*) Perrin and the wolves that come to his call play a large part in Rand's rescue from hostile members of the White Tower at Dumai's Wells, suggesting that he and the wolves will again have a crucial role in the final battle. Jordan's tactic of anticipating a future event through the outcome of a previous one strengthens the threads between the three *ta'veren* youths, and adds to the sense of them forming a triple heroic figure.

HEROIC TRIAD

In his characterisation of each of the *ta'veren*, Rand, Perrin, and Mat, Jordan uses a reduplication of motifs and associations which are intertwined to produce an impressive triple hero figure, and a worthy opponent to the Dark Lord. Each youth has a link to the past that alters and develops his identity and equips him with talents needed to fulfil certain tasks in the focal quest of the narrative. In turn, each of them is linked to a god-figure through imagery or physical attributes which help to define their personalities, and to increase their stature. Through their association with both Christ and the Northern gods, Othin and Thor, the catastrophe facing the world of the Wheel is suggestive of a blend of Armageddon and Ragnarok. Thus, Jordan not only presents a multi-faceted hero figure, but he also intensifies the urgency of the task at hand, and the magnitude of the disaster to be faced by the inhabitants of the Wheel world should the life-thread of any of one of the *ta'veren* trio be snipped from the Pattern.

The textual effect of Jordan's use of the notion of interlace, in relation to his three main male hero figures, is to fold the reader further into their stories, and thus into the imaginary world. For example, through the use of tactics such as echoes and anticipations he provides clues that the reader picks up and interprets and that give a sense of participation in events, which encourages an intimate relationship with the characters and their landscape. The repetitions and variations of themes, whereby the reader's response to Rand's actions is moulded by comparison or contrast to the actions of his two *ta'veren* companions, enhances the concept of them as an interdependent and complex trio. Through a reduplication of the ordeals to be faced by Rand, Perrin, and Mat, Jordan reveals the complicated path that is required in order to resolve moral dilemmas. Thus, the author brings to the fore the ambiguity of moral choice-making in the *WOT* (and by inference in our world) and the complications that are central to moral issues. For in the Wheel world good and evil are both woven into the pattern, and his three young protagonists, whose life-threads have been spun out by the Great Pattern in order to bring change, collectively show that it is only through the overcoming of doubts, fears, and uncertainties that moral choices can be made.

Jordan's splintering of the hero figure, his ability to weave the life-threads of both male and female figures into the heroic paradigm, is a textual strategy that has been enthusiastically taken up by the *WOT* fans in their cyberspace representation of Jordan's imaginary world. It is this fascinating extension of Jordan's texts that forms the focus of my final chapter.

5 VIRTUAL STORYTELLING: *THE WHEEL OF TIME* WORLD WIDE WEAVE

One Page to rule them all,
One Page to find them,
One Page to bring them all
And in the Web to bind them
(The Compleat Index of *Wheel of Time*-Related Net Resources).

Modern fantasy literature has generated an enormous amount of critical and creative response to individual works, and to the genre in general, through fandom communities on the internet. However, it should be noted that the phenomenon of readers' intervention into texts is not entirely new. Literature has long generated a sense of ownership in readers that has at times spilled over into a kind of territorialism, where readers would adopt behaviour characteristics from the beloved text, name children after certain characters, engage in a kind of literary tourism and even demand of authors certain changes to their texts.[1] For example, there is the work of the nineteenth-century author, Anthony Trollope, who reportedly killed off a character (Mrs Proudie, wife of a bishop), following complaints about her from readers (1883).[2] With the upsurge of commercial tourism during the twentieth century, readers from many parts of the world have been able to engage with the landscapes of favourite authors, such as Emily Brontë or Thomas Hardy, through organised tours of the regions in Britain from which these earlier writers drew inspiration. Still recognisable landmarks in the countryside (e.g. Stonehenge) encourage the literary tourist, mentally, to superimpose scenes from these earlier texts onto the landscape in which they stand physically. In a sense such tourists are entering into the fictional world of the texts, just as the fans of Jordan's *WOT*, can imaginatively enter their cyberspace construct of the Wheel world.

The term *fan* (an abbreviation of *fanatic*) has become an accepted colloquialism in our culture, and Henry Jenkins has drawn a similarity between modern fandom and that of earlier times:

> What is significant about fans ... is that they constitute a particularly active and vocal community of consumers ... As such, they enjoy a contemporary status not unlike the members of the 'pit' in 19th century theatre who asserted their authority over the performance, not unlike the readers of Dickens and other serial writers who wrote their own suggestions for possible plot developments, not unlike the fans of Sherlock Holmes who demanded the character's return even when the author sought to retire him. Fans are not unique in their status as textual poachers, yet, they have developed poaching to an art form. (1992b, 27)

By 'poaching' Jenkins is referring to the way in which fans may appropriate or transform a range of texts, and today's computer technology certainly enables fans to achieve this in multiple ways – visual and textual. Although Jenkins is referring to media texts, his words are equally applicable to literary texts, and to the activities of Jordan's *WOT* online fandom communities, which form the focus of this chapter.

WARP AND WEFT – WEAVING A CYBERWORLD

Robert Jordan numbers among a group of contemporary writers of fantasy whose epic series have generated an enormous trans-global following of fans. (Other authors include J. R. R. Tolkien, David Eddings, Ann McCaffrey, Stephen Donaldson, and more recently, J. K. Rowling.) In regard to such modern day fandom the critic Henry Jenkins notes that:

> undaunted by traditional conceptions of literary and intellectual property, fans raid mass culture, claiming its

materials for their own use, reworking them as a basis for their own cultural creations and social interactions. Fans seemingly blur the boundaries between fact and fiction, speaking of characters as if they had an existence apart from their textual manifestations, entering into the realm of the fiction as if it were a tangible place they can inhabit and explore. (1992b, 18)

Although Jenkins is speaking here of fandom in relation to mass media texts (television and film), once again his words can equally be applied to the fans of literary fantasy texts. The phenomenon of the internet has provided a tool whereby enormous numbers of fantasy fans can collectively participate in the virtual construction and on-going development of their favourite Secondary Worlds; actions that constitute in part a rewriting or re-patterning of the texts. In turn this creates a highly imaginative, multi-authored, never-ending story in which they have a satisfyingly creative share.

Over the last two decades, in tandem with the rapid growth of internet usage, Robert Jordan's fans have spawned an ever-increasing network of web sites and online communities devoted to the *WOT* series, all of which can be interpreted as virtual extensions of Jordan's own fictional world. (Jordan has not named his world but it is known to fans as 'Randland', after the main protagonist.) These sites have enabled fans to imaginatively enter the world of the Wheel in a way that is other than their initial experience as readers of the written texts, although both modes require a willingness on the part of the participant to accept mentally the world as an alternative reality. On this point Elizabeth Reid makes the following astute observation in her essay on virtual worlds:

Cyberspace – the realm of electronic impulses and high speed data highways – may be figured as a technological construct, but virtual reality is a construct within the mind of a human being ...Virtual worlds exist not in the technology used to represent them nor purely in the mind of the user, but in the relationship between internal mental

> constructs and technologically generated representations of
> these constructs. The illusion of reality lies not in the
> machinery itself but in the user's willingness to treat the
> manifestations of his or her imaginings as if they were real.
> (1995, 166)

However, the fans' interaction with their cyber-construct of Jordan's literary fantasy world is more dynamic, communal and interactive than that experienced by them as readers of the literary texts; it becomes more an entry of sorts into the Wheel world and not just an immersion in the pages of a finite written story.

As Michael Heim suggests, in his discussion on virtual reality, we have this ability to 'inhabit cyberspace when we feel ourselves moving through the interface into a relatively independent world with its own dimensions' (1993, 79). The fans' virtual construct of the Wheel world provides such a place. Through the web interface they are enabled to step into their cyberworld representation of Jordan's Wheel world and to experience it in ways that are real to them. It also provides a space where they can construct a multi-dimensional and culturally rich community. The Wheel world of virtual reality has many onion-like layers around it that extend the boundaries of Jordan's text and his fantasy world; for instance, the gaming world of role-play and the writing of personalised fan fiction that position the fans within the cyberspace world through the personae of alternative, virtual identities. Thus the hypertext of the internet lends itself to fans opening up new avenues such as these, which are connected to, and yet have the freedom to move beyond, the pages of the written texts.

Fan participation on the internet forms a burgeoning aspect of literary fandom that has received surprisingly little serious critical attention. Scholarly work is largely concerned with fan and cult followings that pertain to mass media (especially film and television), sport and popular music.[3] Although some of this work provides the literary discourse in which to situate my study of the relationship between fantasy literature and web-based fandom, my approach differs as it is conducted not in a sociological context but rather in a literary one. The focus is on the fans' reconstruction of a literary Secondary World on the web and their engagement with it, as constituting a way of extending the world and the meaning of the original text.

Therefore, this chapter seeks not only to explore the phenomenon of internet fandom in relation to the Jordan series of fantasy texts, but also to tie the reading of the labyrinth-like web pages back to the main themes of this thesis, to analyse the coalition that exists between the two different kinds of text – the author's writing and the fans' cyber-community interpretation of his world. It is my intention to show how some aspects of the Jordan novels that have been articulated in the earlier chapters, impact on these sites and on the fan-audience, in particular, in relation to storytelling and pattern making, to rites of passage, and to the heroic quest.

I will not attempt a full analysis of cyber-culture or fandom in general, since such large-scale sociological studies, although worthy, lie outside the scope of this study. As a framework for this present investigation, in particular, I have devised a modification of Nicholas Abercrombie and Brian Longhurst's terms describing popular media fans as being 'skilled', 'active', and 'communal'. In their analysis of such fan audiences and fan practices these scholars argue that:

> fans are: *skilled* or *competent* in different modes of production and consumption; *active* in their interaction with texts and in their production of new texts; and *communal* in that they construct different communities based on their links to the programmes they like. (1998, 127)

For the present purposes I define online *WOT* fans as being *skilled* or *competent* in the way they use the template world of the Wheel to construct the framework of their virtual, mirror world, one complete with detailed maps and diagrams, and compile extensive 'virtual' libraries of encyclopaedic material about Jordan's world. They are *active* in the way they position themselves within the virtual construct of the world through self-authoring, using alternative identities, role-playing games and the writing of pieces of fan fiction. They also produce artwork, and set up forums to analyse or criticise the texts. And they are *communal* in that they have woven an astonishingly intricate, cross-linked and trans-global web of communication that braids each person into the socio-cultural context of Jordan's imaginary world, yet also forms meaningful links to their everyday lives. These ties have proven to be so binding that they stretch out into the Primary World of reality, when fans meet in face-to-face situations, as mentioned earlier, and in some cases produce a blossoming of real life romances. A cross-linking of 'derived' moral and ethical values is also apparent between the fans' cyber Wheel world community and that of reality – as will be shown below in discussion of the Dragonmount web site. Dragonmount.com is one of the largest and most active sites and has provided the basis for my interactive research of an online *WOT* community, and where appropriate comments from participating members will be incorporated.

Web sites devoted to an online portrayal of Jordan's fantasy world provide a unique space that exists both inside and outside the original written texts, and forms an interface between the two. Further the cyberworld constructs a trans-global bridging device for fans whose language and customs may differ in reality. As Jenkins notes:

> Entering into fandom means abandoning pre-existing social status and seeking acceptance and recognition less in terms of who you are than in terms of what you can contribute to this new community.(1992a)

In the cyberspace of the Wheel world it is of no concern which part of the real world one may inhabit, and there is no distinction made based on such issues as race, religion or gender. The essential common denominator that binds participants together is a passionate interest in the *WOT* series. (In relation to virtual communities Henry Jenkins, in a talk given at Michigan University, Spring, 1998, suggested that 'our investment in fictional characters, in effect, gives us a common set of "relatives" or "friends" that become reference points within conversation'. [2004]) Certainly, such sites, which use Jordan's

Secondary World as their template, provide a forum where fans engage in lively debate about various aspects of the texts, as well as a virtual landscape wherein they actively and communally engage with the world of the Wheel.

The pattern of the Secondary World provides the background tapestry upon which the fans' (virtual) life-threads are being creatively embroidered. By means of alternate, online identities, based on the format of Jordan's characters, the fans are empowered to colonise the virtual community of the Wheel world and to take up on-going roles within it. (In role-play game fans may assume multiple identities.) Cross-gendering is not uncommon, and on this subject Fader6818, leader of the Ogier 'Org' on the Dragonmount web community, at the time of my research, offers the following explanation:

> There are both male and female Ogier. But my view ... is that in a completely anonymous medium, people are more apt to react with their true personalities. Many women would not like to conform to the 'puppetmaster' wrap that Aes Sedai have, so they decide to interact as the bold and aggressive Asha'man. This is true of males, who, online, have no shame in expression of having 'Aes Sedai' like tendencies. And for those who have a pleasant mix of both (I stereotype solely to explain, not judge) 'male' and 'female' tendencies, the opportunity to express both without anxiety appreciate the support and acceptance from others who do the same. (2004)

Yet, at times, an interesting melding of disembodied and embodied identities occurs since many of the fans meet in person at fantasy conventions (where they may also participate in role-play gaming), author book signings, or other arranged *WOT* social events. A good example is the annual 'Dragoncon' event in America, which is hosted by the Dragonmount web community. Thus the lines between real and imaginary life have now been blurred or intersected.

Jenkins' hypothesis on media fandom can also be usefully applied to online fantasy fandom in relation to literary texts like Jordan's *WOT*. He suggests that modern day fans:

> actively assert their mastery over the mass-produced texts which provide the raw materials for their own cultural productions and the basis for their social interactions. In the process, fans cease to be simply an audience for popular texts; instead, they become active participants in the construction and circulation of textual meanings. (1992b, 23-4)

Similarly, on the *WOT* web sites, the fans seek to reflect the world as it is found in the written texts, the landscape, political and cultural climate, hierarchical order, societal conventions and morality, to become part of and yet to extend the social organisations depicted in the Wheel world (a point addressed later in the chapter).

As explained in the first chapter, Jordan's world contains 'mirror' worlds, other dimensions of reality that can be accessed by passing through 'Portal Stones', which provide spatially located gateways that are activated by use of the One Power. These 'mirror' worlds form alternative realms of possibility, Wheel worlds that 'might be', or 'might have been', depending on how life-threads are woven into the web of destiny in the primary world of the Wheel. These other dimensions remain empty of human habitation unless entered by one or other of Jordan's characters – or readers – as the Wheel world of cyberspace must be activated or brought to life through the participation of the online users. Thus, the fans have created their own Wheel 'mirror' world, one to which they gain access through the 'Portal Stone' of their online browser. In this realm, although the fans inter-weave their own threads into the patterning of Jordan's world through the introduction of new characters and their exploits, they do so in a context that is not disruptive to the main plot-lines and, as yet, on-going narrative of the author's work.

From my observations of various sites during 2004-5, I believe that the fans seek to find a personal, participatory space for themselves within the Jordan world, but not to destroy the magic of the original story that first brought them all together. In other words they avoid the use of scenarios that, much like an adept's use of 'balefire' in the Wheel world, could burn away threads and cause a fatal unravelling of the Great Pattern of the Third Age. The ingenuity of the cyber-text fan-authoring brings to mind the creative scribblings (and art) of Anglo Saxon monks which embellish the margins of many extant Dark Age manuscripts. For the scribes such actions also constituted a means whereby they could personalise and thus write themselves into the scripts they were copying so laboriously.

Prior to his untimely death in 2007, Jordan's fans had a degree of online interaction with the author (jokingly called the 'Creator'), as he personally answered their questions on the official site of his publishers, Tor Books, and participated in various online interviews. A demonstration of the strengthening cyber linkage between author and his fans is apparent in the way that Dragonmount.com, one of the largest and most diverse cyber communities, continues to work directly with his publisher, and other parties holding licences to the series. In an interesting reversal of roles the author himself became the reader, as he used to visit the various fan web sites, and had a 'very, very long list of sites bookmarked' (Denzel 2004). However, while the author may have read some of the fans' online *WOT* 'prophecies' and 'loony ideas', he denied any possibility of a cross-fertilisation of ideas, insisting that:

> Contact with fans has no effect on my writing with one exception … This is my story; it will play out according to the lines I want. The only exception was regarding the [fan] 'Who Killed Asmodean' question. I was certain that I had enough internal evidence for anyone to work it out … but many fans insisted that they could not, so I attempted to find places where I might put in a few more clues. (Personal communication 2004)

Jordan also advised that, while 'there is no active monitoring [of web sites] by him or his publisher', if unacceptable use of his *WOT* material, such as 'slash' fanfic[4] was brought to his attention – usually by the fans themselves – his publisher's legal department would act to have it removed (personal communication 2004). Karl-Johan Norén, a Swedish fan who over a number of years developed an impressive personal web site, writes that in 1997 Tor Books 'demanded' that he 'remove *The Far Snows Dance*, [his] take of when Rand and Aviendha made love in an igloo in the *Fires of Heaven* (1999). At times, too, fans take up the role of authorship, through the writing of role-playing games and by posting personal theories on the future development of plotlines or on how the sequence of books will finally end. As well as this they write *WOT* related poetry, compose 'filksongs',[5] and create elaborate artwork, which includes comic strips that parody various *WOT* characters. On the potential fluidity between the roles of fan reader and writer, Jenkins observes that:

> Fan reading ... is a social process through which individual interpretations are shaped and reinforced through ongoing discussions with other readers ... [Thus] fandom does not preserve a radical separation between readers and writers. Fans do not simply consume preproduced stories; they manufacture their own fanzine stories and novels, art prints, songs, videos, performances etc.(1992b, 45)

Through their re-authoring of Jordan's Wheel world, his fans are, in a sense, also 'role-playing' the author and becoming storytellers and pattern makers, thus complicating the distinction between the two so that at times one bleeds into the other. These online activities continue to provide the fans with a way to circumvent Jordan's authorial claim that, like an Old Testament god, he is in total control of his Secondary World and of all events portrayed in it.

THREADS THAT BIND:
THE INTERLACED CYBER-REALM OF *THE WHEEL OF TIME.*

Web sites devoted to Robert Jordan's *WOT* series abound. A search on Google during 2004-5 revealed literally thousands of sites. The examples chosen can be classified into a number of distinct types which I will briefly describe and of which I will offer examples (the grouping is a personal one). While this research has not been exhaustive it has gleaned a far richer amount of material than it is possible to include in this book. As the internet is a hypertextual medium some of the inter-connectedness that it displays on screen is lost in the following attempt to describe it on paper.[6] Accessing a web site is not the same as opening a book and leafing through the pages from front to back. Rather the web pages form an intricate series of overlays, a kind of virtual palimpsest where one page becomes superimposed upon another. Web pages can be removed and new ones inserted, or the content of existing pages can be altered over time to include updated information. The online reader can cross-refer between different web pages at random and use provided links to explore pages on other related sites, which in turn can lead to even more links. The effect can be likened to the 'intricately knotted', multi-branching formations of Tolkien's great 'Tree of Tales' (1964, 23) or to a living, ever-expanding coral reef.[7]

TYPES OF WEB SITES

Publisher's official Robert Jordan site: Jordan's publisher, Tor Books, offers fans a range of information on this site including details of the *WOT* series and forthcoming publications and, in the past, news relating to the author, such as interviews, media articles, time slots for forthcoming radio interviews, details of book signing events, or conventions which the author would attend. The site also includes a page that gives stories of real life *WOT*-inspired romances.

Discussion sites: 'The Wheel of Time FAQ' is one of the most comprehensive of these sites. It contains the writing of many fan-authors and is largely devoted to exploring all aspects of the *WOT* series, especially through its 'Frequently Asked Questions' compendium.

Information sites: An extensive site such as 'Encyclopedia *WOT*' contains information on the books, including plot summaries and detailed notes which in turn are cross-linked to an abundance of other sources where such information is also under discussion. The site includes comprehensive alphabetical listings of characters, prophecies, organisations to be found in the Wheel world, as well as historical and geographical material, all of which testifies to the close knowledge and the dedication of the Jordan fans who operate the site. This location also provides links to other information sites that contain complementary material. By contrast 'The Wheel of Time Novice Page' is designed specifically for those who have not yet read the series and offers a synopsis of the story line, details of the main characters, Wheel world organisations and such like, as well as links to other sites that contain similar information. Sites such as 'Ideal Seek' and the '*Wheel of Time* Quote Archive' enable the fans to search the complete Jordan *WOT* texts for specific quotations. The '*Wheel of Time* Character Archive' offers a comprehensive listing of the numerous *WOT* characters.

Cyber-biblio sites: Like written texts that supply bibliographical information related to a particular subject or an author, sites such as these offer comprehensive listings of links to other *WOT* web locations. The most comprehensive of these sites is 'The Compleat Index of *Wheel of Time*-Related 'Net Resources', which groups the links under headings of the type of material to be found on them, for example, 'All Purpose', 'Author Stuff', 'Book Stuff', 'Sources' or 'Games'. Web Rings such as the 'Wheel of Time Webring' provide a further chain of interlinked sites.

Comic site: 'WoT now?' is an online comic that presents a 'somewhat irreverent parody' of the *WOT* series. This online comic is the inspiration of Dave Doyle, a Canadian who confesses to a 'love hate relationship with the series'. Within the comic strips he takes the position that:

> Rand is an idiot, Mat has only brief flashes of intelligence and poor Perrin has to stop his friends from getting him in trouble. You will never see Faile though. She'll be part of the comic as a jealous, ultra-violent entity that always

seems to be just out of the frame. Meanwhile, every sort of evil shadowspawn is out to catch our heroes. The cast will expand over time but I won't be writing storylines that are as complex as Jordan himself. This is for fun after all. (2004)

Figure 1: 'Seuss time' by 'Burnout', No. 181
in comic archive from 'WoT now?'(2005)
(Dave Doyle © aka Burnout)

The comic strips are aimed at an audience that is very familiar with the original texts and are obviously meant to be taken in a light-hearted fashion as shown in Figure 1 (above) where the artist parodies Jordan's narrative by mimicking a Dr Seuss-type rhyme. This comic strip also provides an example of the intertextual 'poaching' that the fans may use in their own creative interpretations of an author's original texts.

Game sites: (Role-playing games, Computer games, Multi User Dimension games etc.) These sites include role-playing games and forums, such as 'The Grey Tower' which is modelled on the world of the Wheel. An image of what the game player sees when they are participating in one such role-playing game is shown in Figure 2, which demonstrates how the narrative of the game is constructed from separate, but interconnected postings that form a web of threads.

The participants take on identities in their virtual world of the Wheel, but they do not use Jordan's actual characters. Instead, they create characters based on his, but who have their own identities and history. Other role-playing sites include 'Silklantern.com', and 'WoTMUD IV'. Another site is used to market a commercial game titled 'The Wheel of Time', and is advertised as a game that mixes 'first person 3D action with strategy and even a bit of role-playing'. One site offers the 'Wheel of Time Word Games', word puzzles based on the Jordan texts.

Figure 2: Role-playing game from 'The Grey Tower'. (2004)

Personal Sites: These are set up and maintained by one person. A good example is 'Abbyland', created by Abigail Goldsmith, a site that offers a range of *WOT* information and artwork and provides links to other sites. The 'Dragonslibrary' is another personal site that is specifically interested in fantasy and Sci-fi fanfic. These sites are not strictly limited to the *WOT*, but both of them have extensive pages on this subject.

Inactive sites: I found two personal sites that are no longer actively monitored but that function as comprehensive archives of *WOT* related material. 'Stone Dog's WOT' contains material on predictions, theories, humour, favourite scenes, discussion forums, and links to other related sites. Karl-Johan Norén began his *WOT* web page in 1995 and it contains extensive plot summaries of the series, reports of interviews held with Jordan during the East of the Sun convention in Stockholm (1995), and various critical articles such as an in-depth exploration of Jordan's borrowings of Old Norse mythology.

Composite sites: These sites are usually described as being 'communities of real people, who simply use a fictional name', where fans of the *WOT* series can meet and interact on line. They offer a wide range of facilities to visitors and members that can be accessed from links on their comprehensive home pages. Facilities may include all or a number of the following: message/discussion boards, individual organisations based on those found in the world of the Wheel, role-playing games, prophecies, theories, humour, artwork, articles and essays, interviews with Jordan, reports on conventions and book signings, plot summaries and analysis, information about the author, up-coming publishing details, fanfic, fan poetry and filksongs, online *WOT* stores, book discounts through Amazon as well as links to further sites that offer similar information. Large, well organised and active sites of this type include 'Dragonmount.com', 'TarValon.net', and 'WoTmania.com'.

WEBSITES FOCUSED ON IN THIS CHAPTER

To explore the notion of Jordan online fans as pattern makers, storytellers and participants in the heroic quest I draw on a variety of *WOT* websites. The analysis of this material will be within the framework of the earlier definition of online fans as being *skilled* or *competent*, and *active* and *communal*. (The definition of the fans as *communal* is dealt with in a discussion of the Dragonmount online community.) Most of the material is drawn from the following sites:

'Dragonmount.com', one of the largest, most comprehensive composite sites; 'The Grey Tower', a well-established role-playing game site; 'Theoryland' and 'Wheel of Time FAQ', both of which contain extensive archives of fan theories and prophecies related to the *WOT*, and 'Dragonlibrary', an extremely rich holding of *WOT*-related fanfic. A more detailed overview of each of these sites follows but as word-pictures fail to do justice to them, images of some of their web pages appear throughout this chapter.

Given the ephemeral nature of Internet websites, it is possible that the sites discussed below no longer exist or have changed web-addresses. Even more likely is the modification of any page's content – additions, deletions, reworking, etc - These comments were made at a time when each was available; the descriptions and analyses are thus couched in the present tense and relate to the content at the time of writing.

Dragonmount.com http://www.dragonmount.com/main.php

'Sound the Horn! The Hunt is on, and may Dragonmount be your hunting-place!'

The Dragonmount site is a perfect example of fans as a *communal* society. It has been in operation since 1998 and within four years of opening its doors to the internet public, it had 'exploded with popularity' to become one of the most 'successful sites on the internet' and the virtual, trans-global home to many thousands of dedicated *WOT* fans. Jason Denzel, one of the original designers of the site, makes the following statement on the home page:

> *Dragonmount* is an online Community of people from all over the world who have come here to experience *The Wheel of Time* series to the fullest. We offer discussions of the books, online Organisations that you can join, an in-depth Role-playing Game, free E-mail, and the chance to buy all of the books at reduced cost through Amazon.com. *Dragonmount*'s goal is to provide web surfers with an online Community to which they may join and belong to. We offer role-playing here, but the true focus of this site is

on the community and friendship we share. We hope that this site will be a place where one may come on a regular basis to socialise and meet new people who also love reading these incredible books.

Faeder6818, the then-moderator of the Wheel of Time General Discussion and *New Spring/Knife of Dreams* forums, promises to 'keep the boards clean. This means no offensive language, slurs of racial, sexual or religious nature'. These promises are an indication of the standard of person-to-person 'netiquette' that is reflected throughout all the pages of this site.

From the home page links are provided to discussions of the books, *WOT* news (including forthcoming publications, Dragoncon convention dates, news in relation to the author), a general Dragonmount community message board, Role-play games, which occur in two virtual 'Portal Stone' worlds, one set at a time very similar to that of Jordan's books, and another in the prehistory of the Wheel world. Links are also available to *WOT* resources, such as plot summaries of the books, members' articles, essays and a *WOT* documentary video, and an alphabetical listing of FAQ, and extensive links to other *WOT* related sites. There is also an online store to promote a range of *WOT* merchandise such as t-shirts and posters (the proceeds help with the running of the site), DM animated movies and the Dragonmount Organisations, which are based on groups and nations of the Wheel world but do not necessarily slavishly mirror them. A good example is 'The Children of the Light' group who, unlike their counterpart in Jordan's world, are not religious fanatics and instead take 'comedy' as their main theme. Another is the Shayol Ghul group who are not, necessarily, evil Darkfriends but are known to be 'non-conformist' and to embrace all that is 'weird and bizarre'. Membership of all the groups (known as 'Orgs'), is open to both sexes which is not always the case in Jordan's Wheel world; for example, the White Tower is the home of Aes Sedai priestesses, and the Children of the Light are strictly male. The 'Orgs' are described as 'the heart and soul' of this web site and include virtual communities of Ogier, The Aiel, The Children of the Light, Shayol Ghul, The White Tower, The Black Tower, The Seanchan, Wolf Brothers and The Band of the Red Hand.

It is the setting up of these individual, but interconnected communities that helps to bring depth and substance to the virtual world, and to increase the sense of fan ability to colonise the space. Members are free to choose the organisation which they believe most suits their needs, although all groups are unanimous in promoting the importance of friendship, sharing, kindness, equality, and community spirit and they all operate according to certain courteous codes of behaviour. The codes of morality and ethics associated with the various groups and nations in Jordan's texts are, to a large degree, endorsed by the individual 'Orgs': for example, the fittingly ecologically-aware Ogier community, or the Aiel community, one which has adopted the concepts of honour and obligation by which the Aiel are defined in the Jordan texts. The hierarchical structure of the 'Orgs' is patterned on that of the Jordan world, and status within the cyberworld is to be earned. As Kathana Sedai, the then leader of the White Tower 'Org' and community administrator explained:

> Each Org is different, but in the White Tower Org you earn rank by participating in the Community actively, taking part in our seminars and doing projects to help out around the site. We don't want it to be a meaningless rank, but for you to have a real sense of accomplishment and progression when you are raised. (2004)

Thus, each participating member gains an added sense of true participation in the cyber-community and an enhanced sense of worth as one of its citizens. I agree with Lawrence Grossberg who suggests that:

> by participating in fandom, fans construct coherent identities for themselves. In the process, they enter a domain of cultural activity of their own making which is, potentially, a source of empowerment in struggles against

oppressive ideology and the unsatisfactory circumstances
of everyday life. (Lewis 1992, 3)

For the Jordan fans their cyberspace identities also effect a cross-over of
the morality and ethics of the virtual Wheel world into reality, such as
with the Ogier Community's discussions and exchanging of ideas on
ways to be more 'green aware' in real time. Similarly, the White Tower
Community, in part, uses its virtual existence to set up Ajah-sponsored
charities or community services to benefit people in the real world.
Thus, the virtual community can be a place where fans are empowered,
not only to engage in a 'domain of cultural activity of their own
making', as Grossberg so rightly suggests, but to instigate actions in
their virtual world that can be transposed to effect positive societal
benefits in their everyday lives.

The Grey Tower http://www.greytowerrp.net/

'May the Light Illumine you all and the Creator shelter you'.

The Grey Tower is a large and well-established role-playing society
based on Jordan's *WOT* series. It is also a site where fans have produced
a large amount of fanfic – stories set in the Wheel world that mostly
concern the exploits of their own online characters. The organisers of
the site have conceived of a time-frame for their virtual Wheel world,
one where a Grey Tower has arisen that is home to both female and
male practitioners (Aes Sedai and Asha'man) of the One Power. The site
organisers advise that the fans are 'making up stories with [their] own
characters', tales set in a period between 'the cleansing of the Taint and
Tarmon Gai'don' and that the Grey Tower runs 'parallel to the books'.
Thus players are instructed that:

> The Grey Tower is located in the Mountains of Mist, near
> a town called Elman's Creek. Your character, who may be
> from anywhere in the world of the Wheel, has made
> his/her way, somehow, to the Grey Tower, to begin
> training as a Warder, Aes Sedai or Asha'man. The exact

details of this will be in your biography, which you write when you join.

Visually, this site is restricted to a portrayal of the Grey Tower and its grounds, while all fan activities take place within the limits of these precincts, but the members bring to this environment their extensive knowledge of the entire Jordan *WOT* world that mentally supplies a richly textured background, enabling them to situate their tower community in the context of the far richer landscape of the author's original Wheel world.

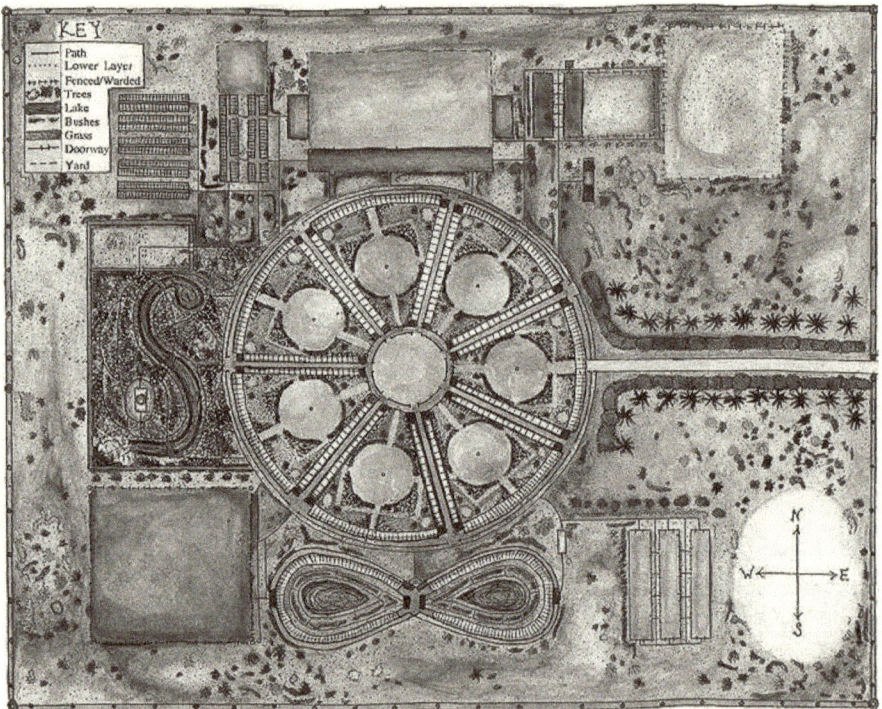

Figure 3: Image from 'The Grey Tower' showing aerial view of Tower and grounds.(Alexandra Bond © 2002 StudioBond.net)

There is a welcoming message for newcomers on the home page who are advised that:

All manner of travellers arrive here hoping to train as Aes Sedai, Asha'man or warders, to meet others and to learn ... Feel free to wander at your leisure around the many halls, chambers and gardens of the Tower and see for yourself.

The home page offers links to a complete listing of the Grey Tower's members, the Warders' yard, Out of Character (OOC) message boards, a listing of current role-plays and guidelines, individual home pages for the seven Ajahs, an archive of frequently asked Tower-related questions, joining information and a guest book. The library link, in turn, links to pages containing guidelines for fanfic, fan biographies, transcripts of fanfic, filksongs, poetry and artwork which include detailed maps and diagrams of the Grey Tower and its grounds. (Figure 3, above, shows one of the images available.) These web pages contain extensive information on the various areas and functions of the Grey Tower. The series of maps and diagrams represent a 'coherent view of how the Tower is constructed and laid out, as well as what it actually looks like'. The images are the work of talented illustrator, painter and concept artist Alexandra Bond. Her work has been inspired by the landscape of the Jordan texts and contains explicit reference to the language of the novels, as the excerpt in the following, attached to the image in Figure 3, notes, 'from the air the Tower would appear as a Great Wheel that weaves the pattern, and the Novice and Soldier Hall appears as the Great Serpent'.

The guidelines to role-play offer general points for the gamers to observe, such as being realistic in terms of Robert Jordan's world, leaving role-playing postings open-ended so other people can join in, not harming each other's characters without their OOC permission, and a reminder not to let In Character (IC) conflicts affect OOC friendships. To encourage new players to feel at home in the community they are assigned an experienced Tower member who acts as a guide and mentor. Role-play games can be short, and are held on the Day-to-Day board while sustained games, referred to as Major Role-plays, are held on separate message boards to which links are provided. Members who will be absent from the site for a period of time may post dates of their intended departure and return on the 'Shara List'.

The other major activity on this site is the writing of fanfic. The site guidelines, in part, specify that:

> Your fanfic **must** be based in the world of the WoT. Where and when it takes place is up to you, but keep it realistic within RJ's world.
>
> Your fanfic does not **have** to be about your own GT character (although most are), but it **cannot** be about characters from the actual WoT books.
>
> The events in your fiction should not change anything drastic about the Tower or the [Wheel] world in general. (eg: writing about how you single-handedly won Tarmon Gai'don is a definite no no.)

A popular theme of fanfic on this particular site is the growth, skill and so the empowerment of the online character, or the telling of a story that fills in the background history of the online character and how they first gained entrance to the Tower.

Abbyland http://www.abbygoldsmith.com/

'Compiled by Abigail of the Brown Ajah. Well okay … I'm not really an Aes Sedai. I'm just an animator'.

Abby is both a creative writer and a graphic artist, and she believes that if you 'blend art and storytelling together … the results are films, comic books, and graphic novels', mediums that are currently becoming an integral part of the work of a growing number of fantasy writers. Abbyland is a personal site that is not exclusively set up for the Jordan fans; however, her *WOT* pages are more extensive and she refers to herself as being 'addicted' to the original series. Abby's *WOT* homepage provides links to Abby's own writings on *WOT* plot synopsis, book reviews, articles and essays, errors and complaints, and her collection of unsolved ponderings and prophecies from the series. As well as these personal compositions she provides links to her favourite *WOT* resources and fan sites. Abby's *WOT* artwork pages include thumbnail images of Jordan's characters, of which she remarks that she 'attempted to capture the personality of each character while remaining true to their literary description'. The artwork pages also display an amusing comic strip featuring Jordan's characters Mat and Tuon that she drew for the 'Wot now?' web comic.

Dragon's library http://www.dragonlibrary.com/fiction/wheel_of_time/

'*Wheel of Time* Original Fan Fiction'

The 'Dragon's library' contains an archive of fan fiction and transcripts of role-play games based on Jordan's *WOT* texts. This library collection is divided into sub categories: 'WoT Third Age', the timeframe of Jordan's texts; 'WoT Ages of Past and Future', 'WoT humour', and WoT Role-playing. Unlike the fanfic on the Grey Tower site, these stories are not based on the exploits of the fan-authors' own alternate virtual identities.

Theoryland of *The Wheel of Time* http://www.theoryland.com/

'More theories than you can stand'.

The home page of this site offers links to reports of media interviews and chats with Robert Jordan, general *WOT* information, and a communal message board where members discuss various aspects of the texts. The site also has links to extensive postings of fan predictions and theories, listed in alphabetical order, many of which are related specifically to a particular character.

The Wheel of Time FAQ http://linuxmafia.com/jordan/

'Surprising what you can dig out of books if you read long enough, isn't it?' (Rand al'Thor).

The organisers of this site describe it as: 'the Wheel of Time Wondrous Masterpiece of Assembled Knowledge, Theories and Discussion'. The site has pages that provide details of possible source material for the *WOT*, such as Norse, Celtic and Christian mythology, However, the site is almost exclusively based on archiving *WOT* theories that have been debated extensively over the years among many fans on the Usenet group. rec.arts.sf.written.robert-jordan The **FAQ** summarises these debates and the conclusions so far reached.

Both 'Theoryland' and 'Wheel of Time FAQ' sites allow the fan-authors a different way to participate in the understanding of the shaping of the *WOT* narrative through their analysis of various aspects of the Jordan texts and imaginative attempts to foretell how the author might well resolve unfinished threads or unresolved prophecies in the plotting thus far.

READING, WRITING, DRAWING AND GAMING IN *THE WHEEL OF TIME* WEB

The patterning of a virtual world

The fans are both *skilled* and *competent* in their setting up of a virtual *WOT* world. In Jordan's terms it is a 'mirror' world, and therefore a realm of 'possibility', where things can be different so they do not have to slavishly follow the patterning of his text. The fans build the virtual world through a combination of literacy tools and visual tools (i.e. maps and artwork). But the tool they most rely on is that of written text and it is largely through their literacy skills and knowledge that their virtual world is brought into being, and the written text also provides the means by which fans can communicate with each other and thus participate in the cyberworld. This is akin to the MUDders' creation of imaginary places, which as Harold Rheingold observes are also produced and sustained by written text. He refers to MUD (Multi-User Dimensions) worlds as being:

> Imaginary worlds in computer databases where people use words and programming languages to improvise melodramas, build worlds and all the objects in them, solve puzzles, invent amusements and tools, compete for prestige and power, gain wisdom, seek revenge, indulge in

greed and lust and violent impulses. (Rheingold 1993,
145)

In the virtual Wheel world the fans already share in a communal story-
hoard of *WOT* knowledge and have no need to build their cyberworld
from scratch, but, rather, can build upon a shared intimate knowledge of
Jordan's *WOT* texts, so that not everything has to be described in detail
online. Thus they produce a kind of virtual overlay of one world upon
the other and are able to create identities for themselves that are derived
from those of the *WOT* texts, and to interpret and use the language of
Jordan's world to give depth and substance to their own creation.

The online fans use a duplication of the Wheel world's histories and
geographies to provide a strong sense of place, and they base their
online personae on Jordan's different races and the ranks. Thus they
emulate the distinctive dress, codes of etiquette, and the range of mores
and ethics of each nation. Yet, in this 'mirror' world of possibility, they
have the power to extend the template of Jordan's imaginary world by
writing themselves into the world through role-play games and fanfic.
They can also introduce contradictions to Jordan's pattern for his world;
for example, the Wheel organisations on the Dragonmount site, which
encourage membership that has no gender restrictions. And the Grey
Tower, a blend of Jordan's opposing White and Black Towers, has
opened its doors to both female Aes Sedai and male Asha'man. As the
ideology of the anti-male Red Ajah of Jordan's pattern (whose main task
is to 'gentle' all males with the ability to channel) would be
inappropriate in this non-gender specific community, it has been
replaced by an Indigo Ajah who seek to uncover lost Talents from the
Age of Legends.

The Grey Tower itself, which has no existence in Jordan's Wheel
world, is given a quality of tangible reality through the provision of a
number of meticulously drawn maps and diagrams of the Grey Tower
and its grounds. This artwork is useful, too, for orientation during role-
play games as the participants choose which routes their characters may

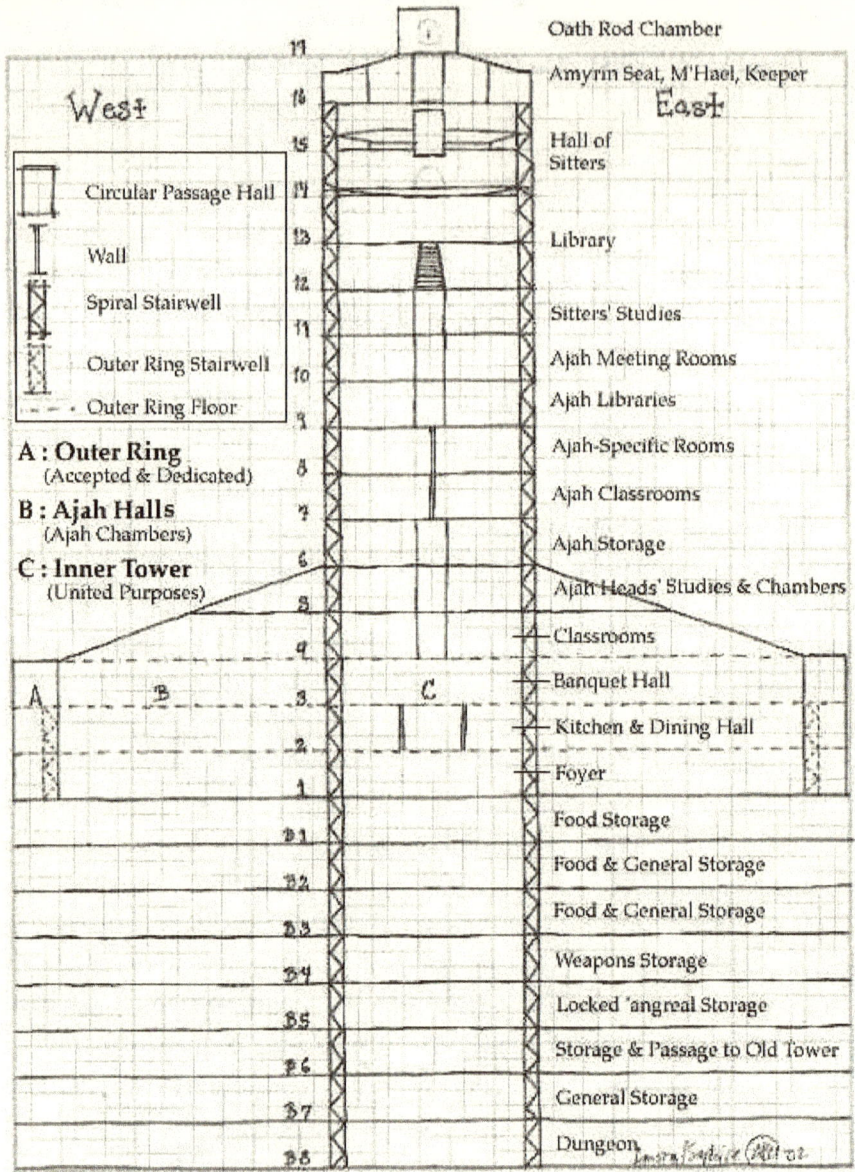

Figure 4: Image of cross-section used in 'The Grey Tower' role-playing. (Alexandra Bond © 2002 StudioBond.net)

feasibly take as they move around the tower. Figure 4 shows a blueprint of the Grey Tower, which is used by participants in active role-playing games, to ensure consistency of the narrative's geography. The levels of the tower are labelled so that characters can name them accurately.

STORYTELLING WITHIN THE VIRTUAL WOsRLD

As was mentioned earlier, the interface of the web enables fans to mentally step into their cyber-representation of Jordan's Wheel world. But it also allows them to become *active* participants within it and, by so doing, to become part of the storytelling process and through alternate identities to have an actual role in the unfolding story itself. The fans' virtual community, which is built on narrative, is a vigorous hybrid formed from their original readings of the texts, and their cyberspace interpretations of them, but one more intertwined with their everyday identities. For instance, even the act of logging into the *WOT* websites and interacting on the general Out of Character (OOC) message boards, or the message boards of a particular organisation based on Jordan's world, necessitates the conscious acceptance on the part of the fans that even at this level they must engage in a form of role-play or performance. They then become part of an enormous, trans-global cast of other *WOT* devotees, which constitutes a braiding of some facets of their mundane existence with those of the imaginary cyberworld.

Yet, in a sense, these realms are the two sides of the same coin as one cannot exist without the other. In an online discussion about the real world and the world of imagination, that sometimes is referred to as the 'true' world, one of the Dragonmount site members captures this duality well with her belief that:

> online communities such as this one help bridge the gap between the [two] worlds. They provide a place where people can enter the 'true' world with others. It adds another dimension to the 'true' world in that it opens it for discussion with others across the 'real' world and, hm, makes it possible to see both worlds in new ways. (Ayeteh el Jara, personal online conversation 2004)

Thus, for this particular fan, the symbiotic relationship that exists between the two worlds is viewed as one that brings enrichment to both, as the suggestion is that involvement in the online community brings an expansion of ideas, attitudes and knowledge that can be applied across both aspects of life – the here and now and the timeless realm of imagination wherein truths can be found.

However, it is specifically through their self-authoring and participation in role-play games and the writing of personalised fanfic that the fans are able to actively project themselves into the fictional and fictive world. Role-play gaming on the *WOT* sites is a form of communally written story, although each major role-play is created and driven by its organiser. The organiser sets up a brief scenario for the game and then asks those who wish to join in to supply their character's name, email, rank within the *WOT* community, and a brief overview of the character's personality. In real time the messages of the players that build the narrative may be posted on the game board over a number of days, weeks, or even months, but within the virtual world events are considered to be constantly unfolding in the present.

A major role-play game (2004) on the Grey Tower site is the 'Indigo Ajah Fair' – a virtual fair designed as an antidote to the tedium of midwinter at the Grey Tower.[8] This fair offers traditional amusements such as music and dancing, a kissing booth, magic, and for 'restless warders', the chance to compete in the Sparring Arena. It is designed to suggest that the Grey Tower is a real community, one where like-minded people can enjoy a festal day of recreational pursuits together. Not all role-play games are as light-hearted as this, for others lay down a challenge to prospective players to join in the on-going *WOT* battle between the Light and the Dark, as is discussed in a later section.

The writing of *WOT*-based fanfic is another avenue that allows the fans to take up the role of storyteller and I have identified three types of this writing. On the Grey Tower site, in general, the stories are personal accounts of the writer's own online character. Many of them concern the ordeals of initiation encountered within the three-arched *ter'angreal* whereby novices of the Grey Tower are 'raised' to the status of Aes Sedai

and Asha'man. This labyrinth-like rite of passage, one in which the
characters must thrice face their worst fears, and to survive the testing
must then return through each arch when summoned, no matter what
situation they find themselves in, closely mirrors the pattern of the
ordeals experienced in the three-arched *ter'angreal* by initiates of the
White Tower within the actual Jordan texts. For instance, in a fanfic
titled 'Zavian's Raising', Zavian must make the choice to abandon his
sister to the mercies of Trollocs, leave a man to be tortured by members
of the Dark, and forego the opportunity to reverse his vows to the Dark
One that had been forced upon him. Fans also each write personal
stories that fill in details of their character's childhood, and the train of
events that sets them on the path to a life at the Grey Tower. Fan stories
such as these are ways of both fleshing out the characters, giving an
indication of how they think and act, and enabling them to gain
increased power and status within the cyber *WOT* tower community.

By contrast, the *WOT* based fanfic held on the Dragon's Library site
is not personalised to the fan-authors' alternative characters. In one story
titled 'The 4th Ta'veren', the fan-author, Michael Sample, has found a
gap in the Jordan narrative of the second volume (*GH*), and inserts an
episode that features new characters and exploits, as is explained in a
short prologue:

> Set during the middle of The Great Hunt, 'The Fourth
> Ta'veren' is a tale taking place within the boundaries and
> parallels of the WoT story, at least how it was for a brief
> period, while Rand, Mat and Perrin still hunted Padan
> Fain and the Horn of Valere, and Egwene, Nynaeve and
> the other girls who they would later befriend have
> journeyed to the White Tower. Much does not happen
> during the four months of the Questors' travel via the
> Stones, and the tutorage of the budding Aes Sedai. It is in
> this period, that a secret quest is undertaken by a small
> band of unsung heroes, following a prophecy which could
> alter the course of Tarmon Gai'don, and give the Dark
> One the upper hand in the last climactic battle. (2000)

It is because the Jordan narrative contains an ever-increasing number of plots and subplots often set in a number of widely dispersed Wheel world locations, and a vast cast of characters, that such an interposed interlude becomes entirely feasible.

Other fanfic on this site is situated in a time before the 'Breaking of the World', or after the Last Battle, which thus allows the fan-authors the freedom to shape the fresh pieces of plot as they wish. One uncompleted story titled 'The Other Side of the Wheel', conceives of a future age which is a mirror-image or reversal of the Wheel world (Sundara 2001). In this turning of the Wheel the dragon is female, while another, titled 'A New Beginning', explores Lan and Nynaeve's return to the ruins of his kingdom of Malkier after the Last Battle (Allanon 1999). Moreover, Jordan fans are not averse to sending up their favourite series; for example, a fanfic titled 'Last Battle Won!' is composed as a contemporary-style media report from the battle site at Shayol Ghul, where the Dark Lord has died before the Dragon can commence battle with him. In part the reporter writes that:

> All over the world, the nations will soon be celebrating at the news that the Light is triumphant. The Last Battle, between the Dragon Reborn and the Dark One has been feared so much over the thousands of years since the Breaking that the outcome seems rather pathetic. Rand al'Thor had an easy victory at 2:30 this morning in Shayol Ghul, the scheduled time and place of the Last Battle. Apparently, Shai'tan himself had a heart attack and died before al'Thor could do much of anything ... Al'Thor sits on a nearby rock with his companions Matrim Cauthon and Perrin Aybara. 'It just happened! Totally unexpected! Shai'tan just keeled over and I didn't even realise what was happening. We were both rather sleepy', says the Dragon (al'Thor), while flipping through a bulging Daily Planner. 'You see, our schedules kept conflicting, so we had to reschedule the possible end of the world more than once

... but now that Tarmon Gai'don is over, I just don't know what to do ... I guess it's time to break the world'. (Mierin 2002)

The humour of this piece comes from not only the flippant journalistic style, but also the juxtaposition of Rand and the Dark One, the protagonist and antagonist of a pre-industrial epic fantasy, with the concept of the modern day corporate highflier whose busy life and 'bulging Daily Planner' make scheduling the Last Battle almost an impossibility. After all, only the end of the world is at stake. A further irony is to have the Dark One die prematurely through the bane of the contemporary Western corporate world – a heart attack.

PLAYERS' DELIGHTS

Part of the pleasure of all the above ways of re-authoring of Jordan's world must arise from the fans' shared, intimate knowledge of the original texts. An extremely detailed knowledge is required to understand and enjoy how cleverly fan stories are being woven into a space in Jordan's pattern of the Wheel world narrative, or how the fanfic can build identifiable additions to his existing texts. Certainly, the humour of the parodying tales would be lost on an audience that is unfamiliar with the original work, as would fan filking songs such as 'Stop the *Wheel of Time*, I want to get off' (sung to the music from the Billy Joel song 'The Longest Time'). In this song, ironically, the singer complains about aspects of the series, yet confesses to his addiction to it.[9] In a sense the writers of such fanfic are taking possession of the Wheel world and obviously enjoy shaping certain aspects of events in it to their own desires.

With regard to such 'organised fandom' Jenkins suggests that it is 'perhaps first and foremost, an institution of theory and criticism, a semi-structured space where competing interpretations and evaluations of common texts are proposed, debated, and negotiated' (1992b, 86). This description fits yet another way in which the *WOT* online fans can become actively involved in the creative process of patterning a story. For they propose numerous theories, prophecies and, in their terminology, 'loony ideas' by which means they can collectively debate, argue and speculate on the ways in which Jordan might possibly tie in the unfinished plot threads, in relation to each successive volume or to the core quest. Another interesting *WOT* web site known as 'The Waygate' (2004) contains archives of the entries written by fans for a contest in which they competed to predict the possible plot for *FOH*, book five of the series, before it was published. These types of interactive discussions and writing processes allow the fans to explore the *WOT* literary texts as both critical readers and creative writers. In the early 1990s in relation to the communal quality and effects of fan reading of texts, Jenkins further observed that:

> Fan reading … is a social process through which individual interpretations are shaped and reinforced through ongoing discussions with other readers. Such discussions expand the experience of the text beyond its initial consumption. The produced meanings are thus more fully integrated into the reader's lives. (1992b, 45)

In the decades following the publication of Jenkins' above-quoted work, the phenomenal growth of fan web sites devoted to particular texts such as Jordan's *WOT*, has provided fans with the tool to communicate as part of a trans-globally linked mind group, which has enhanced their capacity to reshape or extend their personal interpretations of the texts. The web has also given them the means to become participating virtual citizens in their cyberspace construction of Jordan's Wheel world.

WRITING ONESELF INTO THE HEROIC QUEST OF *THE WHEEL OF TIME*

As discussed in chapters one and three, one of the under-pinning themes of contemporary fantasy is the heroic quest, a motif in which the catalyst for the heroic action is the urgent need to rescue the depicted world from some catastrophic event. In reading a book the reader's positioning in such a quest can only be as an onlooker, whereas on the web, through the taking up of alternative personae in role-playing games, the fan-authors are able to project themselves into the cyberworld and feel that they are directly experiencing and changing events. Both mediums are text-based, but in the cyberspace world of the Wheel, the fans are transformed from the position of vicarious readers, to that of totally immersed readers and writers in a way that is dynamic and active.

In their construction of a role-playing narrative the fans initially propose a problem to be solved that endangers the virtual Wheel world, and through their online personae they can write themselves into the action and thus become part of a heroic quest. In keeping with the under-pinning framework of high fantasy, the players are free to choose to fight as champions for either the Light or the Dark. As the narrative of the role-playing game unfolds, the participants must take the initiative to make decisions, develop a range of skills and cunning, and assume positions of power, which is a mirroring of the attributes to be developed by Jordan's heroic figures, and necessary if they are to succeed in carrying out their given task.

A major role-play game on the Grey Tower site, 'The Seals Preserved' (2004), offers a challenge to players to join the on-going battle between the Light and the Dark. This particular quest story commences with the discovery of a 'mysterious *ter'angreal* in the basement of the Grey Tower that could aid in strengthening the remaining seals on the Dark One's prison, thereby allowing humans more time to prepare for the coming of *Tarmon Gai'don*. However, hidden within the Tower community, secret members of the Black Ajah seek to destroy this talisman of Power as it could hinder the plans of their Dark Master, while those of the Light must fight to keep it safe and unlock the secret of how to use it.[10]

Rather like the lives of the characters in Diana Wynne Jones's fantasy novel *Archer's Goon* (2000), in *WOT* role-play games the events are being created as the participants type in the words, and have no existence until the words appear on the web page to bring them to life. Rheingold's observations in regard to MUD worlds seem appropriate to the actions of the *WOT* gamers. He suggests that:

the ability to create places and puzzles for others to explore [is] a form of mastery, a way for people who might lack social status in their real-world community to gain status in their alternate community ... there is a certain attraction to a world in which mastery and the admiration of peers is available to anyone with imagination and intellectual curiosity. (1993, 153)

No one can predict how the narrative of such imaginative games will unfold or how they will end, which adds a certain tension or frisson to the situations but also gives each player a sense of authorial control and power. It also enhances the sense of the reality of events within the game world, since in the everyday world, too, it is impossible to predict how other people will react in a given situation or what the outcome may be.

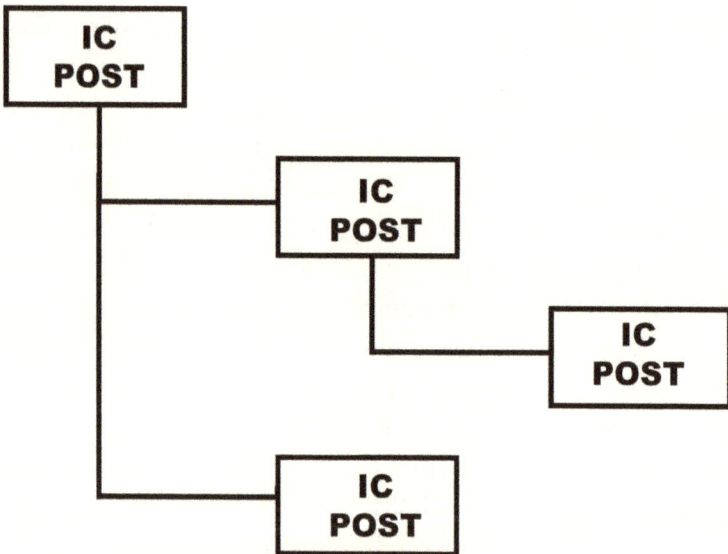

Figure 5: Basic pattern of threads for In Character (IC) posting.

When viewed online (the basic structure is shown in Figure 5), the pattern of the *WOT* role-play games forms a multiple web of threads as players respond to different sections of the postings, thereby producing a number of subplots as they write their characters into the unfolding story. In Figure 5, the first posting begins the story, introducing character or events. As other players respond to this posting, continuing the story or adding new characters, their contribution to the story appears on a lower branch. Players can respond to the original posting or to other branches as they appear, thereby producing a configuration of branching parts. A participant may even have a secondary character, who contributes to the story in separate postings. The multi-threaded storyline that such writing produces is a form that reflects the multi-plotted, interlaced narrative of the Jordan texts, and the role-playing story can seem just as intricate.

As with a literary text, the game narrative is also divided into chapters and in 'The Seals Preserved', the initial chapter begins with a mirroring of the format of the recurring motif as used by Jordan at the start of each volume of his *WOT* series:

> The Wheel of time turns, and ages come and pass, leaving many turned to dust, as many rise from the ashes. In this, it goes the same with powers, as true power lasts not for centuries, but there are rare occasions that a lost power can be found again. Dawn breaks in the mountains, in this age aptly named the Mountains of Mist, and nestled in these simple and wondrous mountains, is the Grey Tower. Aes Sedai and Asha'man alike have learned to live together, and work in harmony toward the greater good. Yet, the wind that blows over the tower on this morning is tainted with one not showing true colors.

The use of this familiar motif provides a trigger that helps imaginatively to situate the players and the Grey Tower within the time and space of the well-known landscape of the story world of the Wheel, and to enhance the sense of a tangible reality.

An interesting aspect of the fans' storytelling and make-believe is the ease with which, as the game progresses, they can step in and out of character. Their Out of Character remarks are signalled on the board through the use of the prefix OOC. As Figure 6 shows, OOC remarks can appear within a single posting together with IC story-telling, or they can appear in separate postings; for example, the following extract from the major role-play, 'The Seals Preserved', demonstrates this narrative interjection within a single posting:

> IC: Riali makes her way across the grounds slowly, and in an almost timid manner. Her heart raced quickly, and had another Aes Sedai glanced at her at this particular moment, they would have been very surprised indeed. She did not hold the grace that all Aes Sedai prided themselves in, her face a stark white colour, and sweatdrops mingling freely with her hair and running down, the droplets stinging her eyes. Light! She hadn't even told anyone anything yet, and she felt like an unarmed Cairhien walking into an Aiel camp!
>
> OOC: I was a bit rushed with this post, as I have to go away for a day and am leaving in just a few moments. I may not have understood a few things in tying the threads up, and if you have any complaints about how this particular post went, feel free to message me … Also, if you need me to help find a way to tie in one of your characters, do this as well … Those that don't have threads concerning Riali in particular, simply pick up below from where you left off below. Thanks. Antar.

Subsequent postings can then include responses to either the IC or OOC text, as the first branch in Figure 6 shows. Rather like the voice of an intrusive author in a literary text, or the stage directions of a theatrical play, this OOC code is used in a variety of ways to inform or influence the other players. It may be used for purposes such as the following: to give added descriptions of a character, or additional information on particular incidents that have not been clarified in the narrative; to correct any perceived misunderstanding in the plotting where the internal inconsistency would break secondary belief; to

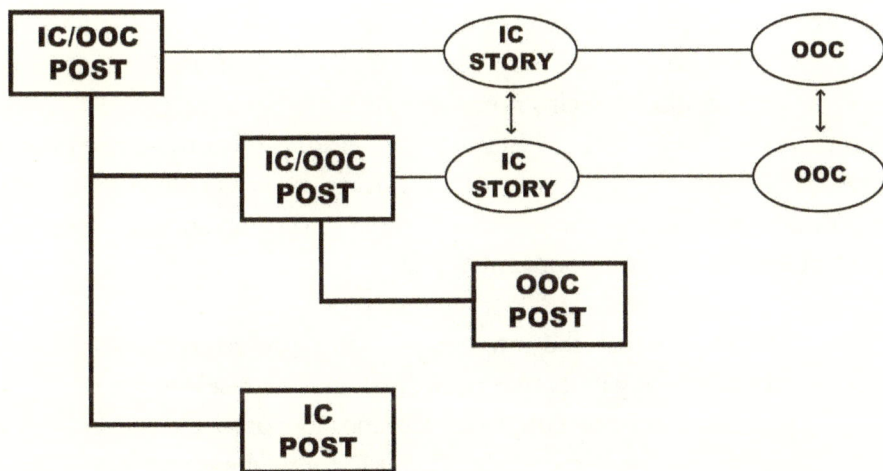

Figure 6: The interweaving of In Character (IC) and Out of Character (OOC) text.

redirect a particular thread; or just to make a cheeky aside. Thus the game participants are always consciously aware that they are taking part in an imaginative story, which is the opposite of the heroic figures in the Jordan texts who often remark that they are not like the heroes in stories. However, this does not seem to detract from the fans' pleasure in the game, or in any way break its spell.

THE NEVER-ENDING STORY

This analysis of the phenomenon of the *WOT* fandom focuses on one fantasy writer's presence and influence in cyberspace, also revealing the way in which Jordan's richly layered and plotted sequence of texts has been 'poached' by his fans, to provide an extension of the author's original and finite texts. And through these fans' activities on the web, their construction of a cyberworld of wonderful choice and possibility, the fans have constructed a 'cultural and social network that spans the globe', one in which the contribution of each and every participant counts (Jenkins 1992b, 45).

In this highly creative fandom response to such a popular continuing series we have remarkable evidence of the power of these stories to fire

218

the imagination, to cause readers to identify with the story situation and even, perhaps, to extend the purposes of the author and spend long periods in a world of their choice and of their fashioning. What is so significant is the enfranchisement of readers-of-print into cyber storytellers, artists and pattern makers in their own right. In response to my question regarding the worlds of reality and of imagination, one of the fans on the Dragonmount site replied:

> The reason that the internet is such a powerful tool for 'bridging the gap' between the 'real and the true' worlds is that it allows the fans to create and add onto the world created by the authors, allowing a deeper submersion into a reality different than the one they currently exist in. People desire more than what the world offers to them … Fantasy can be an escape from the 'norm' that haunts many people. It is a way of dealing with the daily grind of life. The internet simply allows the fan to create and add onto to the 'true world' that they have come to love and enjoy. Unfortunately, an author cannot write a story about their world forever. They move on to new worlds, or they stop writing altogether. The internet allows the continuation of a beloved world into infinity. (Eldar Loial 2004)

The *WOT* fans' interaction on the world-wide web, their capacity to weave new stories collectively about the Wheel world, enables them to keep the author's world alive and thus to imaginatively engage in a type of never-ending story.

AFTERWORD:
'WHEEL' WORLD/REAL WORLD:
THE QUEST OF THE FAN/CRITIC

Charmed magic casements, opening on the foam
Of perilous seas, in faery lands forlorn.
(Keats *Ode to a Nightingale*)

The process of researching and the writing of this book, in which I have sought to find my way through the labyrinth of the Jordan texts, has entailed a quest not unlike that of the hero figure of fantasy. The labyrinth, that place of exploration, testing and self-questioning, is a fitting metaphor for the journey in which the critic, like the hero, is searching for knowledge and a deeper understanding of the texts. But the challenge for the literary critic seeking to reach an understanding of the patterning and meaning within the chosen texts, is to look beneath the surface, to do far more than just vicariously participate in the journey of the story. One of the interesting aspects has been that I am writing as a fantasy fan and critic, and the challenge has been to maintain objective distance from the narrative, resisting the temptation just to step through the 'magic casement' and mentally co-inhabit the author's imaginary world – as would a recreational reader – and to engage with the work not only from the heart but also from the head.

With a background in mediaeval literary studies I was aware that the old story patterns are the quintessence of modern fantasy fiction, and wished to explore how they were being reworked by certain contemporary authors. Tolkien warned that when tracing the conventional motifs and techniques to be found in modern fantasy the critic must be careful not to ignore the way authors use these to new effect:

> It is indeed easier to unravel a single *thread* – an incident, a
> name, a motive – than to trace the history of any *picture*

> defined by many threads. For with the picture in the
> tapestry a new element has come in: the picture is greater
> than, and not explained by, the sum of the component
> threads.(Tolkien 1964, 24, note 1)

Modern fantasy is not just a simple reworking of old story patterns and conventions. Jordan readily acknowledged that in *WOT* he used many sources to form his narrative, which he suggested 'add[ed] resonance to the story', although he took 'great care not to follow the older material in any slavish way' (Korda 2005). Writers of 'second-wave' fantasy from towards the end of the twentieth century have produced a type of story that is both of the literary past and of the contemporary world in which they are writing. In particular, I was interested in their writing of complex epic-style high fantasy series, and the cyberspace fandom that has become attached to, and even extended, the works of some authors. For these critical purposes Robert Jordan's *WOT* has proven to be an excellent example of both aspects.

Moreover, Jordan's *WOT* series enacts the central challenges of contemporary 'second-wave' fantasists. These authors are conscious of writing within an established form, with a rich heritage and a popular appeal. But they are also building their Secondary Worlds in the shadow of Middle-earth and other imaginary worlds of the writers who first followed in Tolkien's footsteps. Jordan and his contemporaries have needed to find ways of telling their fantasy stories that both acknowledge the genre conventions and yet impart a sense of originality to the patterning of their own work. Thus modern fantasists draw on an increasingly eclectic range of cross-cultural material, weaving both the familiar and the strange into necessarily increasingly complex patterns. At first glance large-scale high fantasy can seem like a simple templating of an idea or world, in which the characters appear over and over again in the same landscape. Therefore, these texts may be thought to have less to offer in terms of a critical analysis of the fantasy genre. However, the endurance of a single landscape across multiple texts does not necessarily preclude the play of creative originality in the patterning of narratives, nor the depiction of world-changing interaction between the characters and their depicted environments that may reach a moment of eucatastrophe.

This study has focused on the mediaeval technique of interlacing as the key structuring device of the *WOT* to unlock the intricate patterning of Jordan's narrative. As I have argued, interlace uses multi-threaded plots, echoes, anticipations and repetitions to give a multidimensional quality to the narrative. The device of interlacing allows the writer to encompass a large cast of characters, locations, landscapes and time frames that impart a sense of solidity to the depicted world. The reader's affinity to texts written in such a manner may in part be explained by John Leyerle's theory that 'the human imagination moves in atemporal, associative patterns like the literary interlace' (1967-68, 14). Thus, it constitutes a literary pattern that seems to mimic our own imaginative thought processes. In the *WOT* the threads of connection between the actions and events are also replicated in the characterisation and roles of the three main heroes, Rand, Mat, and Perrin, and in his conception of an interconnected triple hero figure Jordan goes beyond just interlacing as a plotting device. In the complex patterning of his *WOT* he has woven a rich, colourful tapestry of words, a vast panorama that gives the sense of a Secondary World without horizons. It is one in which seven Ages pass and pass again, and wherein the reader can become imaginatively enmeshed in the current portrayal of events, which are to be seen as both history and story in the making. Jordan highlights the process of events being preserved for the future as 'story' through his portrayal of Thom the gleeman, gatherer and 'teller of all tales', and the Ogier historian Loial, who is constantly writing a tale about his own adventures with Rand and his other companions.

As I look back I notice that throughout this study I emphasise the importance of 'story', not only in the Jordan texts, but in our own lives, suggesting that we too live in a story-shaped world. Jordan has privileged the role of the storyteller not only by the inclusion of many embedded stories within his imaginary world, but also through the key role given to Thom, who functions as his alter ego, and there is always a sense of more stories that could be told. Indeed one of the many enjoyable aspects of Jordan's texts is that they are not just simple linear stories, for in the manner of an interlaced medieval tale the narrative proceeds through many separate yet intersecting paths designed to draw the reader into a more intimate relationship with both the characters and the landscape:

> By repetition of pointing signals, or symbols, the author constructs a pattern which guides the interpretation. But in no sense does the writer force the pattern upon the reader ... The story becomes [the reader's] own story to the extent that his imagination interpenetrates the framework of the story and lives for a time in the world of the story. The insights thereby disclosed to one reader may vary from those disclosed to another reader by virtue of the degree of interpenetration. (Timmerman 1983, 8)

Readers thus are encouraged to play an active role, gathering up their own threads of imagination in order to interpret and participate in the patterning of the unfolding narrative – rather like Jordan's magus figures – and so to engage in Secondary Belief for the duration of the tale. And for the readers this is a unique experience, for the extent to which the writer's re-authoring of older motifs and story patterns will resonate with them largely depends on the personal knowledge or cultural inheritance that they each bring to the text. Therefore the layering of the story can be interpreted by the general reader or by those more historically informed critics, at a number of cultural and narrative levels.

Part of the continuing fascination of fantasy is the writer's use of the comfortingly known and the tantalizingly unknown to entice the reader. Readers of modern epic-style fantasy have been drawn to the imaginary worlds of these large-scale texts and have established networks of fan-based communities. I have argued that the internet provides a tool with which fans can share their experiences of the original texts and even extend those texts though their own storytelling, artwork and role-play gaming. Jordan's *WOT* series is the locus of a web of internet sites which intersect with the text. The internet with a plethora of web sites devoted to fantasy texts is a particular feature of modern fantasy that began in the late twentieth century and continues to grow.

As writers such as Jordan produce their texts, fans react and interact with those texts in a complex network of emotional response, critical comment, compliment, anticipation of future plot-lines and re-authorship. *WOT* fans write themselves into the pattern of the heroic quest, model characters on those in Jordan's narrative, and become participating virtual citizens in his Secondary World. The intersection of the fan and the depicted fantasy world is part of the modern appeal of such epic-style stories and encourages a critical reading of these texts which takes seriously the multiple layering of text, reader/fan and scholarship – an exciting and under-explored area for academic study. For to date these kinds of popular high fantasy texts, and the fans' cyberspace representations of them, have received little critical attention, either because of the sheer bulk of the work, or because they have been deemed to be only of passing literary value. But as Northrop Frye so far-sightedly noted more broadly of critical responses, 'scholarship' is a 'process of mutation and metamorphosis [for] subjects regroup themselves and other subjects take shape from the shifting relations of existing ones' (1970, 4). Frye thus suggested that the role of the critic should be to remain open-minded, and willing to embrace different forms of literature as they continue to emerge in society, which itself is constantly mutating, and in this way, perhaps, redefine what we believe literature can offer us. The on-going quest for the critic, like that for the reader of story itself, involves 'the fascination of the desire to unravel the intricately knotted and ramified history of the branches on the Tree of Tales', despite Tolkien's warning that to do so 'is now beyond all skill but that of the elves to unravel it' (1964, 23). Nevertheless, as Thom is so fond of saying, 'that would be something to make a story of'. (*EOTW*, 388)

NOTES

Introduction

1 Lewis himself had a long association with Tolkien, and, it is clear that he took inspiration from Tolkien's ideas. Refer to Carpenter 1978.

2 The Aes Sedai is an order of female priestesses who have the ability to channel the magical 'One Power'.

3 The reader who is unfamiliar with the plot could refer to Karl-Johan Norén's web site which provides extensive *WOT* plot summaries: http://hem3.passagen.se/kjoren/jordan/teotw.html. My own article 'Lore, Myth and Meaning for Post-Moderns: An Introduction to the Story World of Robert Jordan's *Wheel of Time* Sequence', in *Australian Folklore*, 18, 2003, pp. 37-76, is another useful source.

4 Noreen Giffney, personal email. Noreen Giffney, a lecturer at University College, Dublin, is interested in 'the proliferation and commercialisation of medieval apocalyptic beliefs and fears in modern culture, particularly fantasy fiction'.

5 The various terms interlacement, interlacing, and interlace are used throughout this thesis.

6 Shippey (2000) raises the interesting theory that although Tolkien certainly knew the word *interlace* it is 'associated with the structure of French prose romance, in which he took little interest', and that Tolkien 'also knew that the Icelandic word for a short story is a *þáttr*, literally a thread. One could say that several *þáttir*, or threads, twisted round each other, make up a saga … Tolkien may have felt that there had been all along a native version of the French technique of *entrelacement*, even if we no longer know the native word for it' (103).

7 He also notes that 'variations of the form' can be found 'as early as the poet Ovid's *Metamorphoses* and at least as late as Spencer's *Faerie Queen*' (80). West's work shows the earlier influence of Eugene Vinaver's theories on interlace. For instance: *Form and Meaning in Medieval Romance* (1966); *The*

Rise of Romance (1971), in particular chap. 5, 'The Poetry of Interlace' (68ff.).

Chapter 1: Revisiting interlace: the fantasy author as storyteller and pattern maker

1 Leyerle points out that the representation of fate as a 'function of a wheel of fortune' draws on 'an image made popular by Boethius in *De Consolatione Philosophiae* where the goddess Fortuna speaks of the play of her wheel'. See p. 70.

2 It is of interest to note that Leyerle suggests that 'creative criticism itself can be understood as a form of play'. See p. 78.

3 Jordan extended this story and published it as a separate novel, *New Spring: A Wheel of Time Novel*, 2004.

4 The 'long spiral' is an image of progression that is suggestive of the constant cycle of birth, life and death, of spiritual growth, and also of a fluid continuity between past, present and future – as found in Jordan's *WOT* narrative.

5 She is quoting Tolkien's *Beowulf* essay of 1936.

6 The wonderment expressed by protagonists as they journey away from their known environs is of course another matter, as is seen in a later discussion.

Chapter 2: Unravelling the Pattern: The Magus Figures in *The Wheel of Time*

1. Shippey suggests that Tolkien's presentation of evil in *LOTR* is more complex and ambiguous, and could reflect both the Boethian view of evil as 'internal, caused by human sin and weakness and alienation from God', and the Manichaean view that 'evil is a force from outside'. (2000, 112ff).

2. This is equivalent of the Roman myth of the Golden Age of the Gods, the Silver Age of semi-gods, and the Bronze Age of men.

3. This technique may be compared with that of Henry Fielding's use of an overt omniscient narrator in his 18th century 'realist' novel *Tom Jones,* where the narrator interjects and personally addresses the 'Dear Reader', thereby disrupting the flow of the

story and ensuring that the reader takes a more objective or even morally judgmental role. And of course postmodern literature also plays with this device – both metafictively and in terms of exposing the framework/construct of the story.

4. This resonates with the Nordic Skald who, as noted by Karl-Johan Norén (2003) 'had several ways to tell a story, ranging from highly formal styles like drottkvaettr, to pure prose'.

5. Compare the hobbits' first sight of Aragorn/Strider in the inn at Bree. (*Fellowship*, chap. 10)

6. Speaking of the magic quality of words, Le Guin has said that one aspect of her *Earthsea* trilogy is about herself, the 'artist (i.e. the writer) as magician'. See 'Dreams Must Explain Themselves', in Le Guin (1989, 43).

7. The Tarot, like so many fantasy conventions has its origins in 14th century Europe. The designs for the cards are drawn not only from Christian, Gnostic and Islamic imagery, but Celtic and Norse elements as well. (see Douglas 1974, 33.)

8. The supreme head of the White Tower. She is a member of *all* Ajahs, and this is denoted by the seven bands of colour upon her stole.

9. Compare Christ's wish that the cup be taken from him. *The New Testament*, Matthew xxvi, 39.

10. Compare Aragorn's sounding of a silver horn to summon the dead to the 'Stone of Erech', to fulfil their ancient broken vow of fealty to the Dunedain. (*King*, chap. 2)

11. The arch-temptress or white witch reappears in literature in many guises, both secular and religious, stretching from the Middle Ages to the present day. Well-known examples include Malory's enchantress 'Morgan Le Fay', MacDonald's 'Lilith', C. Williams's 'Lily Sammile', S. T. Coleridge's 'Geraldine', J. Keats's 'La Belle Dame Sans Merci', and C. S. Lewis's White Witch, 'Jadis'. More recently this figure resurfaces as Ursula Le Guin's 'Lady Serret', in *Wizard* (discussed later this chapter) and as the wicked 'Mrs Coulter' in Philip Pullman's *His Dark Materials* trilogy.

12. The ongoing temptation of the hero is another element of mediaeval, literary game-play. Compare Malory's portrayal of Gawain and Lancelot.

13. This would make her a female equivalent of the Tolkien's Saruman figure.

Chapter 3: The Patchwork Hero: Jordan's Patterning of Heroic Motifs in *The Wheel of Time*

1. This resonates with earlier philosophical theory of a cosmic Creator of the world who 'set the machine going and then left it'. (Pepper 1996, 137-8)

2. The horror of *Machin Shin* brings to mind J. K. Rowling's Dementors in *Harry Potter and the Prisoner of Azkaban*.

Chapter 4: Heroic Interlace: The Jordan Hero as Destroyer, Builder and Preserver

1. In the Hindu trinity the three principal gods are Lord Brahma (the Creator), Lord Vishnu (the preserver), and Lord Shiva (the destroyer). But they are complex figures who represent many other things at many levels on the physical, mental and earthly planes.

2. Miller suggests that: 'when the hero-child is born and the mother dies in childbirth we may be seeing a kind of imagined sacrifice: a death pays toll for the extraordinary birth'. (2000, 98)

3. These words are part of the Japanese Samurai warrior code.

4. For comparison see: *The New Testament*, Luke xxiii, 44-45; Matthew x, 34-36.

5. Norén also discusses this link to the Northern gods in relation to Mat.

6. J. K. Rowling, in *The Prisoner of Azkaban* uses this trope in the sense of the archetypal good werewolf.

7. Compare the influence of the One Ring over Frodo in *LOTR*.

Chapter 5: Virtual Storytelling: *The Wheel of Time* World Wide Weave

1. In the 19ᵗʰ century there was also a woman's outfit, known as a Dolly Varden that was named after the locksmith's coquettish daughter in Charles Dickens's novel *Barnaby Rudge*.

2. Trollope writes that after overhearing two clergymen complaining about Mrs Proudie he informed them, "'I will go home and kill her before the week is over.' And so I did … I have sometimes regretted the deed, so great was my delight in writing about Mrs Proudie'. (275-76)

3. There is a wealth of critical material in relation to *Star Trek*, *X-Files*, *Star Wars*, *Doctor Who*, *Buffy the vampire slayer*, and numerous soap operas. Major researchers in the area of mass media fandom include Henry Jenkins (1992); Jensen (1992); Fiske (1998); Grossberg (1998); Abercrombie and Longhurst (1998); Hills (2002). And in the area of fan cyber culture, Rheingold (1993).

4. 'Slash fiction' is the term for fan rewriting of the relationships between well-known fictional characters, such as Spock and Kirk of *Star Trek* fame, which are given a romantic or sexual twist that is missing in the original media texts.

5. The term 'filk music' is a derivative of 'folk music'. Fans usually borrow the tunes for their 'filksongs' from well-known popular or folk repertoires, with a theme taken from favourite mass media shows, such as 'Star Trek'. Communal 'filking' sessions are commonly held at conventions which centre around specific fan interests, and in the case of the Jordan fans, they focus on the *WOT*. This type of creative activity is another way in which fans are able to comment on or extend the original texts.

6. Hypertext is a term coined by Theodor Nelson, a computer scientist who described it as: 'non-sequential writing – text that branches and allows choice to the reader, best read at an interactive screen'. Quoted by Landow (1994, 4).

7. J. K. Rowling in her Harry Potter texts is transposing the techniques of the hypertextual medium of the internet to written

texts. Good examples are the people in the paintings at Hogwarts School who magically change location and appear in other paintings or the way entrance to the pupils' dormitories is gained by stepping through the frame of a picture. Characters featured in wizard handbooks, newspapers or on public posters can move and talk; staircases within the school can change location, and Harry's magical map can track the movements of anyone moving around the school by displaying their footprints on the paper.

8. This game has been created by Llewellyn Phyre Sedai and Dedicated Liam Dakred.

9. Co-written by Batya Levin Wittenberg and Merav Hoffman (2004), Other *WOT* 'filksongs' can be found on the Waygate site.

10. This game has been created by Ji'alantin Antar al'Kadar and Amora en'Damier Sedai.

BIBLIOGRAPHY

1. Primary fantasy texts

Cooper, Susan. 1976. *The Dark Is Rising*, London: Puffin Books.

_____. 1979 *Silver on the Tree*, Middlesex: Puffin Books.

Donaldson, Stephen R. 1982. *The Wounded Land*, *The Second Chronicles of Thomas Covenant*, vol. 1, Glasgow: William Collins Son and Co.

Feist, Raymond E. 2002. *Magician*, London: Voyager.

Hobb, Robin. 1996. *Assassin's Apprentice*, London: Voyager.

_____. 1997. *Royal Assassin*, London: Voyager.

_____. 1998. *Assassin's Quest*, London: Voyager.

Jones, Diana Wynne. 1979. *The Spellcoats*, Oxford: Oxford University Press.

_____. 2000. *Archer's Goon*, London: Harper Collins Publishers.

Jordan, Robert. 1991. *The Eye of the World*, London: Orbit.

_____. 1992a. *The Dragon Reborn*, London: Orbit.

_____. 1992b. *The Great Hunt*, London: Orbit.

_____. 1993a. *The Fires of Heaven*, London: Orbit.

_____. 1993b. *The Shadow Rising*, London: Orbit.

_____. 1994. *Lord of Chaos*, London: Orbit.

_____. 1996a. *A Crown of Swords*, London: Orbit.

_____. 1996b'.The Strike at Shayol Ghul', Tor Books. Available from http://www.tor.com/shayol.html

_____. 1998a, *The Path of Daggars*, London: Orbit.

_____. 1998b 'New Spring', in *Legends: Eleven New Works by the Masters of Modern Fantasy*, edited by Robert Silverberg,

London: Voyager. 519-91.

_____. 2000. *Winter's Heart*, London: Orbit.

_____. 2003. *Crossroads of Twilight*, London: Orbit.

_____. 2004. *New Spring: A Wheel of Time Novel.* London: Orbit.

_____. 2005. *Knife of Dreams*, London: Orbit.

Jordan, Robert and Patterson, Teresa. 2000. *The World of Robert Jordan's 'The Wheel of Time'*, London: Orbit.

Le Guin, Ursula K. 1971, *A Wizard of Earthsea*, London: Penguin Books.

_____. 1974. *The Farthest Shore*, London: Penguin Books.

_____. 1990. *Tehanu: The Last Book of Earthsea*, New York: Macmillan..

_____. 2001a. *The Other Wind*, Orlando, Florida: Harcourt.

_____. 2001b. *Tales from Earthsea*, New York: Harcourt.

Silverberg, Robert, ed. 1998. *Legends: Eleven New Works by the Masters of Modern Fantasy*, London: Voyager.

Tolkien, J. R. R. 2001. *The Fellowship of the Ring*, London: Harper Collins.

_____. 2001. *The Return of the King*, London: Harper Collins.

_____. 2001. *The Two Towers*, London: Harper Collins.

2. *The Wheel of Time* web sites

(Few websites have 'publication dates' and are subject to constant modification (as well as occasional disappearance. In most instances, the dates given below are those on which the writer accessed the website in question.)

'Dragonmount.com'. 2004. Available from
http://www.dragonmount.com/main.php

'Encyclopaedia Wot'. 2004. Available from
http://www2.photeus.com:8090/~ewot/main/welcome.html

'Robert Jordan and the *Wheel of Time* series'. 2004. Available from
http://www.tor.com/jordan/index.html

'Seven Spokes: A *Wheel of Time* Chronology'. 2004. Available from
http://www.sevenspokes.com/

'Silklantern.com'. 2004. Available from http://www.silklantern.com/

'Tarvalon.Net'. 2004. Available from http://www.tarvalon.net

'The Grey Tower'. 2004. Available from http://www.greytowerrp.net/

'Theoryland of the *Wheel of Time*'. 2004. Available from
http://www.theoryland.com/

'The *Wheel of Time* Novice Page'. 2004) Available from
http://www.hotcom.net/users/lawrence/wot.html

'The *Wheel of Time* Org'. 2004. Available from
http://www.wheeloftime.org/index.html

'Wotmania.com'. 2004. Available from http://www.wotmania.com/

'Wotmud IV'. 2004. Available from http://www.wotmud.org/

'Wot Now?' Available from http://shadowburn.binmode.com/wotnow/

'Dragon's Library'. 1998 . Available from
http://www.dragonlibrary.net/

Butler, Leigh, Korda, Pam and Sadun, Erica, 'The *Wheel of Time*
FAQ'. 2004. Available from http://linuxmafia.com/ jordan/

Clark, Rob. 'Stonedog's *Wheel of Time* Page'. 2004) Available from
http://stonedog.org/wot/index.html

Craig, '*Wheel of Time* Quote Archive'. 2004. Available from
http://www.geocities.com/jalapeno425/WoT2.html

Doyle, Dave. 'Wot Now?' 2004) Available from
http://www.shadowburn.com/wotnow/

en'Damier, Saphire. 'Maps and Diagrams of the Grey Tower'. 2004. Available from http://www.greytowerrp.net/ GTAdmin/Library/grey_tower_art.html

Garrett, Bill. '*Wheel of Time* Word Games'. 2004 Available from http://www.linuxmafia.com/~garett/jordan/ wordgames.html

Geyer, Helmut. 'The Waygate'. 2004. Available from htp://www.linuxmafia.com/waygate/jordan.html

Goldsmith, Abigail. 'Abbyland'. 2004. Available from http://www.abbygoldsmith.com/

Korda, Pam. 'The Compleat Index of *Wheel of Time*-Related 'Net Resources'. 2004. Available from http://www.ece.umd.edu/~dilli/WOT/WOTindex/

Mercury, Marek, 'The *Wheel of Time* Character Archive'. 2004. Available from http://dmt.customer.netspace. net.au/home.htm

Norén, Karl-Johan. 'My Robert Jordan Page'. 2004. Available from http://hem.passengen.se/kjnoren/

Posey, Daniel, 'Ideal Seek'. 2003,. Available from http://idealseek.no-ip.com/

3. Secondary sources

New Encyclopaedia Britannica. 2002. vol 4, 15th edition, Chicago: Encyclopaedia Britannica.

Abercrombie, Nicholas, and Longhurst, Brian. 1998. *Audiences: A Sociological Theory of Performance and Imagination*, California and London: Sage Publications.

al'Kadar, J'altantin Antar, and en'Damier Sedai, Amora. 2004. 'The Seals Preserved'. Available from http://disc.server.com.Indices/220380.html

Allanon. 1999. 'A New Beginning'. Available from http://www.dragonlibrary.com/1999/story218.htm

Attebery, Brian. 1980. *The Fantasy Tradition in American Literature: From Irving to Le Guin*, Bloomington: Indiana University Press.

_____. 1992. *Strategies of Fantasy*, Bloomington and Indianapolis: Indiana University Press.

Balfe, Myles. 2004. 'Incredible Geographies? Orientalism and Genre Fantasy', *Social and Cultural Geography*, 5.1: 75-89.

Basney, Lionel. 1980. 'Tolkien and the Ethical Function of "Escape" Literature', *Mosaic*, 13.2: 23-36.

Baum, M. D. 2000. 'Robert Jordan's *Wheel of Time*: Fantasy Epic-Style'. Available from wysiwyg://9/http://www.cnn.com/2000/books/news/12/07/rob ert.jordan/

Bell, Mary Ann, Berry, Mary Ann, and Van Roekel, James, L. 2004. *Internet and Personal Computing Fads*, Binghamton, New York: The Haworth Press.

Benford, Gregory. 1996. 'Alt.Fans', *Reason* 27.8, 1996: 43-44.

Bloomfied, Morton W. 1975. 'The Problem of the Hero in the Later Medieval Period', in *Concepts of the Hero in the Middle Ages and the Renaissance: Papers of the Fourth and Fifth Annual Conferences of the Center for Medieval and Early Renaissance Studies. State University of New York at Binghamton, 2-3 May 1970, 1-2 May 1971*, edited by Norman T. Burns and Christopher J. Reagan, Albany: State University of New York Press: 27-47.

Boyer, Robert H. and Kenneth Zahorski, J., eds. 1984. *Fantasists on Fantasy: A Collection of Critical Reflections by Eighteen Masters of the Art*, New York: Avon Books.

Brombert, Victor, ed. 1969. *The Hero in Literature*, New York: Fawcett World Library.

Brooke-Rose, Christine. 1981. *A Rhetoric of the Unreal: Studies in*

Narrative and Structure, Especially of the Fantastic, Cambridge: Cambridge University Press.

Brooks, Peter. 1984. *Reading for the Plot: Design and Intention in Narrative*, Oxford: Oxford University Press.

Brunel, Pierre, ed. 1992. *Companion to Literary Myths, Heroes and Archetypes*, translated by Wendy Allatson, Judith Hayward and Trista Selous, London: Routledge.

Bull, M. ed. 1995. *Apocalypse Theory and the Ends of the World*, Oxford: Blackwell Publishers.

Burns, Norman T. and Reagan, Christopher J., eds. 1975. *Concepts of the Hero in the Middle Ages and the Renaissance: Papers of the Fourth and Fifth Annual Conferences of the Center for Medieval and Early Renaissance Studies. State University of New York at Binghamton, 2-3 May 1970, 1-2 May 1971*, New York: State University of New York Press.

Butler, E. M. 1993. *The Myth of the Magus*, Cambridge: Canto, (1948).

Caillois, Roger. 1961. *Man, Play and Games*, translated by Meyer Barash, New York: The Free Press of Glencoe.

Cameron, Eleanor. 1962. *The Green and Burning Tree*, Boston: Little, Brown and Co.

Camille, Michael. 1992. *Image on the Edge: The Margins of Medieval Art*, London: Reaktion Books.

Campbell, Joseph. 1973. *The Hero with a Thousand Faces*, 2nd ed., Princeton, NJ: Princeton University Press.

Canon, Peter and Zaleski, Jeff. 2002'.The Wheel Turns Another Notch: Publishers Weekly Talks with Robert Jordan', *Publishers Weekly*, 249.51: 19-20.

Carpenter, Humphrey. 1978. *The Inklings: C. S. Lewis, J. R. R. Tolkien, Charles Williams and their Friends*, London: Allen and Unwin.

Carter, Lin. 1973. *Imaginary Worlds: The Art of Fantasy*, New York: Ballantine Books,.

Cavendish, Richard. 1995. *Man, Myth and Magic: The Illustrated Encyclopedia of Mythology, Religion and the Unknown*, revised ed., vol. 5, New York: Marshall Cavendish Corporation.

Clark, George, and Timmons, Daniel, eds. 2000. *J. R. R. Tolkien and His Literary Resonances: Views of Middle-Earth*, Westport, CT: Greenwood Press.

Clute, John and Grant, John, eds. 1999. *The Encyclopedia of Fantasy*, New York: St Martin's Griffin.

CNN Interactive Chat Transcripts. 2000. 'Robert Jordan Chats about His *Wheel of Time* Series'. Available from http://www.cnm.com/COMMUNITY/transcripts/2000/12/12/jordan/index.html

Colebatch, Hal G. P. 2003. *Return of the Heroes: The Lord of the Rings, Star Wars, Harry Potter, and Social Conflict*, 2nd ed., Christchurch, N.Z: Cybereditions Corporation.

_____. 2004. 'The Magic Ingredient'. Available from http:www.abc.net.au/compass/s1120233.htm

Coleridge, Samuel T. 1907. *Biographia Literaria*, 2 vols. Oxford: Oxford University Press.

_____. 1971. *Samuel Taylor Coleridge: Selected Poetry and Prose*, 2nd ed., edited by Elizabeth Schneider, San Francisco: Rinehart Press.

Comoletti, Laura B. and Drout, Michael D. C. 2001. 'How They Do Things with Words: Language, Power, Gender, and the Priestly Wizards of Ursula K. Le Guin's *Earthsea* Books', *Children's Literature*: 113-41.

Cook, Elizabeth. 1976. *The Ordinary and the Fabulous: An Introduction to Myths, Legends and Fairy Tales*, Cambridge: Cambridge University Press, 2nd ed.

Cooper, J. C. 1992. *An Illustrated Encyclopaedia of Traditional Symbols*, London: Thames and Hudson.

Cornwell, Neil. 1990. *The Literary Fantastic: From Gothic to Postmodernism*, Hertfordshire: Harvester Wheatsheaf.

Davian. 2005. 'Dragonmount Message Boards'. Available from http:/www.dragonmount.com/Boards/ viewtopic.Php?t=17420

Davidson, Hilda Ellis, ed. 1989. *The Seer in Celtic and Other Traditions*, Edinburgh: John Donald Publishers.

Denzel, Jason. 2004. 'About Us'. Available from http://dragonmount.com/about_us.aspx.

_____. 2004. 'ComicCon Wrap-Up'. Available from http://www.dragonmount.com/Community/ Events/comicCon2004.php

Donaldson, Stephen, R. 1986. *Epic Fantasy in the Modern World: A Few Observations by Stephen R. Donaldson*, Ohio: Kent State University Libraries.

Douglas, Alfred. *The Tarot: The Origins, Meanings and Uses of the Cards*, Middlesex: Penguin Books., 1974.

Doyle, Dave. 2004'.About the Comic'.. Available from http://www.shadowburn.com/wotnow/about.html.

_____. 2005. 'Suess time' comic strip. Available from http://www.shadowburn.com/wotnow/comic. php?comic_id=194

Dunn, Margaret. 1986. 'The Dragon Is Not Dead: Le Guin's *Earthsea Trilogy*', in *Forms of the Fantastic*, edited by Jan Hokenson and Howard Pearce, Westport, CT: Greenwood. 175-80.

Eilers, Michelle L. 2000. 'On the Origins of Modern Fantasy, *Extrapolation*, 41.4. 317-37.

Elgin, Don D. 1985. *The Comedy of the Fantastic: Ecological Perspectives on the Fantasy Novel*, Westport, CT: Greenwood Press.

_____. 2004. 'Literary Fantasy and Ecological Comedy', in *Fantastic Literature: A Critical Reader*, edited by David Sandner, Westport, CT: Praeger. 255-70.

Eliade, Mircea. 1965. *The Myth of the Eternal Return, or Cosmos and History*, translated by Willard R. Trask, Bollingen Series 46, Princeton, NJ: Princeton University Press.

_____ ed. 1987. *The Encyclopedia of Religion*, vol. 4. New York: Macmillan.

Evans, Gwyneth.1990. 'Three Modern Views of Merlin', *Mythlore: A Journal of J. R. R. Tolkien, C. S. Lewis, Charles Williams, and the Genres of Myth*, 16.4, Summer. 17-22.

Fader6818. 'New Moderator'. 2004. Available from http://www.dragonmount.com/Boards/viewtopic.php?t=9639

Fine, Gary, Alan. 1983. *Shared Fantasy: Role-Playing Games as Social Worlds*, Chicago and London: The University of Chicago Press.

Fiske, John. 1992'.The Cultural Economy of Fandom', in *The Adoring Audience: Fan Culture and Popular Media*, edited by Lisa A. Lewis, London: Routledge. 31-65.

Frye, Northrop. 1967. *Anatomy of Criticism*, Princeton, NJ: Princeton University Press.

_____. 1963. *Fables of Identity: Studies in Poetic Mythology*, New York: Harcourt, Brace and World.

_____. 1970. *The Stubborn Structure: Essays on Criticism and Society*, London: Methuen.

_____. 1990. *Northrop Frye Myth and Metaphor: Selected Essays, 1974 – 1988*, edited by Robert D. Denham, Charlottesville and London: University Press of Virginia.

Graves, Robert. 1959. *The White Goddess: A Historical Grammar of Poetic Myth*, London: Faber and Faber.

Grossberg, Lawrence. 1992. 'Is There a Fan in the House?': The Affective Sensibility of Fandom', in *The Adoring Audience: Fan Culture and Popular Media*, edited by Lisa A Lewis, London: Routledge. 50-65.

Hayward, Jennifer. 1997. *Consuming Pleasures: Active Audiences and Serial Fictions from Dickens to Soap Opera*, Kentucky: The University Press of Kentucky.

Heim, Michael. 1993. *The Metaphysics of Virtual Reality*, New York and Oxford: Oxford University Press.

Herbert, Tim. 2001. 'Fantasy Island', *Australian Author*, 33.3. 16-20.

Hills, Matt. 2002. *Fan Cultures*, London and New York: Routledge.

Hourihan, Margery. 1997. *Deconstructing the Hero: Literary Theory and Children's Literature*, London and New York: Routledge

Huizinga, Johan. 1970. *Homo Ludens: A Study of the Play Element in Culture*, London: Maurice Temple Smith., (1949).

Hume, Kathryn, 1984. *Fantasy and Mimesis: Responses to Reality in Western Literature*, New York and London: Methuen..

Huppé, Bernard F. 1975. 'The Concept of the Hero in the Early Middle Ages', in *Concepts of the Hero in the Middle Ages and the Renaissance: Papers of the Fourth and Fifth Annual Conferences of the Center for Medieval and Early Renaissance Studies, State University of New York at Binghamton 2-3 May 1970, 1-2 May 1971*, edited by Norman T. Burns and Christopher J. Reagan, Albany: State University of New York Press. 1-26.

Irwin, W. R. 1976. *The Game of the Impossible: A Rhetoric of Fantasy*, Chicago: University of Illinois Press.

Isaacs, Neil D. and Zimbardo, Rose A., eds. 1981. *Tolkien: New Critical Perspectives*, Kentucky: The University Press of Kentucky.

Jackson, Rosemary. 1988. *Fantasy: The Literature of Subversion*, London and New York: Routledge.

Jayaram, V. 2000. 'The Trinity of Gods'. Available from http://hinduwebsite.com/trinity.htm

Jenkins, Henry. (2004) 'The Poachers and the Stormtroopers: Cultural Convergence in the Digital Age', *Red Rock Eater Digest*, (accessed 13 September, 2004). Available from http://www.strangelove.com/slideshows/articles/The_Poachers_and_the_Stormtroopers.htm

_____. (1992a) '"Strangers No More We Sing": Filking and the Social Construction of the Science Fiction Community', in *The Adoring Audience: Fan Culture and Popular Media*, edited by Lisa A. Lewis, London: Routledge, pp. 208-36.

_____. (1992b) *Textual Poachers: Television Fans and Participatory Culture*, New York: Routledge.

Jenson, Joli. 1992. 'Fandom as Pathology: The Consequences of Characterization', in *The Adoring Audience: Fan Culture and Popular Media*, edited by Lisa A Lewis, London: Routledge. 9-29.

Jones, Diana Wynne. 1983. 'The Shape of the Narrative in *the Lord of the Rings*', in *J. R. R. Tolkien: This Far Land*, edited by R. Giddings, London: Vision Press.

Jones, Steven G., ed.1994. *Cybersociety: Computer-Mediated Communication and Community*, Thousand Oaks, California: Sage Publications..

Jung, Carl, 1956. *Symbols of Transformation: An Analysis of the Prelude to a Case of Schizophrenia*, translated by R. F. C. Hull, London: Routledge & Kegan Paul.

_____. 1978. *Man and His Symbols*, introduction by John Freeman, London: Pan Books.

Kerr, Walter. 1967. *Tragedy and Comedy*, New York: Simon and Schuster.

Korda, Pam. 2005. 'Trivial Pursuits'. Available from http://linuxmafia.com/waygate/no-haunt/preLoC-3.html

Kroeber, Karl.1992. *Retelling/Rereading: The Fate of Storytelling in Modern Times*, New Brunswick, NJ: Rutgers University Press.

Lancaster, Kurt. 1996. 'Travelling among the Lands of the Fantastic: The Imaginary Worlds and Simulated Environments of Science Fiction Tourism', *Foundation: The Review of Science Fiction*, 67. 28-47.

Landow, George, ed. 1994. *Hyper-Text-Theory*, Baltimore and London: John Hopkins University Press.

Le Guin, Ursula K. 1989.*The Language of the Night*, edited by Susan Wood, revised ed., London: The Women's Press.

Lewis, C. S. 1965.*An Experiment in Criticism*, Cambridge: Cambridge University Press.

_____. 1966. *Of Other Worlds: Essays and Stories*, edited with a preface by Walter Hooper, New York and London: Harcourt Brace Jovanovich..

Lewis, Diane.2004. 'Understanding the Power of Fan Fiction for Young Adults', *KLIATT*, March. 4-6.

Lewis, Lisa A., ed. 1992.*The Adoring Audience: Fan Culture and Popular Media*, London: Routledge.

Leyerle, John. 1967-68. 'The Interlace Structure of Beowulf', *University of Toronto Quarterly*, 37. 1-17.

_____. 1973. 'The Game and Play of Hero', in *Concepts of the Hero in the Middle Ages and the Renaissance: Papers of the Fourth and Fifth Annual Conferences of the Center for Medieval and Early Renaissance Studies. State University of New York at*

Binghamton, 2-3 May 1970, 1-2 May 1971, edited by Norman T. Burns and Christopher J. Reagan, Albany: State University of New York Press. 49-82.

Lilley, Ernest. 2003 'Robert Jordan Interview', *SFRevu*. Available from http://www.sfrevu.com/ISSUES/2003/0301/Feature%20Intervi ew%20-%20Robert%20Jordan/Interview.htm

Lindahl, C., McNamara, J. and Lindow J., eds. 2000. *Medieval Folklore: An Encyclopedia of Myths, Legends, Tales, Beliefs, and Customs*, California: ABC-CLIO .

Lobdell, Jared, ed. 1975. *A Tolkien Compass*, La Salle, IL: Open Court.

Manlove, C. N. 1975. *Modern Fantasy: Five Studies*, Cambridge: Cambridge University Press.

_____. 1983. 'On the Nature of Fantasy', in *The Aesthetics of Fantasy Literature and Art*, edited by Roger C. Schlobin, Notre Dame, Indiana: University of Notre Dame Press. 16-35.

_____. 1999 *The Fantasy Literature of England*, London: MacMillan Press.

Mathews, Richard. 2002. *Fantasy: The Liberation of the Imagination*, London and New York: Routledge.

Matthews, W H. 1970. *Mazes and Labyrinths: Their History and Development*, New York: Dover Publications.

McGillis, Roderick F. 1979. 'George MacDonald and the Lilith Legend in the XIXth Century', *Mythlore: A Journal of J. R. R. Tolkien, C. S. Lewis, Charles Williams, and the Genres of Myth*, 6:1, no. 19, Winter. 3-11.

Melabrid Asha'man. 2004. 'Guidelines and Tips for Fanfics'. Available from http://www.greytowerrp.net/ GTAdmin/ Library/fanfiction/guidelines.html.

Mierin. 2002. 'Last Battle Won!'. Available from
http://www.dragonlibrary.com/fiction/data/2002/
last_battle_won.php

Miller, Dean A. 2000. *The Epic Hero*, Baltimore: The John Hopkins
University Press.

Mobley, Jane. 1974-4. 'Toward a Definition of Fantasy Fiction',
Extrapolation, 15. 117-28.

_____. 1974. *Magic Is Alive: A Study of Contemporary Fantasy Fiction*,
PhD Thesis, University of Kansas.

Molson, Francis J. 1979. 'The Earthsea Trilogy: Ethical Fantasy for
Children', in *Ursula, K. Le Guin: Voyager to Inner Lands and
Outer Space*, edited by Joe De Bolt, Port Washington: Kenikat
Press. 128-49.

_____. 1982. 'Ethical Fantasy for Children', in *The Aesthetics of Fantasy
Literature and Art*, edited by Roger C Schlobin, Notre Dame,
Indiana: University of Notre Dame Press. 82-104.

Moorcock, Michael. 1987. *Wizardry and Wild Romance: A Study of
Epic Fantasy*, London: Victor Gollancz.

n.a. 2000. 'Robert Jordan: The Name Behind the Wheel', *Locus: The
Newspaper of the Science Fiction Field*, issue 470, 44.3, March,
7.

Norén, Karl-Johan. 1999a. 'Norse and Germanic Mythology in the
Wheel of Time'. Available from
http://hem3.passagen.se/kjnoren/jorden/norse.html

_____. 1995. 'Summary of the Robert Jordan Interview Made at the
East of the Sun Fantasy Convention, Stockholm, 17 June 1995
by Helena Löfgren'. Available from http://hem3.passagen.se/
kjoren/jordan/rj-talk1.html

_____. 199b. 'The Rand-Mat-Perrin Tripod'. Available from
http://hem3.passagen.se/kjnoren/ jordan/tripod.html

Organ, Troy Wilson. 1974. *Hinduism: Its Historical Development*, New York: Barron's Educational Series.

Parkes, Henry B. 1981. 'Critical Approach to Story', in *Tolkien: New Critical Perspectives*, edited by Neil D. Isaacs and Rose A. Zimbardo, Kentucky: The University Press of Kentucky: 133-149.

Pepper, David. 1996. *Modern Environmentalism: An Introduction*, London and New York: Routledge.

Phyre Sedai, Llewellyn, and Dakred Dedicated, Liam. 2004. 'Indigo Ajah Fair'. Available from http://disc.server.com/Indices/218131.html

Potts, Stephen. 1991. 'The Many Faces of the Hero in *The Lord of the Rings*', *Mythlore: A Journal of J. R. R. Tolkien, C. S. Lewis, Charles Williams, and the Genres of Myth*, 66: 4-11.

Pratchett, Terry. 1999. 'Imaginary Worlds, Real Stories: The Eighteenth Kathrine Briggs Memorial Lecture, November 1999', *Folklore*: 159-68.

Propp, V. 1990. *Morphology of the Folktale*, translated by Laurence Scott, Austin, revised and edited by L. A. Wagner, Texas: University of Texas Press.

Rabkin, Eric S. 1976. *The Fantastic in Literature*, Princeton, NJ: Princeton University Press,

_____, ed. 1979. *Fantastic Worlds: Myths, Tales and Stories*, New York: Oxford University Press.

Rasliev, Zavian. 2004. 'Zavian's Raising'. Available from http://www.greytowerrp.net/ GTAdmin/Library/ fanfiction/savians_raising.html

Rees, A. and Rees, B. 1961. *Celtic Heritage: Ancient Tradition in Ireland and Wales*, London: Thames.

Reid, Elizabeth. 1995. 'Virtual Worlds: Culture and Imagination', in *Cybersociety: Computer-Mediated Communication and*

Community, edited by Steven G. Jones, Thousand Oaks, California: Sage Publications.: 164-83.

Rheingold, Howard. 1993. *The Virtual Community: Homesteading on the Electronic Frontier*, New York and Ontario: Addison-Wesley Publishing Company.

Riali. 2004. 'Misguided Information or Dangerous Truths?' Chapter 4, 'The Seals Preserved'. Available from http://disc.server.com/Indices/220380.html

Ringel, Faye 1979. *Patterns of the Hero and the Quest: Epic, Romance, Fantasy*, PhD Thesis, Brown University.

_____. 2000. 'Women Fantasists: In the Shadow of the Ring', in *J. R. R. Tolkien and His Literary Resonances: Views of Middle-earth*, edited by George Clark and Daniel Timmons, Westport, CT: Greenwood Press, 2000: 159-71.

Rothstein, Edward. 1996. 'Flaming Swords and Wizards' Orbs'. *The New York Times*, 8 December: 60.

_____. 1998 'An Adored Fantasy Series Now Hints at 1990's Angst', *The New York Times*, 26 October: 2.

Ryan, J. S. 1961. 'Folktale, Fairy Tale, and the Creation of a Story', in *Tolkien: New Critical Perspectives*, edited by Neil D. Isaacs and Rose A. Zimbardo, Kentucky: The University Press of Kentucky: 19-39.

Saciuk, Olena H., ed.1990. *The Shape of the Fantastic: Selected Essays from the Seventh International Conference on the Fantastic in the Arts*, Westport, CT: Greenwood Press,.

Sample, Michael. 2000. 'The Fourth Ta'veren'. Available from http://www.dragonlibrary.com/2000/story319htm

Sanborn, John Newell, 1987. 'Malory's Reduction of Interlace', *Quondam et Futurus Newsletter*,7.2, Winter. 5-10.

Sanders, Joe, ed. 1995. *Functions of the Fantastic: Selected Essays from the Thirteenth International Conference on the Fantastic in the Arts*, Westport, CT: Greenwood Press.

Sandner, David, ed. 2004. *Fantastic Literature: A Critical Reader*, Westport, CT: Praeger Publishers.

Saycell, K. J. 1979. 'Organic Unity and Interlace: Some Aspects of Malory's Morte D' Arthur', *UNISA English Studies, Journal of the Department of English*, 17.2. 1-7.

Schaafsma, Karen. 1987. 'The Demon Lover: Lilith and the Hero in Modern Fantasy', *Extrapolation*, 28.1. 52-61.

Schakel, Peter, J. 1979. *Reading with the Heart: The Way into Nardia*, Grand Rapids, Michigan: William B. Eerdmans Publishing Company.

Schlobin, Roger C. 1979. *The Literature of Fantasy: A Comprehensive, Annotated Bibliography of Modern Fantasy Fiction*, New York: Garland.

_____, ed. 1982. *The Aesthetics of Fantasy, Literature and Art*, Notre Dame, Indiana: University of Notre Dame Press.

_____. 1987. 'From the Old on to the New: New Directions in Fantasy Criticism and Theory', *Extrapolation*, 28.1. 3-9.

Seeman, Chris.1995. 'Tolkien's Revision of the Romantic Tradition', in *Proceedings of the J. R. R. Tolkien Centenary Conference 1992*, edited by Patricia Reynolds and Glen Goodknight, Altadena: Mythopoeic Press. 73-83.

Segal, Robert A., ed. 2000, *Hero Myths: A Reader*, Oxford: Blackwell Publishers.

Senior, William. 1995. 'Oliphaunts in the Perilous Realm: The Function of Internal Wonder in Fantasy', in *Functions of the Fantastic: Selected Essays from the Thirteenth International Conference on the Fantastic in the Arts*, edited by Joe Sanders, Westport, C.T.: Greenwood Press. 115-23.

Shea, John. 1978. *Stories of God: An Unauthorized Biography*, Chicago: The Thomas More Press.

Shippey, Tom. 2000. *J. R. R. Tolkien: Author of the Century*, London: Harper Collins Publishers.

_____. 2003. *The Road to Middle-earth*, expanded and revised ed., New York: Houghton Mifflin Company.

Storr, Anthony, ed.1983. *The Essential Jung*, Princeton, NJ: Princeton University Press.

Sturlason, Snorre. 1990. *Heimskringla or The Lives of the Norse Kings*, edited with notes by Elking Monsen, translated by A. H. Smith, New York: Dover Publications,.

Sukul, Vishad. 2004. 'Spokes of the Wheel: An Analysis of Robert Jordan's Writing'. Available from http://www.dragonmount.com/articles/Downloads/wot_paper_Vishad.pdf

Sundara.2001. 'The Other Side of the Wheel'. Available from http://www.dragonlibrary.com/fiction/data/2001/other_side.php

Swinfen, Ann. 1984. *In Defence of Fantasy: A Study of the Genre in English and American Literature since 1945*, London: Routledge and Kegan Paul.

Thompson, Bill. 2003. 'Local Author's Fantasy Fiction as Loved as Tolkien's', *Charleston Post and Courier*, 9 February, 2003. Available from http://www.charleston.net/stories/020903/art_09jordan.shtml

Thompson, William. 2003. 'Crossroads of Twilight: A Review by William Thompson', 2003, *SF Site Featured Reviews*. Available from http://www.sfsite.com/03a/ct147.htm

Timmerman, John H. 1983. *Other Worlds: The Fantasy Genre*, Bowling Green, Ohio: Bowling Green University Press.

Tolkien, J. R. R. 1964. *Tree and Leaf*, London: Allen and Unwin.

Trckova-Flamee, Alena. 'Thrice-Hero', 2004. Available from http://www.pantheon.org/articles/t/thrice-hero.html

Trollope, Anthony. 1883. (1950) *Anthony Trollope: An Autobiography*, edited by Michael Sadleir and Frederick Page, London: Oxford University Press.

Trubshaw, Bob. 2003. *Explore Mythology*, Wymeswold, Loughborough: Heart of Albion Press.

Trumble, William R. and Stevenson, Angus, eds. 2002. *Shorter Oxford English Dictionary*, 5th ed. 2 vols. Oxford: Oxford University Press.

Tuve, Rosemond. 1996. *Allegorical Imagery: Some Medieval Books and their Posterity*, Princeton, NJ: Princeton University Press.

Vinaver, Eugene. 1966. *Form and Meaning in Medieval Romance: The Presidential Address of the Modern Humanities Research Association, 1966*, Cambridge: Modern Humanities Research Association.

_____. 1971. *The Rise of Romance*, Oxford: Oxford University Press.

West, Richard C. 1966-67 'The Interlace and Professor Tolkien: Medieval Narrative Technique in the *Lord of the Rings*: A Paper Read to the U. W. Tolkien Society April 17, 1967', *Orcrist, Annual Bulletin of the University of Wisconsin J. R. R. Tolkien Society*, 1.1, 19-31.

_____ 1975. 'The Interlace Structure of the *Lord of the Rings*', in *A Tolkien Compass*, edited by Jared Lobdell, La Salle, IL: Open Court, 7-94.

Weston, L. Jessie. 1957. *From Ritual to Romance*, New York: Doubleday, (1920).

Wicker, Brian. 1975. *The Story-Shaped World: Fiction and Metaphysics: Some Variations on a Theme*, London: The Athlone Press of the University of London.

Wilson, R. Rawdon. 1990. *In Palamedes' Shadow: Explorations in Play, Game, and Narrative Theory*, Boston: Northeastern University Press.

Wittenberg, Batya Levin, and Hoffman, Merav. 2004. 'Stop the *Wheel of Time*, I Want to Get Off'. Available from http://wwwfortunecity.com/tattooine/challenger/3/stopthewheeloftime.html

Wolfe, Gary, K. 1986. *Critical Terms for Science Fiction and Fantasy: A Glossary and Guide to Scholarship*, Westport, CT: Greenwood Press.

Wollert, Edwin. 2003. 'Wolves in American Indian Culture'. Available from http://www.wolfsongalaska.org/wolves_in_american_culture.html

Zanger, Jules. 1982. 'Heroic Fantasy and Social Reality: *ex nihilo nihil fit*', in *The Aesthetics of Fantasy Literature and Art*, edited by Roger C Schlobin, Notre Dame, Indiana: University of Notre Dame Press. 226-36.

ABOUT THE AUTHOR

Heather Attrill's lifelong interest in Anglo-Saxon and Mediaeval literature and her passionate reading of authors such as J.R.R. Tolkien, C.S. Lewis, Ursula Le Guin and Robert Jordan, have led her to the study of ancient influences on modern fantasy literature. Born in New Zealand she moved to Australia in her early twenties, living in several cities and towns before settling in Armidale, NSW. Heather completed her PhD at the University of New England, where she has taught in a number of English literature courses. Heather currently lives with her husband and a large black cat in a house she was inspired to buy because it reminded her of the hobbit houses of Tolkien's Middle-earth.

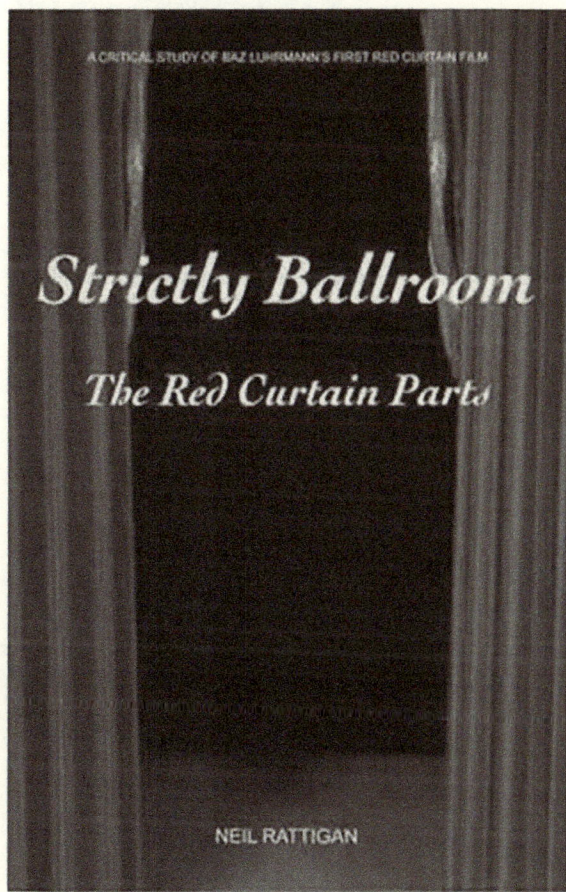

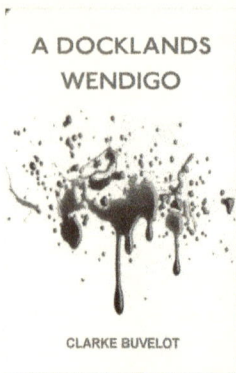

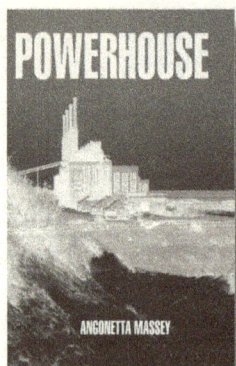

www.ingramcontent.com/pod-product-compliance
Lightning Source LLC
Chambersburg PA
CBHW021047090426
42738CB00006B/231